ANDREA COHEN
and NIGEL EASTMAN

Assessing Forensic
Mental Health Need

Policy, Theory and Research

GASKELL

Gaskell is an imprint of the Royal College of Psychiatrists
17 Belgrave Square, London SW1X 8PG

British Library Cataloguing-in-Publication Data
A catalogue record for this book is available from
the British Library.
ISBN 1-901242-42-0

Distributed in North America
by American Psychiatric Press, Inc.

Printed by Henry Ling Ltd, Dorset, UK

Contents

Figures and tables

Foreword

For the first time, taking action to improve mental health services and to address the very real social exclusion felt by those experiencing mental health problems has been made a shared national priority for health and social care agencies. While developing a new policy framework will not in itself change the type, level or equity of access to service support, it does create an impetus and opportunity for real advances. The National Service Framework, published last year, sets a challenging agenda for all mental health services and draws into the mainstream of commissioning and provision previously isolated areas such as high security services.

As a group, mentally disordered offenders (MDOs) must be high on anyone's list of those who suffer social exclusion; being at least doubly excluded by reason of their disorder and offending and, for a significant group, because of their ethnic origin. In any reasonable world it is through society's understanding and response to an individual's needs that social exclusion starts to be addressed. This book provides a wealth of information that will be of use to policy makers, commissioners, clinicians and researchers, all of whom are critical players in developing our society's attitudes to and actions on exclusion.

In their introduction to the subject of needs assessment for MDOs the authors make an important contribution to both theoretical and methodological thinking about needs assessment in general. The book clearly describes needs assessment as a complex, inherently political process which is necessarily embedded in both historical and current policy objectives. As a consequence the authors correctly perceive an endeavour that is as much about art as it is about science, about subjective choices rather than objective certainties. It is this understanding which forms a major theme of the text and which makes reading it both enlightening and enjoyable.

At a practical level we are given a systematic framework for understanding differing approaches to needs assessment, an appraisal of their relative strengths and weaknesses and a useful understanding of the historical context in which UK forensic mental health services have developed. This, in conjunction with a wide-ranging review of UK literature relevant to needs assessment for MDOs, offers a basis for more rational planning of services and for the translation of the new policy framework into action.

No discussion of needs assessment can be complete without some understanding of what outcomes are sought. For any health or social care intervention this presents considerable theoretical and practical difficulties. However, there are special difficulties in relation to MDOs, where the need for public protection runs alongside, and at times is in tension with, the needs of the individual for appropriate and ethical treatment and care. The discussion in the book of these issues emphasises that there is an absence of indicators that properly reflect the multi-dimensional nature of outcome for this population.

The conclusion of this work gives a very clear message to all those involved in service planning. Policy makers, providers, commissioners and researchers have a duty to understand the complexity of needs assessment as a dynamic and multi-faceted process. Above all, in taking decisions to commission services or research it is crucial that both the underlying value base and the assessment that is being made of available evidence are made explicit. The same applies to evaluating existing services. We owe it to the people who are excluded from the services that they need to ensure that this central message of the book is not ignored.

Eddie Kane
Director of Mental Health and Learning Disabilities, NHSE London
and Director, High Security Psychiatric Services Commissioning Team

Preface

As all health care planning and provision have become more rational, so greater attention has properly been paid by commissioners to the assessment of need. Rationality is embodied in the Department of Health's definition of need (NHS Management Executive, 1991), which stipulates that something is a 'need' only if there is a service response which can meet it, at least partially. That is, it must be treatable, or at least 'careable'. This definition of 'need' is closely related to the economic concept of 'cost-effectiveness'. Rationality is then expressed through the use of data describing different types of need in order to allocate resources. In this context, therefore, needs assessment is closely related to cost-benefit or cost-utility analysis, themselves bases for resource allocation.

The application of health care needs assessment to the mentally disordered is no less problematic, and in many ways more problematic, than its application to those with physical medical conditions. Even in the latter field, the difficulties of coping with subjectivity in the evaluation of health status, and the value of 'improving' health status, are great. Hence, even the attempt to measure, in relative terms, the quality of life in different physical health states, by way of 'quality-adjusted life-years' (QALYs), serves sometimes to hide what is, ultimately, profound subjectivity. However, any similar attempts at measurement applied to mental health status are even more fraught with subjectivity. When it comes to measuring the needs of MDOs, both the level and scope of subjectivity enter new dimensions. The high level of subjectivity is illustrated, for example, by posing the question "How 'needy' is a man with schizophrenia who now also suffers from post-traumatic symptoms relating to his killing of another?" The unusual scope of subjectivity is emphasised by the obvious fact that need related to an MDO is not restricted to the offender. Society also has a 'need' to be protected from him or her. That takes 'particular need' into a new and uncharted sea. It also emphasises starkly not just subjectivity *per se* but the sensitivity of definition of need to public policy. Indeed, that sensitivity is a core feature of the review of the field which is offered in this book.

The origins of the work presented here go back to the early to mid-1990s, when, in the context of the 'internal National Health Service market', purchasers were encouraged by the Department of Health (DoH) to pursue a 'value for money' approach to commissioning. They were also required to "assess the health needs of their populations", and then to take rational decisions on how to allocate their resources between competing needs. A new service could be commissioned only if it was justified by a 'needs assessment' and even an existing service was safe only if it could be shown to be 'needed'. In practice, of course, given the very limited resources available to district and regional health authorities, needs assessment was highly restricted in both its scope and method. As a result, there was a danger of more rhetoric than reality in practice.

The new era of rational service planning based on need coincided with political demands for increased service provision for MDOs. This originated in a welfare-based philosophy which dated back to the Butler and Glancy reports of the mid-1970s (DoH and Social Security, 1974*a*; Home Office/DoH and Social Security, 1975). Both emphasised the need to respond to the *mental health* needs of MDOs, although they were influenced by a public protection agenda and by social demands for 'secure places' for the mentally disordered, including sometimes for the mentally disordered who perhaps did not 'need' it. However, the political and DoH pressure on health commissioners to respond to MDO need implied a substantial resource commitment. It also set up a natural tension between their required duty rationally to assess need, including for MDOs, and what seemed to be a political imperative to 'buy' more beds. This tension nicely represents, in fact, core aspects of needs assessment. It was introduced as a rationally based, and rationality-pursuing, technique and yet there was a political imperative to commission new beds. This almost implied that any needs assessment had to come up with the right (political) answer, that is, to commission more secure beds. An illustration of this is provided by the influential *Review of Health and Social Services for Mentally Disordered Offenders and Others Requiring Similar Services* (Reed report) (DoH/Home Office, 1992). In line with the rhetoric of the time it advised that, of course, health authorities would carry out their own assessment of MDO need – gone were the days of norms and indicative planning, represented by the Glancy and Butler report recommendations of 20 and 40 medium-security beds per million population. And yet the Reed report still could not resist adding that the authors would be surprised if at least 30 beds per million were not to be 'needed' in any district or region (their 'averaging' of the Glancy and Butler indicative figures was itself of interest).

Turning more specifically to this book, its origins lie in questions put to one of its authors (NE) by health authorities from one regional health authority, which asked, in the mental health political climate just described, "What is known about the need for MDO services?" Interestingly, an immediately supplementary question was "Does medium-security service stop MDOs from subsequently reoffending?" The latter question, implicitly equating 'need' with public protection, clearly emphasised the importance of a (rational) debate about the core definition of MDO need *per se*. Was it, in fact, to be equated with the need for public protection, both during secure care and after 'release'? Indeed, the fact that it was *health* commissioners asking such a criminological question further emphasised the need for a rational theoretical review of the field.

The response of both authors to health authority questions about MDO needs assessment went beyond the theoretical. Clearly, they wanted to know what was the empirical knowledge base relevant to such assessment. Yet, it was evident both to them and us that there was no available comprehensive review of empirical studies relevant to commissioner assessment of MDO need. As a result, the authors were asked, as part of their work in the Mentally Disordered Offenders Policy Research Unit (MDO PRU) of St George's Hospital Medical School, itself commissioned by regional and district health authorities, to conduct a comprehensive literature review. That review was produced in the form of a report to the regional health authorities. Subsequently, the High Security Psychiatric Services Commissioning Board of the DoH expressed an interest in the work and requested of the authors an expanded 'update'. In offering to underpin the work financially, the Board enabled the production of this book.

The book is published at a time when the political health agenda has developed somewhat differently from how it was when the work was begun. The internal National Health Service market has gone. However, its shadow still clearly persists in the form of 'commissioning' rather than 'purchasing', and the new era of providers in commissioner cooperation and joint working still emphasises commissioning-based needs assessment. The book is also published at a time when the High Security Board has itself just been merged into a framework of 'regional specialist commissioning groups', which will be responsible for both high-security and medium-security care. This offers great advantages, both in terms of making the Special Hospitals less 'special' and isolated, and in terms of reducing or abolishing perverse financial incentives which lead to commissioners leaving patients receiving care in high-security environments which they do not 'need'. However, the risk is now that the perverse incentives will operate at the interface between medium-security care and general mental health care. Although it is to be hoped that the government's new National Service Framework will ameliorate this problem, by properly and explicitly defining the boundary between specialist forensic care (high-security and medium-security in-patient care and specialist forensic community care) and general mental health care, the separation and 'top-sliced' funding of the former may distort the proper balance of quasi-response to need by forensic and general services. So, the new commissioning world offers opportunities better to meet real need, for example to relocate high-security patients who do not need high security, but with attendant risks.

It is hoped that this book offers a theoretical framework for conducting needs assessment for MDOs in the new commissioning era the National Health Service now faces. It also provides a systematic review of empirical studies relevant to MDO needs assessment, presented within the chosen theoretical framework. That review is not comprehensive but it is hoped that it is comprehensive *enough* to give a grounding in the available data and studies and, more particularly, to illustrate how the theoretical framework functions, in terms of integrating information from both the studies presented and any other studies the reader may address as time and research unfolds.

Finally, the book emphasises above all a note of heavy caution. Needs assessment is value-laden and fraught with subjectivity, and the main message here is therefore that the definition of terms and the chosen method of conducting needs assessment must substantially determine the result. There are dangers of simply demonstrating that what current policy implies is actually wanted (politically). Needs assessment, like cost-benefit or cost-utility analysis within economic science, is only as good as its assumptions and method. Ultimately, it offers a view, or a range of views, of need. A judgement then has to be taken by policy makers on those views and a subjective decision is made about what to weight and by how much. As with cost-benefit analysis, numbers do not imply decisions – they give the *bases* for decisions. Indeed, in the authors' view the very term 'needs assessment' is profoundly misleading. It implies 'an answer'. A far better term we would suggest is 'perspectives on need'. That properly suggests, first, that there are general perspectives on any individual 'need problem' and that a judgement then has to be made which goes beyond the data, and which is not inherently implied by the data. The ultimate caution is, therefore, that you can demonstrate a need for almost anything you want to commission. What is needed is sufficient understanding of the technology of needs assessment to be able to review critically any given needs assessment or data which are offered as relevant to it. This book attempts to offer a framework for both critically interpreting and also conducting MDO needs assessments.

A.C. & N.E., London

Acknowledgements

We are grateful to all those in the South Thames Region of the National Health Service, now divided between the London Region and the South East Region, who supported the work which lies behind this book. In particular, we thank David Morris for initiating the work several years ago. Tony Thake and Dr Dilys Jones of the High Security Psychiatric Services Commissioning Board (HSPSCB) of the Department of Health were responsible for the idea of extending the work and bringing it up to date. We are also grateful to the HSPSCB, which provided necessary funding for completion and publication of the work. Without the Board, the work would not have become a book. We would also like to thank all those who responded to our national survey of needs assessment for MDOs and who sent relevant articles and reports. Dr Sian Rees was extremely generous with her time in agreeing to edit parts of the text and she made numerous important suggestions. Finally, thank you to Jane Horne for her work in correcting a late version of the text.

Dedicated to
Jack and Sheila Cohen
and to
Rachel Eastman

Abbreviations

ACSeSS	Admission Criteria to Secure Services Schedule
ADM	alcohol, drug and mental health [services]
BCS	Behavioural Coding System
CAN	Camberwell Assessment of Need
CPA	Care Programme Approach
CPQ	Community Placement Questionnaire
DHA	district health authority
DSPD	Dangerous Severe Personality Disorder
GP	general practitioner
HSPSCB	High Security Psychiatric Services Commissioning Board
MDO	mentally disordered offender
MINI	Mental Illness Needs Index
NFCA	Needs for Care Assessment
NHS	National Health Service
QALY	quality-adjusted life-year
RAWP	Resource Allocation Working Party
RHA	regional health authority
RMO	responsible medical officer
RSU	regional secure unit
RUT	rates under treatment
SCU	special care unit
SHSA	Special Hospital Service Authority
YPI	York Psychiatric Index

1 Needs assessment policy

The assessment of 'need' has always been at least a tacit component of all modern health service planning and delivery (Butler, 1992). Only that which is 'needed' should be provided. However, after the introduction of the National Health Service (NHS) internal market, the assessment of individual and population needs became an explicit and central principle of both health and social services policy. Service purchasers – the district health authorities (DHAs) – were directed by the DoH both to become more explicit and transparent about priority-setting and to make needs assessment and service planning more publicly visible (Butler, 1992).[1] Hence, needs assessment has been propounded within recent government policy as the proper tool with which successfully to plan, commission and deliver health and social services of all kinds. It has thus become a major responsibility of purchasers (including their public health advisers) always to base their purchasing on explicit assessments of need.[2] Providers of these services have also necessarily become directly implicated in the practical pursuit of the policy. This is partly because there is an insufficient repository of knowledge within purchasing authorities to cover the myriad of health 'specialties' which they purchase and partly because the process of needs assessment, at both the population and individual level, is inherently linked to clinical concepts and questions. Indeed, the process of accurately assessing and meeting the individual clinical needs of service users is one of

---

[1] The change of government in 1997 and/or further reorganisation of the NHS by way of the abolition of general practitioner fundholding and the replacement of the 'internal market' by a group commissioning approach (Department of Health, 1997) have not reduced the drive towards explicit priority-setting or needs assessment.
[2] Since the 1997 White Paper (Department of Health, 1997), it has been policy of the Labour government to abolish the internal market and so the term 'commissioning' rather than 'purchasing' seems increasingly to be more appropriate. Throughout this text, however, the two terms should be read as interchangeable since, in terms of needs assessment, the distinction is of little direct relevance.

the central tasks of service providers acting strictly within their own role. Hence, although formally it is specifically a commissioner function, needs assessment tends automatically, and properly, to become a joint activity.[3]

Needs assessment sits somewhat uncertainly between being seen as a practical means of improving service responses to patient need and a tightly defined and pursued research field. Such uncertainty gives rise, in turn, to important questions about the validity and reliability of the purchasing decisions that are made on the basis of only 'quick and dirty' assessments of need that lack scientific rigour, and about whether it is right to direct purchasing policy on such a basis. However, as will become apparent, 'scientific' needs assessment is a costly activity which, if pursued in a widespread fashion, would divert substantial resources away from the very patients whose needs are to be estimated. There is, therefore, an important 'cost-effectiveness' aspect to needs assessment which raises questions about whether the policy of 'purchasing based on needs assessment' is too expensive and ultimately even self-defeating, in terms of patient benefit; or, at least, whether it would be if it were pursued validly and reliably. The dilemma is, therefore, whether to adopt a cheap and potentially invalid and/or unreliable version of needs assessment, which will be at risk of allocating resources to patients inefficiently (in welfare terms) but which will divert few resources away from direct patient care, *or* whether to pursue valid and reliable, and therefore expensive, needs assessments which will allocate resources efficiently between patients but at the expense of a lower total budget for direct health care. The choice is therefore between pursuing welfare efficiency in the allocation of resources and maximising the aggregate level of service provision.

The foregoing dilemma is, of course, predicated on the assumption that needs assessment can be 'policy neutral' in a broader sense. That is, that the way in which it is constructed and carried out is not biased by tacit policy objectives, in particular by the definition of need adopted or by virtue of its chosen methods of inquiry. Even if not intended to be so, and however 'scientific' it is in its technical pursuit, if needs assessment is, in fact, biased in the way it is individually constructed then even scientific needs assessment cannot be seen as necessarily welfare efficient (see generally de Graaf, 1967). It is simply that, by contrast with unscientific needs assessment, its

---

[3] The reforms proposed in the 1997 White Paper (Department of Health, 1997) have formally abolished provider competition, further reinforcing commissioner–provider cooperation in needs assessment.

scientific cousin results in welfare inefficiency not via invalidity and unreliability but via inherent assumptions which underlie its operation.

Thus although, on the face of it, needs assessment is a logical and sensible policy basis to adopt in order to determine purchasing decisions, its operation is fraught with fundamental difficulties. In spite of this, however, even though health service researchers have also become involved in the field, there has been surprisingly little critical analysis of the practical and theoretical problems involved in assessing need. This book attempts to offer something to fill that gap. Although it is focused specifically on needs assessment for forensic mental health care, it may also infer a more general critique of needs assessment, going beyond the rather narrow field of needs assessment in relation to mentally disordered offenders (MDOs).

Mental health care has been given priority by governments in recent years, and since the early 1990s the 'needs' of MDOs have been highlighted for special attention. This dates particularly from the Reed report (DoH/Home Office, 1992), which became perceived as the 'blueprint' for the development of MDO services and which itself featured needs assessment as one of its central principles. However, this narrow field of needs assessment has very special aspects to it, arising out of necessary consideration of the welfare of others, in addition to that of patients. It also sits in a very particular public policy context. That context is worthy of some attention in its own right since, as already suggested, it is impossible to divorce the practice of needs assessment from underlying policy assumptions and thinking. Also, particular aspects of recent MDO policy clearly have direct and obvious implications specifically for needs assessment. Further, some more recent aspects of government policy towards some MDOs are inherently in conflict with the predominantly welfare approach of earlier government policy as epitomised and informed by the Reed report (see Chapter 8).

This chapter outlines, therefore, how the concept of needs assessment is woven through current health and social policy, as well as related legislation, initially in relation to general and mental health. It will then provide a descriptive and analytical framework for current government policy specifically regarding MDOs, with particular reference to needs assessment. All of this will be pursued in historical order but an attempt will be made both to draw out themes and to address issues that are inherent to the systems and issues under consideration. The bias towards an historical approach, which is pursued throughout the book, will allow us to provide a summary compendium of both individual reports and research projects, while not eschewing consideration of broad themes. These themes will be drawn together in the final chapter, in which the inherent linkage between (narrow) needs assessment and (broad) policy on MDOs will also be used to expand the discussion so as to incorporate a general consideration of MDO policy in the post-Reed era.

Needs assessment in general health and mental health policy

The central position given by recent governments to needs assessment can be traced back to various government publications which appeared in the late 1980s and early 1990s and which made explicit the importance of both 'need' and 'needs assessment'. These publications were concerned primarily with the delivery of community care and focused mainly on the organisation, resourcing and efficiency of the health and social services.

The Griffiths report (Griffiths, 1988) examined the effectiveness of use of public funds for community care. It recommended that local authorities should act primarily as purchasers of non-health care and that, in so doing, they should assess community care needs and then target resources so as to meet individual needs on the basis of local priorities. It also proposed that local authorities should work in collaboration with health authorities in order to assess health care needs and to deliver care packages, while maximising the use of the voluntary and private sectors so as to widen consumer choice and encourage efficiency. The following year, the White Paper *Caring for People* (DoH, 1989*a*) focused on reform of the organisation and funding of social care. It stated that the key component of community care should be "services that respond flexibly and sensitively to the needs of individuals and their carers ... and that concentrate on those with the greatest needs" (p. 5). Proper assessment of need was proposed as the cornerstone of high-quality care, and local authorities were directed to collaborate with health and other providers in the process of identifying and meeting individual needs. In the same year, the health service equivalent of *Caring for People*, *Working for Patients* (DoH, 1989*b*), formally gave health authorities the responsibility for identifying the health needs of their resident populations and for ensuring that those health needs were met. The importance of effective inter-agency collaboration was also re-emphasised. Both *Caring for People* and *Working for Patients* were then together expressed in the National Health Service and Community Care Act 1990. This introduced the public policy novelty of a purchaser–provider split and outlined the functions and legal responsibilities of local purchasing authorities. The Act also made it mandatory for local authorities to carry out individual needs assessments for community care services and to involve DHAs and other agencies in the process, wherever they might be involved in the delivery of care.

In the same year that the NHS and Community Care Act was passed, the government issued guidelines, in the form of the Care Programme Approach (CPA), specifically regarding community care for those mentally ill people being cared for by specialist psychiatric services (DoH, 1990). This has, of course, become the cornerstone of community mental health care. According to the DoH (1993*a*), the CPA was designed both to secure improvements in community services and to ensure that the mentally ill received community care (as opposed to hospital care) only if there were adequate health and social services available to meet their needs. In keeping with general health policy, the assessment of individual need was identified as central to the operation of the CPA. Health and local authorities were instructed to cooperate in order to ensure "systematic arrangements for assessing the health [and social] care needs of patients who could, potentially, be treated in the community". They were also given responsibility "for regularly reviewing the health [and social] care needs of those being treated in the community" (DoH, 1990).

The following year, the NHS Management Executive (1991) instructed DHAs to assess the needs of their resident populations and then to use those assessments to establish local purchasing priorities. Up until this stage, the DoH had not provided any practical guidelines about *how* to assess need. However, it now attempted to fill this gap. It provided a specific definition of 'need', which it suggested was "the ability to benefit from health care", and proposed a needs assessment strategy based primarily on an epidemiological approach (this model will be discussed in detail in Chapter 2). The NHS Management Executive also announced a programme of research reviews aimed at testing the feasibility of its needs assessment approach; one of these research reviews was to cover mental illness.

One year later, the government published its major White Paper *Health of the Nation* (DoH, 1992*a*). This stated that its policy targets could be met through the provision of high-quality services. These, in turn, could be achieved "by identifying and meeting the health needs of local populations and securing the most appropriate balance between health promotion, disease prevention, treatment, care and rehabilitation" (p. 14). Joint working between NHS purchasers was encouraged as a means both of identifying local targets and of integrating local services to meet specific needs, and joint purchasing between authorities within and outside the NHS was encouraged. Meanwhile, providers were instructed to reassess the services they provided and to confirm with purchasers and local people that they were meeting local needs and improving health. *Health of the Nation* also listed five key areas for action, one of which was mental illness. It went on to set targets both for the overall improvement of the health and social functioning of the mentally ill and for the reduction of suicide rates. It further identified MDOs as a particularly vulnerable group and warned that, if their health and social care needs were not recognised and met, they might slip into a vicious cycle of imprisonment, reoffending and deteriorating mental health. *Health of the Nation* supported the Home Office (1990*a*) policy (see below) of achieving the appropriate and rapid diversion of MDOs from the criminal justice system. It also emphasised the consequent need for inter-agency cooperation between health services, social services, the criminal justice system, and the private and voluntary sectors. It stated that strategic and related purchasing plans should include the necessary range of health and social services (both secure and non-secure) in order to respond to the 'special needs' of MDOs. The inclusion of MDOs in this general mental health policy document was mirrored in later documents (e.g. DoH, 1995). This serves to illustrate the priority given to MDOs in an era when, in a context of developing community care, the risk of violence by the mentally disordered was becoming a subject of major political concern.

In the same year (and indeed thereafter), a number of serious incidents involving psychiatric patients brought the government's care in the community policy to more highly focused media and political attention. Two cases in particular, those of Ben Silcock (a man suffering from schizophrenia who jumped into the lions' den at London Zoo) and Christopher Clunis (a man also suffering from schizophrenia who killed a stranger, Jonathan Zito, at Finsbury Park tube station) (Ritchie *et al*, 1994), focused public and political attention, in a highly publicised way, on the quality and safety of community care. The publication of the Reed report on health and social services for MDOs (DoH/Home Office, 1992) also occurred in 1992 (see below) and so the needs of violent mentally ill people like Christopher Clunis were especially prominent in the minds of both the government and the public. These cases thus provided the impetus for the government's 'ten-point plan' for community care for the mentally ill (DoH, 1993*b*). The plan included an outline of the government's intention to develop a new legal power of supervised discharge (subject to parliamentary approval), as well as its intention to issue fresh clinical guidance regarding the achievement of appropriate and safe discharge and after-care of psychiatric patients. The plan also announced the government's intention of introducing supervision registers for patients most at risk and in greatest need of service support. These were to be aimed at further targeting community resources where they were most 'needed', even though the government resisted the less publicly reassuring label 'priority registers'. The aim was thereby to reinforce the CPA.[4]

In January 1993, the government set up the Mental Health Task Force to promote and assist a more concerted, comprehensive and speedy implementation of its policies for mental health, with particular regard to the creation of more locally based and accessible services (Home Office/DoH, 1995). In the same year it published a *Health of the Nation* handbook (DoH, 1993c) which related specifically to the key area of mental illness. The handbook expressed concern that mental health services appeared fragmented and poorly coordinated, and that alliances between health and social services had not been developed to their full potential. It concentrated on providing practical advice to managers within the health and social services regarding the implementation of the changes necessary to achieve the targets in the mental illness key area. One of the principal themes it identified was "a systematic approach to needs assessment and review of current service provision" (p. 13). It recommended that managers should focus not only on the general mental health needs of the population but also on the needs specifically of MDOs, black and ethnic minority groups, women, the elderly, children and adolescents and other 'disenfranchised' groups (e.g. the homeless, lesbians and gay men). In terms of MDOs, the handbook encouraged local assessments of their needs and emphasised that this should include the need for secure hospital provision at all levels, as well as for non-secure provision. The importance of inter-agency working between health, social services and the criminal justice system was again emphasised. The handbook also recommended a minimum data set approach to assessing need and provision which, it was suggested, should include a socio-demographic profile of the local population and a profile of local service availability and capacity (including special hospitals, NHS and private medium-security and local low-security facilities). It further recommended that epidemiological data about the prevalence and incidence of mental illness should be extrapolated to local populations (while taking local socio-demographic and

---

[4] There was widespread resistance both to supervised discharge (Thompson, 1995; Eastman, 1995, 1997a) and to supervision registers (Caldicott, 1994). The subsequent guidance on discharge (NHS Executive, 1994a) was largely welcomed.

health factors into consideration). It also recommended that the assessment of need should include surveys of users in the local catchment area, focus groups and in-depth interviews, as well as process information, such as general practitioner (GP) referral patterns, GP morbidity surveys, GP and in-patient data by diagnosis. This advice incorporated, in fact, a number of the categories of needs assessment which we shall later delineate and explore in great detail.

The next year, the government issued its detailed clinical guidelines about discharge which it had promised in the ten-point plan (NHS Executive, 1994*a*). These guidelines grounded discharge decisions in the CPA, and hence in the assessment of need. Providers were particularly instructed to discharge patients only after they had conducted a thorough risk assessment. This, it was stated, should take place in the context of a "systematic assessment of health and social care needs (including accommodation) bearing in mind both immediate and longer term requirements ... [and] ... regular review of the patient's progress and of his or her health and social care needs". Information-sharing and inter-disciplinary and inter-agency working were encouraged, including (where consistent with confidentiality guidelines) close contact between the health and social services and the criminal justice system. Particular concern was expressed about discharges from special hospitals and medium-secure units in this regard.

The same guidance on discharge also required mental health providers to hold supervision registers, listing those patients considered to be most at risk to others or themselves (including by way of serious self-neglect). The government then issued separate guidelines about this later in the year (NHS Management Executive, 1994).[5] The discharge guidance, combined with the introduction of supervision registers, would, the government claimed, help to ensure proper working of the CPA and prevent people from 'falling through the net'. However, these guidelines about discharge were largely clinical in nature and would not, or should not, have been unfamiliar to providers (particularly psychiatrists), since they echoed many of the recommendations already made by the Royal College of Psychiatrists (1989) in its own guidelines issued five years earlier.

---

[5] As already described in footnote 4, supervision registers were the subject of fierce criticism by many, including the Royal College of Psychiatrists (Caldicott, 1994). Their use is still being researched, but there is some evidence to suggest that they are being applied very inconsistently geographically and, therefore, potentially in 'political' or 'defensive' fashions (Cohen & Eastman, 1996). This implies that it is unlikely that they are being applied in accordance with relative need.

The NHS Executive discharge guidelines also introduced requirements for the investigation of violent incidents perpetrated by psychiatric patients, with particular reference to the effective use of the CPA. It mandated an independent inquiry in all cases of homicide by psychiatric patients recently in touch with health and/ or social services. The remit of such inquiries was to be to examine at least: (a) the care the patient was receiving at the time of the incident, (b) the suitability of that care in view of the patient's history and assessed health and social needs, (c) the extent to which that care corresponded with statutory guidelines, relevant guidance from the DoH, and local operational policies, (d) the exercise of professional judgement, and (e) the adequacy of the care plan and its monitoring by the key worker (NHS Executive, 1994*a*). Again, the assessment of need was put forward as being central to the content of any inquiry, the assumption being that a valid assessment of the needs of the mentally ill would lay the foundation for the provision of high-quality services and reduced risk to the public. Indeed, inquiries which have followed the guidelines have tended explicitly to include an examination of the appropriateness of the care plan and care provided, viewed in the context of the patient's assessed health and social care needs (cf. Sheppard, 1996; see also Peay, 1996).

The Mental Health (Patients in the Community) Act 1995 enacted the government's promise in the ten-point plan to establish a 'supervised discharge order'.[6] This gave a power to mental health professionals to convey a discharged psychiatric patient back to some designated place for treatment, but no power of compulsory community treatment *per se* or of recall to hospital. However, arguably its most important aspect, certainly in terms of the CPA generally, was to place a legal obligation on the clinicians responsible for the patient's care to provide the services described in the order as needed and to require certain responses on the part of (particularly) the 'supervisor', should the patient renege on his or her receipt of the care package. Hence, response to need became, for patients on 'supervised discharge', legally sanctioned (Eastman, 1997*a*). This was a novelty. As to whether there was, in reality, any principle of reciprocity enshrined in the 1995 Act which ensured that patients whose civil liberties were restricted by supervised discharge had a right to the resources they needed, the DoH argued that there was (Calman, 1995), but others were more sceptical (Eastman, 1995).

---

[6] This power was like the supervision registers, resisted by the Royal College (Thompson, 1995) and many others (see Eastman, 1997*a*).

The government's close attention to mental illness was again reflected in 1995, when another *Health of the Nation* document, entitled *Building Bridges*, was published (DoH, 1995). *Building Bridges* stated that specialist mental health services should "target their resources and efforts first and foremost on severely mentally ill people" (p. 8) and that this policy should be pursued on the basis of the assessment of individual need. This should then be reflected in a tiered approach to the CPA. The tiered approach, the DoH argued, would help to target resources on the most severely mentally ill but would also ensure that those with 'lesser needs' would still receive the basic elements of the CPA. In *Building Bridges*, the DoH acknowledged the difficulties involved in defining 'severe mental illness' and provided a 'framework definition' which focused on three key elements, namely, disability, diagnosis and duration, with the addition of two further dimensions, safety and the need for informal or formal care. It also stated, however, that "local health and social services will wish to agree with other agencies their own operational definitions, in line with local needs and priorities, consistent with this framework definition" (p. 13). Overall, *Building Bridges* promoted close and effective inter-agency working aimed at ensuring well coordinated and flexible service delivery capable of responding to changing needs over time. It stated that "such co-ordinated care will only come about when patients receive a detailed needs assessment, a comprehensive care plan, and have their care monitored and reviewed on a regular base ... these elements represent the core of the Care Programme Approach" (p. 14). However, the mechanisms for identifying need were explicitly left to local teams to determine. As in other *Health of the Nation* documents (DoH, 1992*a*, 1993*c*), MDOs were again singled out for special mention and inter-agency working in relation to this group was reiterated, especially cooperation between health, social services and criminal justice agencies (e.g. police, courts, probation, prison). This was seen as one way to ensure that the needs of MDOs were taken properly into account, albeit the notion of needs assessment across agencies which included those in the criminal justice system was inherently ethically controversial.

The next year, another *Health of the Nation* document, *The Spectrum of Care* (DoH, 1996), summarised the range of care which should be offered to the mentally ill at a local level. It pointed out that some mental health services still appeared to be poorly coordinated and that some providers were not making full use of the CPA (and, by implication, were not assessing need). It emphasised that local purchasers could "find solutions" to meeting local mental health needs by coordinating planning with all local service providers, by offering a flexible approach to meeting needs, and by adopting a clear definition of their responsibilities. *Spectrum of Care* offered a definition of mental health problems ranging from the mild to the severe. It defined a list of needs that should be taken into consideration, including the need for services to be available when required and for services to be suitable for the needs of both patients and the general community. The latter had obvious implications for MDOs, the boundaries of whose needs tended automatically to expand in order to incorporate the benefit of their potential victims.

Needs assessment for MDOs

The preceding discussion provides a general background against which to examine policies regarding needs assessment specifically for MDOs. Indeed, the high priority given to MDOs in recent years by the government has meant that policy documents relating to general mental health have frequently singled out MDOs for special mention. Public (and, it seems, sometimes even government) perception of community mental health care has also become profoundly intertwined with questions of public safety. However, in parallel with the general policy developments outlined above, there have been a number of government publications aimed specifically at addressing the service needs of MDOs. This is epitomised by the Reed report (DoH/Home Office, 1992), still the current blueprint for the development and operation of MDO services in the UK. However, the Reed report was not the first to focus specifically on the needs of MDOs, and many of its recommendations were not new. Indeed, the needs of MDOs have long been a cause of specific public and professional concern, and many issues currently debated, as well as problems experienced, can be traced back at least into the nineteenth century (Eastman, 1993). Hence, in 1830, John Connolly wrote:

"The present regulations for the protection of the insane are at once inefficient for the protection of the insane themselves, and dangerous to the public; that it results from them, that some are improperly confined, and others improperly at large; that whilst the eccentric are endangered, those actually mad are often allowed a dangerous liberty; in that the public are dissatisfied, and medical men are harassed and perplexed." (Cited in Greenland, 1978, p. 211)

This said, the political profile of MDOs and the extent of any action taken to address the problems they pose both to themselves and to society has tended to fluctuate over time. Indeed, the Reed report and its service consequences represent a 'new wave' of government and public interest in MDOs and their needs. A 'previous wave' of interest (arising perhaps rather more out of government than public concern) culminated in the Butler and Glancy reports of the mid-1970s (Home Office/DoH and Social Security, 1975; DoH and Social Security, 1974a). Hence, before outlining the contents of the 'new wave', it is necessary to place them in their historical context by examining in some detail that pre-Reed era. This will help to illustrate the enduring nature of many of the concerns currently expressed about MDOs and about services for them. It will also highlight the difficulties involved in converting policy guidelines into practice.

Pre-Reed policy and service developments

The origins of the Butler and Glancy reports lie in broad changes to the pattern of general mental health care provision dating back to about the mid-1950s. The deinstitutionalisation movement, as well as pressure for a stronger civil rights approach to mental health law and a wish to destigmatise and 'normalise' psychiatric patients, resulted in open-door policies and, to a degree, closure of psychiatric hospitals. This presaged the much more rapid closure programme in the 1980s and 1990s, which was directly associated with the implementation of the policy of care in the community. Both the 'open-door' policy and the gradual closure of psychiatric hospitals in favour of community care eventually led to a 'security gap' between special hospitals and local (often wholly unlocked) psychiatric facilities. This gap was first recognised as early as the mid-1950s and led the Percy report (Royal Commission on the Law Relating to Mental Illness and Mental Deficiency, 1957) to recommend that secure psychiatric facilities should be provided in order to fill it. The recommendation was repeated in 1961 by a working party looking at the special hospitals, which produced the Emery report (Ministry of Health, 1961), and again in 1971 (DoH and Social Security, 1971). However, no secure units were established (Parker, 1985). Additional pressure to establish secure NHS psychiatric facilities also came from the Home Office, alongside concern that there should be better psychiatric provision within the prison service itself (Parker, 1985). The Gwynne report (Home Office, 1964), which commented on the organisation of the Prison Medical Service, recognised the need for specialist psychiatric input to prisons and suggested closer links between the Prison Medical Service and the NHS. It also recommended that consultant forensic psychiatrist posts be established and jointly funded by the Home Office and the NHS. Indeed, between 1966 and 1975 seven such posts were established in England, although the pattern of their work varied considerably and their success was limited (Snowden, 1990).

Despite the pressure from a number of sources to develop secure services, there was general inertia and disinterest (Snowden, 1990) and well-recognised need largely went unmet. Indeed, Parker (1985) argued that it required a politically high-profile case in order for adequate attention to be focused on the issue of security needs. In this regard, the case of the poisoner Graham Young is of particular historical note.[7] Young reoffended while on conditional discharge from Broadmoor Hospital, and thereby provided the political impetus for the setting up of the Butler Committee (Snowden, 1990). The terms of reference of this committee were:

(a) to consider to what extent and on what criteria the law should recognise mental disorder or abnormality in those accused of a criminal offence as a factor affecting their liability to be tried or convicted, and their disposal;

(b) to consider what, if any, changes are necessary in the powers, procedure and facilities relating to the provision of appropriate treatment, in prison, hospital or the community, for offenders suffering from mental disorder or abnormality, and to their discharge and after-care; and to make recommendations (Home Office/DoH and Social Security, 1975, p. 1).

The interim Butler report (Home Office/DoH and Social Security, 1974), like its predecessor reports, recognised that the 'open-door' policy embraced by NHS psychiatric hospitals had created a 'yawning gap' between 'non-secure' NHS hospitals and the special hospitals. It therefore recommended that 2000 medium-security places be established urgently to fill the gap. This, it claimed, would encourage a more fluid system both within the health service and between the health service and the criminal justice system. It would therefore prevent both mentally abnormal offenders from being over-contained within the special hospital system and the inappropriate containment of mentally abnormal offenders in prisons, as well as facilitating the diversion to mental health care of mentally abnormal offenders from the criminal justice system. However, the interim Butler report also encouraged local services to maintain their capacity to deal with difficult patients and warned against the potential silting-up of medium-security beds with difficult long-stay patients, that is, 'bed-

---

[7] The parallel with the much later case of Christopher Clunis, and his impact on community service provision and operation, is both stark and politically instructive.

blocking'. Due to the urgency of the situation, the establishment of temporary interim secure units was recommended pending the establishment of permanent units.

The DoH and Social Security (1974*b*) only partly accepted the Butler report's recommendations, in that it confirmed capital funding for 1000 regional secure unit (RSU) beds, with the potential for increasing this to 2000 beds dependent upon resources and 'local requirements' (for which read, in modern terminology, 'need'). However, it was only in January 1976, and arising out of the Glancy report (DoH and Social Security, 1974*a*) (see below), that the government attempted further to encourage the development of RSUs. It provided both capital funding for building RSUs, also known as medium-secure units, and an annual special revenue allocation, based upon the estimated need of 20 beds per million (Bluglass, 1985).

One year after the interim report, the final version of the Butler report (Home Office/DoH and Social Security, 1975) was published. It expressed concern that, despite earlier recommendations, little progress had so far been made in establishing interim (or permanent) medium-secure units and that some regional health authorities (RHAs) appeared to have *no intention* of establishing such units. The final Butler report also addressed other issues relating to the needs of mentally abnormal offenders. It stated that the overriding concern should be to provide the best possible treatment for the patient's mental disorder, with proper regard for the requirements of public safety. It further stated that patients should have full access to treatment in the location best suited to their needs, preferably as close to their home as possible. It also identified the need for better coordination between the agencies involved with the treatment of mentally abnormal offenders, including social services, the Probation Service and the Prison Medical Service. The report recommended that forensic psychiatric services, based in medium-secure units within all the RHAs, should be fully integrated with local psychiatric services and should also play a key role in facilitating inter-agency working. It also identified a need for "vigorous and substantial up-grading of the medical resources in the prisons ... including specialised psychiatric training" (p. 283). Further, it noted a need for longer-term care for single homeless people and for the provision of social support and 'after-care' in hostels, particularly for 'socially inadequate' mentally abnormal offenders. All of these recommendations were to be echoed in the Reed report (DoH/Home Office, 1992) nearly 20 years later (see below).

In 1974, a working party of the DoH and Social Security was instructed to review the existing guidance on security within NHS psychiatric hospitals and to make recommendations on the present and future need for security (Snowden, 1990). The working party, led by Glancy, did its work in parallel with the Butler Committee. It also identified the need for medium security and the Glancy report (DoH and Social Security, 1974*a*) noted that despite the 'open-door' policy of NHS psychiatric hospitals, many were over-containing the majority of their patients in order to cater for a small minority who did require security. All regional hospital boards were surveyed to determine "how many patients were considered to present such difficult behaviour problems that they could not be managed in an ordinary psychiatric ward". Interestingly, this inferred a criterion for admission to medium-security facilities based not on patient characteristics *per se* but on service failure at a lower level of care (Eastman & Bellamy, 1998). A total of 1258 patients were identified. The Glancy report stated that "without believing that the figures can be regarded as in any sense absolute ... the number who in 1970 were in NHS psychiatric hospitals, and required treatment in secure accommodation, lies somewhere around 1000 patients" (i.e. 20 beds per million population) (p. 7). However, the Glancy report described this figure as having a "flimsy statistical base" and warned that the survey results were "so varied and inconsistent that it is difficult to make use of them as a reliable base for planning" (p. 7). Such disparities, it claimed, could be explained by varied interpretations of the survey question and diverse thresholds for 'difficult behaviour problems', both within and between hospitals and regions. Indeed, it seems likely that such definitional problems persist in current NHS and researcher thinking (see Chapter 2). The Glancy report also noted that the accuracy of its 1000-bed estimate of need could be affected by the development of psychiatric facilities at a district level, advances in the treatment and management of difficult patients, and by potential additional demand from "persons presently in special hospitals, prisons, in care or the community". The estimate also took no account, of course, of differential regional psychiatric morbidity and criminality by geographical area. However, the Glancy report did recommend that RHAs and the DoH and Social Security should together review the ability of new secure services to meet emerging demand, and expand secure services accordingly. It also warned, as did the Butler report, against the potential silting-up of NHS hospitals with difficult patients and suggested that this might result in (further) reduced tolerance of such patients within mainstream services, a concern echoed later by one of the regional leaders of service development (Gallwey, 1990).

Despite the Butler and Glancy recommendations, there were still considerable delays in developing and opening medium-secure units, and the overall development of RSUs was patchy and idiosyn-cratic (Snowden, 1983, 1985; Parker, 1985, Bluglass, 1985; Grounds *et al*, 1993). In fact, the development of both forensic psychiatry services generally, and of medium-secure units in particular, depended largely on local 'product champions' (Stocking, 1985), usually forensic psychiatrists who lobbied for the establishment of specialist forensic psychiatric services. The nature of forensic psychi-atric services that were established varied, therefore, according to the service philosophy of the local 'product champion', often widely and even sometimes so as to challenge the core Butler/Glancy RSU model (e.g. see Gallwey, 1990). Service development was also either helped or hindered by 'gatekeepers' (e.g. DHAs) (Stocking, 1985). Such 'gatekeepers' were in a position to help or to hinder the acceptance of any proposed new service, which was always hindered by 'blockers' (Stocking, 1985) who were likely to be affected directly by a change of their job, work philosophy or environment. The differential rate of development of RSUs across the country was largely determined therefore by local politics, with 'blockers', such as local communities and local branches of health unions, having a major impact on whether and where RSUs were developed (Snowden, 1985; Eastman, 1993). Indeed, frequently, RHAs, the 'gatekeepers' to which the supposedly 'ring-fenced' revenue was allocated by the DoH and Social Security, applied the funds to other mental health services (sometimes, but not always, under some very broad defini-tion of the word 'forensic'), or even to other types of medical service entirely (Bluglass, 1978; Parker, 1985). This tended to confirm Scott's (1970, 1974) argument that local psychiatric services would never substantially accept difficult mentally disordered patients and that the money was more likely to be used effectively if applied to the improvement of mental health care within prisons.

Some six years after the Butler and Glancy recommendations, the Royal College of Psychiatrists (1980) reviewed the progress that had been made in establishing secure facilities for psychiatric patients, and also considered the role of security across the complete spectrum of psychiatric care. It identified the slow and varied progress of RSU development across regions and also recognised that a diverse range of services (including secure treatment units in psychiatric hospitals, local sub-regional units, and regional units) was required in order to meet the security and intensive treatment needs of many different categories of patient. It stated further that the proper development of such services would depend on local needs and difficulties and on existing resources. The College also recommended that secure services at every level should be integrated with general and forensic psychiatric services and community facilities, and that these should be closely linked with the special hospitals, social services, the Probation Service and the Prison Medical Service. The overall aim should be one of facilitating the smooth movement of patients across the various links in the chain of security and care. The College went on to repeat the Butler report recommendation that patients should be admitted to secure units on the basis of behaviour, treatability and need for care, rather than on the basis of psychiatric diagnosis or legal classification. The College report further recognised that some patients requiring security would not be offenders in the strict legal sense of having been convicted. It suggested that "such patients would be those identified as creating continual difficulty in management and with a potential to respond to treatment facilities offered by special units" (p. 6). This broader definition was reflected later in the Reed report (see generally Chapter 2 concerning definition of the term 'mentally disordered offender'). Specifically as regards levels of need for secure beds, the College recognised the short-comings of previous estimates of need and recommended urgent research, including epidemiological work. However, there was no response from the DoH and Social Security to these recommendations, beyond that already initiated by the Butler and Glancy reports. It was only much later that the need for medium-security beds, as well as other recommendations from the Royal College of Psychiatrists (1980), were, again, addressed in the Reed report (DoH/Home Office, 1992) (see below).

The Reed report and its aftermath

It was not only the assessment of need that was lacking in sophistication in the practical development of services for MDOs after the Butler and Glancy reports. The medium-security services themselves were only crudely defined. Indeed, as already described, the service model varied greatly between regions. Also, many services were ring-fenced not only and most obviously in terms of their funding but effectively also often in their operation. Hence, many RSUs tended to occupy, clinically, a discrete position between general mental health and high-security mental health facilities and to exhibit little integration or direct connection with them (Eastman, 1993). As one practical result, patients could still fall through service gaps; for example, a patient might be perceived as too difficult to manage in an open ward and yet insufficiently dangerous for an RSU. If the relevant general mental health service possessed no locked ward then 'placement stalemate' occurred. In like manner, if patients were deemed insufficiently dangerous to require a special hospital bed, because they were not a "grave and immediate danger to the public" – an example of a patient-based rather than service-based access criterion (Eastman & Bellamy, 1998) – but would need (medium-security) treatment beyond the 18 months to two years written into the service definition of RSUs, then, again, they would fall between services. This would often occur to the puzzlement of judges wishing to make hospital orders under Section 37 of the Mental Health Act for defendants clearly suffering from severe mental disorder warranting treatment. In both examples, there is an evident 'service gap' measured against 'patient need'. This serves to emphasise the importance of ensuring that service definitions and operational policies at different security levels are established in an interlocking fashion, so as to achieve 'seamless' operation of services which, in security terms, are adjacent to one another (Eastman & Bellamy, 1998).

It was Home Office circular 66/90 (Home Office, 1990a) which began, or at least represented the beginning of, the 'new wave' of specific government interest in the treatment and security needs of MDOs. It emphasised that mentally disordered individuals in contact with the criminal justice system should receive care from health and social services. It stated that arrangements should be made between all agencies concerned to ensure the immediate diversion of mentally disordered individuals from the criminal justice system to appropriate mental health or social services whenever that was in the public interest. At the same time, concerns were raised about the high suicide rate among prisoners (Home Office, 1990b) and a group of voluntary organisations petitioned the Home Secretary to improve conditions for mentally vulnerable prisoners (Home Office, 1991). The Woolf report (Home Office, 1991) examined the 1990 prison disturbances in England and Wales, and itself made a number of recommendations relevant to MDOs. It supported circular 66/90 and again highlighted the shortfall in medium-security beds and in other psychiatric and social services required for successful diversion.

Also in 1990, the NHS Management Executive (1990) instructed RHAs, DHAs and the Special Hospital Services Authority together to give special attention to services for MDOs and difficult-to-manage patients. The NHS Management Executive recognised the difficulties involved in predicting demand for services (distinguished, of course, from 'need' – see Chapter 2). It therefore instructed purchasing authorities to maintain at least the current capacity of providers to meet the treatment needs of MDOs and difficult-to-manage patients (specifically referrals from prisons, courts and special hospitals) after April 1991. Purchasing authorities were also specifically instructed to arrange adequate medium-security provision in the interests of public safety.

Later that same year, DoH and Home Office ministers established the Review of Health and Social Services for Mentally Disordered Offenders and Others Requiring Similar Services, chaired by Dr John Reed. At least part of the driving force behind establishing the review was the need for a response to the somewhat narrow operation of some of the RSU services which had been developed after the Butler and Glancy reports, including lack of integration with general and special hospital psychiatric services. The Reed Committee therefore explicitly emphasised the widening of its field of view to include *all* MDOs, that is, including those requiring only general mental health services. Indeed, by including in the group of patients they considered, beyond MDOs *per se*, 'others requiring similar services', the Committee clearly and explicitly removed any requirement even for specialist forensic services to be directed solely at those who were, or had recently been, in contact with the criminal justice system. Further, the Committee addressed more energetically than had Butler and Glancy the issue of integration of different services, emphasising a policy of smoothing the passage of MDOs ('and others requiring similar services') between elements of (ideally) a unified and seamless 'pyramid' (our term) of secure and non-secure in-patient, and also out-patient, services. It also specifically addressed mechanisms for smoothing and making more efficient the transfer of MDOs from elements of the criminal justice system to elements of the mental health system, the most visible bridge between the two systems being court diversion schemes. These represent the health system 'going into' the criminal justice system in order to 'find' one example of MDOs needing mental health care. They therefore also represent individual clinical needs assessment (see particularly Chapter 3). Surveys of prison populations, also described later in this book (in Chapter 3), represent aggregate needs assessments conducted within the criminal justice system in a similar vein. Hence, both individual and aggregate needs assessment can be conducted either between elements of the mental health system or between that system and the criminal justice system.

The specific terms of reference of the Reed Committee were: (a) to review English health and social services for MDOs and others requiring similar services, (b) to determine the necessity for change in the current level, pattern or operation of services, and (c) to identify ways of promoting these changes. The review had to take into account: (a) the effects of the internal market, (b) the government's proposals for community care for the mentally ill, (c) recommendations of recent reports relevant to the Prison Medical Service (e.g. the Woolf report), (d) service developments and potential improvements, and (e) relevant research studies. Given that the assessment of need was embedded within its terms of reference, the Reed Committee focused specifically on the spectrum of care necessary to meet the varied needs of MDOs. It also examined the mechanisms required to estimate the number of MDOs in need of specialist services and/or diversion from the criminal justice system (DoH/Home Office, 1992).

Three advisory groups examined separately services provided in the community, hospitals and prisons (DoH/Home Office, 1993*a*). They concluded that medium- and low-security provision was inadequate to meet both existing and projected need, and estimated a national need for at least 1500 medium-security beds; although they emphasised that local provision should always be based on local needs assessment and subject to future assessment. It is unclear quite how the national average figure of 1500 beds was arrived at, although it is perhaps noteworthy that it sits exactly at the mid-point between the earlier Butler and Glancy estimates. The advisory groups also identified a need to diversify medium-security provision so as both to take into account the needs of certain 'special groups' (see below) and to offer medium-security provision beyond the generally accepted 18–24-month limit. Further, the report identified short-comings in the availability of information on the current level of services for MDOs, particularly for MDOs outside of specialist or secure provision and those inappropriately placed in prison or elsewhere. Not only was it not known across the country how many beds of various types were needed, it was not even known how many beds currently existed.

A second tranche of two advisory groups (finance, staffing and training; academic and research development) carried forward the framework established by the first three groups and looked at the resource implications of their proposals (DoH/Home Office, 1993*b*, 1993*c*).

Special working parties were also established to examine issues relating to 'special needs' groups. One such working party examined the need for services for people with brain injury, hearing impairment, drug and alcohol misusers, sex offenders with mental health care needs, potential suicides, children and adolescents, elderly people, and women (DoH/Home Office, 1993*d*). Another working party focused on services for MDOs with learning disabilities and autism (DoH/ Home Office, 1994*a*). Both recommended that agencies should adopt a 'positive' and 'non-prejudicial' attitude to identifying and meeting the 'special needs' of these MDOs, and that services must be flexible enough to respond appropriately to individual needs. They also emphasised that a key requirement was to ensure effective links across all services and agencies involved with 'special needs' groups. A further advisory group, on race, gender and equal opportunities, endorsed a proactive approach to equal opportunities within all agencies dealing with MDOs (DoH/Home Office, 1994*b*). It also recommended that service development and professional training should explicitly address racial and cultural issues, and should encourage ethnic minority involvement in service development and provision, as well as in professional training and research.

In light of the reports of the various advisory groups, government ministers announced a large increase in the capital allocation for RSUs for the financial year 1992/93 (DoH, 1992*b*). As regards existing services, since the purchaser–provider split had created some uncertainty about what would be the future of services for MDOs, the Reed Committee recommended a 'steady-state' policy. Hence, nine months before its final summary report was published, the DoH extended the length of its previously implemented steady-state policy (NHS Management Executive, 1992*a*). The intention of this was to ensure a stable base from which to develop MDO services following publication of the Reed report (DoH/Home Office, 1992). The instructions stipulated that RSUs and associated services should be maintained at least at their 1990/91 levels, including for patients with 'special needs' such as mentally disordered adolescents and those with learning disabilities or personality disorders. The circular reiterated the importance of diversion from the criminal justice system and the consequent need for joint working between the NHS, local authorities and other agencies. It also instructed RHAs to ensure adequate local facilities specifically for patients admitted from special hospitals and from the criminal justice system.

While the Reed review was still under way, the DoH also instructed regional directors of public health to assess the needs of their resident populations for special hospital, medium-security and local secure provision. Health authorities were directed to time this such that the information would be available just before the end of the Reed review and therefore available to inform its final recommendations (NHS Management Executive, 1992*b*). RHAs were instructed to carry out the exercise in conjunction with other relevant agencies and, in addition to the mentally ill, other 'special needs' groups (those MDOs with learning disability, psychopathic disorder, and those requiring longer-term treatment) were singled out for particular attention. The broader aims of this exercise were to enhance local planning and coordination of services across agencies, to foster and encourage local purchasing responsibility for special hospital and RSU patients, and to switch the emphasis from nationally set targets for medium-security beds to an approach based on local population needs (Jones & Dean, 1992). The *Final Summary Report* of the Reed review (DoH/Home Office, 1992) recommended that

this exercise should be repeated in future, with necessary adapta-
tions, and that it should be broadened to cover a wider range of
services; indeed, this recommendation was adopted in 1993 (NHS
Management Executive, 1993*a*) (see below).

While the Reed review was under way, a number of violent deaths
caused by discharged psychiatric patients (cf. Sheppard, 1996) raised
concerns about the safe application of the care in the community
policy and specifically about MDOs. As one consequence, the
government also announced that the Royal College of Psychiatrists
would conduct a confidential inquiry on behalf of the DoH into
homicides and similar incidents by any psychiatric patients cared
for or recently discharged by specialist psychiatric services (DoH,
1991). The rationale of the inquiry was that lessons might be learned
from such incidents so as to prevent or reduce their recurrence. In
establishing the inquiry the Secretary of State for Health laid
particular emphasis upon the role and importance of the CPA in
accurately identifying and meeting the specific needs of the mentally
ill, especially those at risk of committing harmful acts. The assumption was that such tragedies could be prevented if "the specific needs
of each mentally ill person are accurately identified and ... also met"
(DoH, 1991). The remit of the resulting Confidential Inquiry was
later extended to include suicides by the mentally ill. However, this
was done only at the request of the chairperson of the Steering
Committee (Steering Committee of the Confidential Inquiry into
Homicides and Suicides by Mentally Ill People, 1996).

While the Reed review was progressing, attention was also focused
on the special hospitals. In 1992, the *Report of the Committee of Inquiry
into Complaints about Ashworth Hospital* (Blom-Cooper *et al*, 1992) and
the *Report of the Committee of Inquiry into the Death in Broadmoor Hospital
of Orville Blackwood* (Special Hospital Service Authority, 1993) raised
concerns about the treatment of MDOs in special hospitals. Although
outside the remit of the Ashworth Inquiry, its chairperson, Louis
Blom-Cooper QC, wrote a letter to the Secretary of State for Health
alongside the report, questioning whether secure hospitals as large
as the British special hospitals were capable of managerial control
so as to provide high-quality care. This raised fundamental questions
about the future of the special hospitals. The more recent inquiry
into Ashworth, the Fallon Inquiry, has again brought into question
the ability of special hospitals to respond to patient (and public)
need with high-quality, and even secure, care (Fallon *et al*, 1999).

The *Final Summary Report* of the Reed review was published in 1992.
As already emphasised, it is noteworthy that many of its recom-
mendations echoed those made in the Butler and Glancy reports.
It proposed a set of guiding principles for service provision for

MDOs. Significantly, the assessment of need featured in the first principle. The principles were:

(a) MDOs should be cared for "with regard to the quality of care and proper attention to the needs of individuals" (p. 7) to ensure that patients receive the level and type of care they require.
(b) MDOs should be cared for in the community whenever possible, rather than in institutional settings.
(c) MDOs should be contained under conditions of security no greater than is justified by the degree of danger they present to themselves or others.
(d) MDOs should be contained in such a way so as to maximise rehabilitation and their chances of sustaining an independent life.
(e) MDOs should be contained as near to their homes and families as possible.

The *Final Summary Report* stated explicitly that the starting point for determining future service patterns should be regular needs assessments carried out on a multi-agency basis. It also endorsed government policy regarding diversion from the criminal justice system, although acknowledging the difficulties involved in converting policy into practice. It concluded that the majority of MDOs would require in-patient or out-patient treatment by general mental health or learning disability services, rather than by specialist services. In this recognition its focus of attention was therefore much broader than the service developments which followed the Butler and Glancy reports. It therefore suggested that multi-agency planning and resourcing of general services would have to take proper account of the needs of MDOs, in particular those diverted from the criminal justice system. The *Final Summary Report* also recommended a seamless service for MDOs, whereby they could move between and within services without financial or other hindrance and according to their treatment and security needs.

In August 1993, the DoH called for a repetition of the 1992 national needs assessment exercise (NHS Management Executive, 1993*a*) and set a deadline in October the same year. Sections were added to the 1992 exercise to include the needs of prisoners and adolescents, as well as sections addressing requirements for medical staffing. Unfortunately, the data obtained from this exercise were never fully analysed because DoH resources were not available so to do (personal communication, DoH, April 1997). Responses also varied in form and quality so widely that it was questioned whether further repetition of the exercise would be worthwhile. Consequently, national needs assessments coordinated by the DoH were abandoned (personal communication, DoH, June 1994). By way of justification, the DoH indicated that it believed that communication between RHAs and local purchasers had developed sufficiently to make such centrally led assessments of need unnecessary (again, personal communication, DoH, April, 1997). However, the experience of highly variable needs assessment performance by RHAs and districts was hardly encouraging of such a belief. It seemed likely that needs assessment would be pursued less rather than more effectively and vigorously by districts in the absence of central direction or pressure.

Also in 1993, NHS authorities were instructed to work with local authorities and criminal justice agencies in order to develop strategic and purchasing plans based on the principles embodied in the Reed report (NHS Management Executive, 1993*b*). The mental health care needs of transferred and discharged prisoners were singled out for special attention, and DHAs were also instructed that patients no longer in need of high security should be transferred to alternative care within six months.

The need for further work specifically on psychopathic disorder was identified by the Reed Committee, and this resulted in the establishment of the Working Group on Psychopathic Disorder (DoH/Home Office, 1994*c*). Aside from some limited service and research recommendations, an important legal recommendation of this group was the creation of a 'hybrid order' (essentially combining a hospital order with a penal tariff) for the purposes of sentencing in criminal courts. This was designed to take account of uncertainty about the treatability of many psychopaths and, therefore, about the type of individual health need they represented, or indeed whether they had any health need at all. The latter was directly reflected in the criterion that the Working Group recommended should be utilised for the making of such an order (by comparison with a hospital order), namely 'uncertain treatability'. In a very substantially altered form, the hybrid order was proposed in a 1996 discussion paper on sentencing (Home Office, 1996), and passed into law within the Crime (Sentences) Act 1997. The new 'hospital and limitation direction' (as it is called in the Act) became legally effective on 1 October 1997 in relation to psychopaths. Ministers were given the power to extend its application to the mentally ill and mentally impaired (in Scotland it was made immediately available for all three categories of disorder). The order is likely to be used by sentencers, however, on the criteria of 'culpability' and 'public protection' rather than 'uncertain treatability' (Eastman & Peay, 1998). The 'hospital and limitation direction' has been the subject of heavy criticism (Eastman, 1996a, 1997a; Royal College of Psychiatrists, 1996), including via the combined opposition of the Royal College of Psychiatrists, the Law Society and the mental health charity MIND. The same Act also extends the mandatory life sentence (currently restricted to defendants convicted of murder) to all defendants convicted of a second 'serious offence' in a way that can include any mentally disordered defendant.

The two provisions of the Crime (Sentences) Act 1997 relevant to MDOs, that is, the 'hospital and limitation direction' and the extension of the mandatory life sentence, could have profound implications in relation to the defined 'need' for services for MDOs. First, detention in hospital of a patient who, from a joint health and risk perspective, is ready to move to the community solely in order to complete a tariff, does not represent a 'health need' (Eastman, 1996a). Indeed, it is hard to see why a NHS purchaser should attach any priority at all to such a 'prisoner-patient' who merely has to be held for reasons of punishment. Second, it seems likely that, over time, significant numbers of hospital directions will be made in preference to hospital orders. This will allow judges apparently to maximise public safety while also having regard to the welfare of the MDOs. If the order is extended to the mentally ill and impaired in England and Wales, such orders will likely result in detention in hospital for longer periods than would apply under hospital orders. This will increase the 'need' (or rather the 'demand', since there would be no 'health need') for secure beds, particularly high- and medium-security beds (Eastman, 1996a).

The implications of the Crime (Sentences) Act 1997 extend, in fact, far beyond the specific need implications just considered. The Act involves a substantial shift, at least for some MDOs, away from a centuries old welfare approach to sentencing to a predominantly justice approach. It is not even correct to call it an approach that 'hybrid-ises' welfare and justice, since justice, in the form of the persisting tariff, always ultimately trumps welfare. Hence, the Act represents a partial challenge to the primacy of the welfare approach embodied in the policy line represented by Butler, Glancy and, especially, Reed. Albeit that MDOs made the subject of hospital directions will still be placed in a (secure) hospital, the custodial aspect of such placement will necessarily be emphasised at the expense of the therapeutic aspect. Put in 'need' terms, clinical staff will have to decide whether to send patients on to prison to complete their sentences when they no longer need hospital care (by comparison, for example, with community care), or whether to maintain them, to their comparative advantage in mental health terms, in hospital care which they do not 'need'. More broadly, an increasingly justice-based sentencing policy may open up again the debate about whether MDOs should be cared for in hospital, as it has been public policy for more than 30 years that they should be so, or in hospital wings of prisons. This debate will be fuelled if the present policy of keeping separate DoH and Home Office budgets for MDOs persists, and if longstanding NHS pressure to encourage the Home Office to send not only patients but their cost from prison to hospital continues to fall on deaf ministerial ears.

Another special report of the Reed Committee was also produced by the Working Group on High Security. This examined the future specifically of the special hospitals (DoH/Home Office, 1994d). Its main recommendation was the disbandment of the Special Hospital Services Authority as a provider body and the devolution of purchasing of special hospital services to DHAs. In response, the then Under-Secretary of State for Health announced changes in the organisation and funding of high-security psychiatric services (i.e. special hospitals) (NHS Executive, 1995a), although falling far short of devolution to DHAs. The High Security Psychiatric Services Commissioning Board (HSPSCB) was established within the NHS Executive to commission high-security services, and three new special health authorities were established to manage the special hospitals.[8] The aim of this reorganisation was to separate responsibility for commissioning and provision of high-security services in line with the NHS internal market. There was also an intention to integrate high-security services more closely with mainstream mental health services (NHS Executive, 1995a). More recent Labour government policy on the future organisation of all health care has transferred from central responsibility the purchasing of special hospital care to the new regional specialist commissioning groups. Although DHAs clearly have a role in relation to such commissioning, it seems likely to be limited. Indeed, the joining together of the commissioning of high- and medium-security services could lessen their influence overall since, in the context of the previous 'internal market', many had exerted very direct control over commisionning, albeit sometimes within consortia.

The future of the special hospitals and the needs of MDOs who require high security is again in the spotlight as a result of the Fallon Inquiry (Fallon *et al*, 1999). This was an inquiry specifically into

---

[8] The Board was transformed into a Commissioning Team in April 1999, in conjunction with the introduction of Regional Specialist Commissioning.

the personality disorder unit at Ashworth Hospital, concerning allegations of imported pornography, child abuse and lack of adequate staff control. However, although the terms of reference of the Inquiry were fairly narrowly drawn, the interconnections of personality disorder issues with other aspects of the hospital inevitably substantially widened its scope. Yet again this Inquiry also recommended closure of the whole hospital. The Reed Committee finding regarding the poor research evidence in relation to the treatability of psychopathic disorder(s) (Dolan & Coid, 1993) left it a live issue as to whether such MDOs 'need' hospital care rather than prison custody (perhaps in association with limited prison-based mental health care). The more recent proposals of the Home Secretary for new law and services for those with 'severe personality disorder' who pose a grave danger to others hiked this issue to the top of the forensic mental health care agenda (Home Office/DoH, 1999). At the time of writing, two sets of alternative proposals are being consulted upon. The possibility of achieving (under option A) adequate services in not only hospitals but prisons looks challenging, given the history of prison mental health care. The alternative proposal (under option B) for a new form of 'hybrid service' looks innovative but not only costly but problematic where many prisoner-patients will have been deemed untreatable (these proposals are explored in some detail in Chapter 8).

Following publication of the *Final Summary Report* of the Reed Committee, the Home Office/DoH (1995) further promoted inter-agency cooperation and the development of local inter-agency arrangements for MDO services by organising a series of conferences for local stakeholders in each RHA. These took place in 1992 and 1993. They also introduced a wide range of initiatives both centrally and locally to encourage and promote diversion and inter-agency working with MDOs, including providing pump-priming money for court diversion schemes. Finally, the government appointed a committee to advise on the implementation of the Reed recommendations and other issues related to service provision for MDOs (Home Office/DoH, 1995), although the success of the latter was limited.

In 1995, the NHS Executive (1995*b*) issued a circular that reiterated previous directives regarding effective inter-agency working to facilitate the provision of services to MDOs. However, after 1995, there was something of a 'tailing off' of the flurry of government and NHS activity which surrounded and followed the Reed review, except with regard to legislation about criminal sentencing. Although this tailing off may have been, so to speak, a natural process, it seemed likely that the abolition of the RHAs and their replacement with greatly slimmed down 'regional offices' of the NHS Executive, with only limited abilities to influence local health authorities in a detailed way, would continue to reinforce such a natural process. Indeed, specifically as regards needs assessment, the Reed report presaged the decline of central pre-cipitation or control of service development by emphasising the importance of local needs assessment as the basis of local service development and purchasing. A risk developed, therefore, of repeti-tion of the apathy and inertia that preceded, and gave rise to, all three of the Butler, Glancy and Reed reports. The only counter-vailing force was perhaps continued fear, both on the part of the public and (by reflection) on the part of health authorities, of serious offending by the mentally disordered. However, this was hardly a laudable basis for action, nor was it likely to be a basis that encouraged either rational needs assessment or purchasing. In any event, a related concern must remain even now that individual health authorities are unlikely to contain within them sufficiently detailed purchaser knowledge about MDO needs and service responses so as effectively to link the two. There is some risk, therefore, in the future, of a disjointed combination of continued central DoH concern about MDO need and services, based upon the continuing high profile of some MDO cases, and local health authority confusion about the most effective way to respond to that DoH concern. It may be, however, that this risk will now be reduced by the construction of regional commissioning of specialist (includ-ing MDO) health services. Indeed, some DHAs even fear that there will be too much 'central control'. They also fear disjunction of specialist forensic and generic mental health care services arising from separate commissioning, the very disjunction which the Reed Committee intended to overcome.

Some of the developments just described flowed naturally from the Labour government's 1997 White Paper entitled *The New NHS* (DoH, 1997). This announced the abolition of the internal market in favour of "integrated care, based on partnership and driven by per-formance". *The New NHS* retained the rhetoric of need. It stated that "the starting point for the new NHS is the needs of patients" and that:

> "the Government is committed to the historic principle that if you are ill or injured there will be a national health service there to help, and access to it will be based on need and need alone – not on your ability to pay or on who your GP happens to be or where you live." (p. 1)

The 1997 White Paper announced new roles for health authorities, NHS trusts and the DoH, and offered incentives for high-quality services. It also announced the abolition of GP fundholding and the introduction of primary care groups, which would assume responsibility for commissioning services for the local community. However, the White Paper noted that primary care groups would not be expected to take responsibility for commissioning specialised mental health care, although they would be expected to work closely with specialist mental health trusts. The White Paper also emphasised partnership among providers as opposed to competition, and placed a strong emphasis on improving and demontrating the quality and clinical effectiveness of services.

Conclusions

Needs assessment is, both explicitly and implicitly, a concept central to government policy and it appears repeatedly in statements of government health and social care policy. It is seen as underpinning both good commissioning (in the aggregate) and good clinical practice (at the individual patient level). Valid assessment of need, combining a population and an individual basis, is assumed to be necessary in order to ensure both that the 'correct' aggregate level of services is commissioned and that the 'right' types of service are delivered to the appropriate patients. It is also assumed that valid needs assessment will help both commissioners and providers to prioritise patient groups, thereafter guiding scarce resources to the 'right' patients and, overall, being welfare efficient. Further, it is assumed that needs-led commissioning will, together with separation of commissioning from provision *per se*, help to provide high-quality services and that this will, in turn, lead to safer care in hospital and in the community for both the patient and the public. However, there has been very little guidance from the DoH about what 'need' really means, about how to 'do' needs assessment, or about how to translate needs assessment into commissioning plans and high-quality services. This is so despite the central place of needs assessment in health and social policy, and despite continued instructions that population-based and individually based needs assessment should be carried out in order to inform both the commissioning and provision of health care. This is true both of needs assessment in general and specifically in relation to mental health. It is certainly true in relation to services for MDOs. The following chapters attempt therefore to address such needs assessment and related service definition issues in relation to MDOs and to offer a structured framework for thinking about, carrying out and interpreting MDO needs assessment.

In constructing each chapter one important decision which we had to take was whether we would try to write a review of studies which was entirely constructed around the content of the studies or whether we would, in part, adopt largely an historical approach. As can easily be guessed from reading this first chapter, we decided to adopt the latter approach, even though, within each chapter representing a particular 'needs approach', there is some further categorising of the studies. We adopted this approach largely because we concluded that there was some advantage, especially in a study that was focused, in policy terms, on the UK, in demonstrating the development of thinking which itself emerges from an historical presentation. Also, a review constructed solely by content would not have allowed us to describe each study in detail. Since we know of no other publication which draws together and presents all of the available studies, we thought that such a detailed compendium might also be useful to planners and clinicians, even if at times the text is a little heavy to read. So, Chapters 3–6 will review the empirical studies, under headings of particular categories of needs assessment approach described in Chapter 2, while Chapter 7 will deal with the definition of outcome and of 'ability to benefit'. Finally, Chapter 8 will attempt to summarise all of the preceding chapters. It will include offering a theoretical review of the relationship between needs assessment and outcome, as well as setting that review in a broader forensic mental health services and policy context in a post-Reed era. The book will also address the 'politicisation' of need. It will end by offering recommendations to policy makers and providers about future needs assessment for MDOs.

2 Definitions

Introduction

Despite the central role given to both 'need' and 'needs assessment' in the planning and delivery of health and social services, both concepts have been poorly defined and operationalised. Indeed, Baldwin (1986) argues that the terms are used in a woolly and uncritical fashion, without regard to clarity or precision, and Royse & Drude (1982) suggest "it is time that all those currently conducting and funding needs assessments acknowledge that the term is fraught with ambiguity" (p. 103). This chapter attempts, therefore, both to distinguish different constructs of 'need' and to distinguish 'need' from other constructs to which it is closely related. As in Chapter 1, the analysis is conducted initially in relation to all services, but then narrowed down to MDO services.

The social construction of 'need'

The field of health needs assessment is mired in confusion in part because there is no single accepted operational definition of the core term 'need'. Hence, "doctors, sociologists, philosophers and economists all have different views of what needs are" (Wright et al, 1998). Indeed, the construct is extremely difficult to define, because it is inherently subjective and relative rather than objective (Fryers & Greatorex, 1992; Robinson & Elkan, 1996). However, despite its subjective and even nebulous quality, the concept of need has been widely attributed to individuals, populations, subpopulations (e.g. ethnic groups, social classes) and organisations (Sheaff, 1996). When the concepts 'health' and 'mental health' are used to narrow 'need', the definitional problem is exacerbated, because the concepts of health and mental health are themselves difficult to make objective and to operationalise, even though "most doctors are used to assessing the needs of their individual patients" (Wright *et al*, 1998). Indeed, like 'need', both 'health' and, specifically, 'mental health' are social concepts which vary across cultures and societies (Wing *et al*, 1992).

Definitions of need are necessarily rooted in the sociocultural, philosophical, moral, political and temporal contexts in which they are defined and assessed (Bell *et al*, 1988; Fryers & Greatorex, 1992). Hence, texts which trace the history of psychiatry illustrate how state and public attitudes and responses to mental disorder and its treatment have changed (Scull, 1979; Porter, 1987; Fennell, 1996; Shorter, 1997). What is considered a mental health need in the early twenty-first century is not necessarily what would have been considered to be such a hundred years ago. Indeed, both the definition of health need generally and the attention given to it has changed even over the past few decades. During the 1970s and 1980s, attention was directed particularly towards rational planning and resource allocation at a population level (Stevens & Gabbay, 1991). Aggregate, including indirect, measures of health status were used to compare health needs between different geographical areas and populations, and this implied that only aggregate rectification of health need problems was possible, via the overall allocation of resources to large populations (Stevens & Raftery, 1994). Such a general approach to need is reflected, in fact, specifically in the Butler (Home Office/DoH and Social Security, 1975) and Glancy (DoH and Social Security, 1974*a*) approaches to allocating resources for medium-secure units, although no attempt was made within them to allow for differential geographical forensic psychiatric morbidity (see Chapter 1). In the 1990s, government policy led to a further shift in focus from the measurement of 'need for health' to the more refined and specific 'need for health care'. This refers to the ability to improve the population's health by way of health care rather than through other routes to health improvement (Stevens & Raftery, 1994). The corollary of this is that 'need' becomes inherently linked to the 'outcome' specifically of health care intervention.[9] The distinction between 'health need' and 'health care need' is of particular importance in relation to MDOs, given the many and substantial influences on outcome which are likely to have little to do with health care. More generally, the focus of needs assessment has also shifted partially towards the assessment of individual need, including using individual needs assessment directly as a basis

---

[9] The close interconnection of 'need for health care' and 'outcome' of health care intervention is explored in Chapter 7, with some exploration specifically of the state of knowledge about the outcome of mental health care interventions for MDOs.

for service delivery (DoH, 1992*a*). Again as regards MDOs, this approach is explicitly reflected in the Reed report (DoH/Home Office, 1992) (see Chapter 1). Finally, the way that need is perceived and defined is also influenced by the dissemination of information, advancements of knowledge, current research agendas and scientific and technological developments (Stevens & Gabbay, 1991; Wing *et al*, 1992). These factors must, in turn, be influenced by public policy, which provides the social, philosophical and practical framework for such developments.

Clearly, perceptions of need (and, therefore, inferred definitions of need) are likely to vary also between individuals, groups and societies, depending on personal or professional opinions or vested interests (Murphy, 1992). One group's definition of need is therefore no more objective or 'true' than that of another (Bowling, 1992), even though relative positions of power within a group or society will determine not only how needs are defined and measured but also how they are prioritised and met, and by whom. The latter is perhaps of particular importance in relation to mental health needs, because the various stakeholders in the mental health system are clearly very unequal in their power and influence (Sedgwick, 1982). Users of mental health services are, by their disorder and social situation, relatively powerless. This is so even more in relation to MDOs. MDOs may also have very different beliefs from mental health professionals, criminal justice system agencies or the general public about what their needs are (Wing, 1993). Further, there is likely to be disagreement even between these three groups about what are the needs of MDOs, both as a group and as individuals. Even at a very general level, there may be fundamental disparities between mental health professionals, the criminal justice system and the lay public concerning the relative weights that should be given to the principles of 'welfare' and 'justice', as well as concerning the balance to be set between individual and societal welfare. Professionals, researchers and lay people can also be seen frequently to hold very different beliefs about who should receive care and under what circumstances (Klerman *et al*, 1992). For example, in recent years the media have frequently questioned the appropriateness of care delivered to the mentally disordered (e.g. in well publicised cases such as that of Christopher Clunis) and, in so doing, have usually invoked a public safety imperative as properly overriding the welfare principle. By contrast, mental health professionals are inherently, by their professional background, inclined to give greater weight to patients' welfare, albeit, arising from such media or social attitudes, profess-ionals are likely sometimes to be drawn excessively towards public protection (regardless of need) because of understandable concern for career and reputation. The introduction of mandatory inquiries after homicides by psychiatric patients (NHS Executive, 1994*a*), which directly reflected media pressure and public concern, has probably strongly reinforced this tendency (Eastman, 1996*b*, 1996*c*).

Mental health service professionals may also disagree among themselves about what are the needs of MDOs (as a group or individually), sometimes mirroring the lay public in holding conflicting views. Such disagreement may be compounded by ambiguity in the definition of mental disorder and by disputes between mental health professionals about the appropriateness of treatment for particular groups or individuals (Klerman *et al*, 1992). Hence, according to Holloway (1994), "there is a lack of clarity over the nature of severe mental illness and the problems of the mentally ill, with no conceptual framework agreed by all stakeholders in community care" (p. 321). An obvious example of a profound dispute relating to MDOs concerns the diagnosis and treatment of 'psychopathic (personality) disorders'. The debate includes questions about whether or not people with these 'conditions' can or should be treated at all and, if so, what form such treatment should take and in what setting it should occur (Cope, 1993; Dolan & Coid, 1993; Reed, 1996). To add further complexity, in the context of NHS purchasing or commissioning, authorities are given a role which requires them to form their own judgements about what need means, and these judgements may be dissimilar from those of service providers or users.

The politics of 'need'

It is clear from the foregoing general discussion that perceptions of need are based fundamentally on value judgements, as are responses to need (Holzer *et al*, 1988; Bowling, 1992). Such perceptions depend on what is valued by a society, including what are considered desirable health gains or outcomes (Robinson & Elkan, 1996).[10] Sheaff (1996) has argued that, since the introduction of the NHS, and arising out of the clear individual welfare principle underpinning the Beveridge report (Beveridge, 1942), government

---

[10] Of course, in relation to MDOs, the gains or outcomes which are valued by the government or by society may go far beyond health, including reduced future offending. There may, therefore, be inherent conflict between pursuit of health gains and of other (societal) gains. The 'gainers' may also extend beyond MDOs themselves (see Chapter 7).

policy has invoked the idea of needs as founding an entitlement to health care, independent of commercial or financial considerations. Indeed, current DoH policy states that "the key objectives of the NHS ... [are] ... to provide a health service for all, on the basis of clinical need, regardless of ability to pay ...[and] to ensure that treatment and care are targeted to meet local needs" (NHS Management Executive, 1993*c*, p. 5). However, such a statement hides an inevitable contradiction between welfare rhetoric and consumer reality. In NHS economic reality, and regardless of what measures of need are used, finite resources have to be spread (in theory) equitably and productively across services (Butler, 1992). Decisions have to be made about which needs to prioritise and how to ration services. The phrase "regardless of ability to pay" refers to the patient's ability and not the ability of the relevant district purchasing authority. Hence, some patients' welfare is seen as worth more than that of others (irrespective of whether this is decided on grounds of relative relief of subjective individual suffering or on grounds of societal economic advantage). Such prioritisation of need, and choices about where to place resources, represent essentially political decisions, and this must be explicitly acknowledged in the course of any needs assessment (Holzer *et al*, 1988). Indeed, decisions of this kind properly belong to the domain of political rather than scientific discourse and cannot be resolved by recourse to needs assessment data *per se* (Klerman *et al*, 1992). Otherwise, Butler (1992) argues, a 'myth' of planning services on the basis of need may allow (or rather give the illusion of allowing) difficult political issues of rationing to be side-stepped. As Butler states, use of the language of needs assessment in policy documents such as *Working for Patients* (DoH, 1989*b*)

> "not only fails to ring true (since the NHS will continue to be funded on an annual cash-limited basis that has nothing to do with meeting a specified amount of need but everything to do with the political and economic spirit of the times) but also shirks the tricky question of which services should be provided through the NHS and which should not." (p. 125)

As described in Chapter 1, the commissioners of health and social services have been formally charged with the responsibility of making these political decisions, and providers are also necessarily caught up in that process. However, central government intervenes to 'guide' commissioners and providers about which services and patient groups to prioritise, both by way of general guidance and sometimes even in individual cases. For example, *The Health of the Nation* (DoH, 1992*a*) was explicit in identifying five key areas for action, one of which was mental illness, and later guidance was clear about the need to target resources at the most severely mentally ill (DoH, 1995). Specifically as regards MDOs, the DoH has identified services for such patients as a high priority (NHS Management Executive, 1990, 1993*b*) and has frequently encouraged both commissioners and providers to focus attention on the needs of MDOs (see Chapter 1).[11] The DoH has even intervened in individual cases. This has occurred either proactively or in response to expressions of judicial concern. On occasion, it has occurred directly in response to attempts to call the Secretary of State for Health to court under Section 39 of the Mental Health Act in order to explain why a bed cannot be provided for a particular MDO. This overall prioritisation of MDOs has been reinforced by provision of additional funding by central government to commission such services, as well as by giving providers specific financial incentives to expand their services so as to accommodate MDOs (see Chapter 1). Such mechanisms of guidance and encouragement may have resulted, even in the context of greater apparent commissioner autonomy through the operation of the NHS internal market, in more resources being applied to the care of MDOs than occurred in the 1970s under a 'planned economy' for health care. If true, this may have occurred partly because of the introduction, under the internal market, of explicit 'contracts' relating to specific services. This perhaps made it less easy for local NHS authorities to operate hidden prejudices, such as those that previously resulted in the idiosyncratic and patchy development of RSUs (again, see Chapter 1). However, it would be naive to suppose that such DoH or commissioner attention and prioritisation arises simply out of the needs of MDOs *per se* rather than out of consideration of public protection and pressure from both the Home Office and the media. It already seems clear that there has been little change effected here through movement under the Labour government away from 'purchasing' and towards 'commissioning' of MDO services.

Returning specifically to the potential for ambiguity or lack of clarity in defining and measuring need, this also has important political implications. The implementation of government policy in a consistent manner requires stable agreement on how different needs are to be defined and prioritised (Slade, 1994). Such stable agreement is also essential if services are to be purchased and

---

[11] The Labour government's White Paper on health (DoH, 1997), in describing an increased role for NHS Executive regional offices through, for example, arranging for regional commissioning of some highly specialised services, even makes reference to medium-secure units as a specific example of such commissioning.

provided in an equitable manner, since explicitness and clarity, while not guaranteeing equity, are prerequisites of it. However, particular *versions* of 'equity' will flow from particular definitions of need. Hence, the definitions of need adopted in any needs assessment will determine the results, in terms of both the extent and types of need elicited in the inquiry (Rabkin, 1986). That is, different operational definitions of need will result in different data with different implications. The selection of particular definitions, as well as of any particular methodology, is thus a political choice (Royse & Drude, 1982). Needs assessments should not be regarded, therefore, as the panacea for planning. Nor should they be regarded as a means of 'telling' health agencies what services they ought to commission or provide (Royse & Drude, 1982). Rather, they may give planners a range of different types of information that must be interpreted and then translated, by way of value judgements, into service and commissioning plans. Such a task of translating assessments of need into local commissioning requirements capable of expression in explicit terms is, both ethically and technically, an extremely complex activity (Butler, 1992).

The economics of 'need'

Some economists are critical of the concepts of both 'need' and 'needs assessment' in general, arguing that 'economic evaluations' have important advantages over 'needs assessments' (Mooney, 1994). They suggest, therefore, that health care priorities should be based on economic evaluations and not on total needs assessments (Donaldson & Mooney, 1991). Economic evaluation, it is argued, is more relevant to contracting or commissioning because it ensures that, no matter what total needs are, health care resources will be allocated in such a way as to maximise the benefits from them (Donaldson & Mooney, 1991). Of course, health economists are particularly concerned not only with the benefits of health care but also with its costs and with the rationing of resources between activities and, clearly, needs assessment does not directly offer any particular solution in terms of relative resource allocation between competing needs. Hence, Stevens & Raftery (1994) argue that, if health care resources are allocated without a formal analysis of *both* benefits and costs, then waste and lost potential benefit are inevitable. Inefficient services may go undetected and resources may be used in a less than optimal fashion (McCrone & Weich, 1996). Economists also tend to emphasise that the capacity to benefit from health care will always exceed the resources available to provide every possible beneficial intervention (Robinson & Elkan, 1996): "No society can afford to offer all its members all the health care that might possibly do them some good. Each society has therefore to establish priorities, that is, it has to decide who will get what and, by implication, who will go without" (Williams, 1993, cited in Robinson & Elkan, 1996, p. 18). Rationing and prioritisation are thus inevitable, and the resources used to address one health problem will necessarily deny society the opportunity to use those resources to address alternative health problems (i.e. opportunity costs will be incurred) (Donaldson & Mooney, 1991). The aim of priority setting from an economic perspective is, therefore, to maximise aggregate health benefit and to minimise opportunity costs. This can be achieved only by comparing different health care interventions with each other in terms of health gains produced for resources spent (Donaldson & Mooney, 1991). From an economist's perspective, decisions about which needs to meet and how best to meet them involve, therefore, comparing the costs of interventions with their benefits, as well as weighing up the relative costs and benefits of competing interventions (Robinson & Elkan, 1996). This goes beyond analysis of 'cost-effectiveness', which aims merely to minimise the cost of achieving an already chosen and defined single type of health gain. It implies, rather, the need to analyse 'cost-utility' or 'cost-benefit', which weigh the relative benefits and costs of different interventions aimed at different health gains, one health intervention and gain against another.[12] In this context, economists have developed a number of 'generalisable' measures of health gain (e.g. 'quality-adjusted life-years', or QALYs) (Mooney, 1994). Such generalised numeraries allow comparisons between very different types of achievable health gain and therefore facilitate such 'simultaneous equation' solutions for aggregate commissioning.

Different types of cost must be taken into consideration in any economic evaluation (McCrone & Weich, 1996). Direct (financial and resource) costs are incurred when contacts are made, for example, with specialist mental health providers. Indirect costs may accrue as a result of contacts with services which are not primarily part of the mental health care system (e.g. criminal justice system agencies, social services) and may result from lost production caused by health problems. Hidden costs are those which arise from the burden on families and carers, those associated with unemployment and also those incurred by the patient travelling to receive

---

[12] Strictly defined, 'cost-benefit' goes beyond 'cost-utility' by allocating a money value to any utility measured so that it can be compared directly with (money) costs.

treatment. The cost of conducting the therapeutic or services research should also be included in any economic evaluation. Finally, there are 'non-measured costs', which represent aspects of care to which it is impossible, or unethical, to attach a cost.

Cost-benefit analysis applied to MDOs is further complicated because consideration has to be given to the potential benefit arising from avoiding the *dis*benefits of crime to or the *dis*benefits arising from the costs of crime prevention, aside from any reference to benefits arising from treatment of mental disorders *per se*.[13] However, it is, in fact, very difficult to 'cost' crime in terms of victim costs and costs to families (and, therefore, in terms of potential benefit arising from avoidance of victim and family damage). The core problem is that of having to put a monetary value on life or disability (de Graaf, 1967). Also, the lost benefit to patients (through loss of liberty) of being detained has to be weighed against the benefits to society of them being detained. Relevant questions here are whether involuntary detention contributes to quality of life (of either the MDO or others), what the evidence is that it does it and, if so, how it does it. A further question is whether such detention 'adds life to years'. That is, does detention improve quality of life, prevent further deterioration in mental disorder or prevent the adverse effects on the MDOs themselves of committing further crimes. Another relevant question is whether detention 'adds years to life' by, for example, preventing the person from being killed or injured (by self or other). Responses to these questions cannot be ethically or politically neutral and will not be determined solely on the basis of the benefits potentially accruing to, or the needs of, the individual MDO. Also, some policy objectives will tend in practice to transcend strict benefits or needs analysis, for example, those of personal or public safety (albeit that, in the aggregate, there will ultimately be resource rationing which does not fully minimise the risk of death to MDOs or others).

Turning from benefits to costs, Knapp & Beecham (1990) present four rules for determining the costs of mental health services. First, costs should be measured comprehensively, so that the full range of relevant service components is included (e.g. the multi-agency perspective, in-patient and out-patient services, home visits). Second, the cost variations between patients, facilities and geographical areas should be fully acknowledged. Hence, it may be more expensive to treat some patient groups; for example, the cost of treatment in medium security may exceed that in minimum

---

[13] The weight given to victim costs is emphasised by the strong tendency of researchers to measure the 'outcome' of MDO services in terms of recidivism or reoffending (see Chapter 7).

security, or it may be more expensive to treat patients in rural than in inner-city areas. Third, only 'like-with-like' comparisons should be considered as fully valid, even though insights can be gained from less than perfect comparisons. For example, it probably makes little sense to compare the costs of MDO services with the costs of general psychiatry services, albeit that some comparative 'benefit–cost' ratio might be applied in balancing commissioning decisions between the two. Fourth, cost information should not stand in isolation from other relevant data but should be integrated with outcome information. Both high-quality outcome and cost data are thus required to assist policy makers, commissioners and providers in making the best use of their limited resources (McCrone & Weich, 1996). McCrone & Weich have reviewed a number of studies that attempted to cost mental health care. They conclude that, contrary to the rules of good practice we have just described, economic evaluations frequently fail to measure costs at all, or do so in incomplete and inappropriate ways. In fact, few effective cost instruments have been described, and probably only one in the UK (cf. Beecham & Knapp, 1992). Notably, in our own search of the literature pertaining to the costs and benefits specifically of MDO services, few economic evaluations were found (cf. James *et al*, 1998), and this represents an important gap in knowledge.

It is important to emphasise that the economic perspective is, like the needs assessment perspective, not divorced from policy weighting or choices. Indeed, policy considerations – such as the principles contained in the Reed report (DoH/Home Office, 1992) or Home Office circular 66/90 (Home Office, 1990a) – may be so important that, essentially, they transcend any reasonable analysis of cost-benefit or cost-effectiveness. Of course, a cost-benefit analysis of MDO care *could* weight the benefits of containment and treatment of MDOs so heavily as to *ensure* that stated public policy goals are matched by resource application. However, taken to an extreme, this may 'invalidate' or, at least, marginalise any formal cost-benefit analysis. Similarly, in terms of cost-effectiveness analysis, if the objective for which costs are to be minimised were to be stated simply as that of 'MDO containment' (rather than containment and treatment) then it would, of course, be possible to compare prison containment with a given hospital containment. However, recent government policy has been such that it should automatically exclude any analysis in favour of prison (assuming all MDOs under consideration are detainable under the Mental Health Act). Indeed, there is much anecdotal evidence that health purchasers have, from the mid-1990s, increasingly responded to government MDO policy almost irrespective of the cost.

Definitions of 'need' and of related constructs

Despite the many difficulties already described, a number of different disciplines have attempted to define and measure need as a general concept, from a range of theoretical and methodological perspectives. However, it is doubtful whether some of these very different approaches can ever be reconciled (Robinson & Elkan, 1996).

Bradshaw (1972), a sociologist, developed a 'taxonomy of social need', which is frequently referred to in texts on mental health needs assessment. He defined four types of need, all of which may overlap with one another. 'Normative need' is identified by measuring existing provision against a desirable standard, while 'comparative need' is identified by measuring the gap between service provision in one geographical area and that in another, weighting for differences in local morbidity. 'Normative need' and 'comparative need' are both defined by experts. By contrast, 'felt need' is what is wanted or desired by service users, and 'expressed need' is 'felt need' which is expressed as a 'demand' for services. These various distinctions emphasise the widely varying potential perspectives on need and, taken together, they represent contrasting 'pictures' of need. This highlights the practical and ethical difficulties involved in translating measures of need into service plans.

Bradshaw's conceptual framework identified the concept of need as being closely related to, but distinct from, those of 'demand', 'service utilisation' and 'supply'. It is important to spend some time disentangling these concepts. This is necessary because many researchers and planners have tried to estimate need by measuring one or more of the other constructs (Warheit *et al*, 1977) *and* because the NHS Management Executive has, itself, in its discussion paper on needs assessment, been careful to distinguish need from demand and supply (NHS Management Executive, 1991).

Demand

Matthew (1971) suggests that "a demand for care exists when an individual considers that [s]he has a need and wishes to receive care" (cited in Wing, 1990, p. 4). This clearly identifies both that the two concepts of need and demand are closely related and that they are ultimately distinct from one another. In spite of this, some researchers have assumed that measuring the demand for health services (defined in this or some other way) provides a valid measure of the need for those services. Such an approach assumes that there is a direct and predictable relationship between underlying need and demand, based upon the presumption that individuals will actively seek treatment when they need it. Although in some medical conditions such an assumption may well be valid (e.g. in the case of broken bones), in many medical conditions, including mental disorder, it may frequently be invalid. This said, the demand for a service or treatment must at least be influenced by many of the same variables which influence need, because need and demand do clearly overlap. For example, demand, reflecting need, may be mediated by knowledge about treatments available, 'fashions' in treatment, the social and educational backgrounds of those making the demands, and by third parties such as the medical and related professions (Stevens & Gabbay, 1991). The seeking of health care may also be influenced by clinical factors such as symptoms and subjective distress, as well as by predisposing or enabling factors. The latter may include socio-demographic (e.g. age, gender, race, education), geographic (e.g. rural versus urban), economic (e.g. ability to pay) or attitudinal (e.g. fear of stigmatisation) factors (Klerman *et al*, 1992).

Specifically as regards mental disorder, no clear relationship has been shown between the presence of a psychiatric disorder and help-seeking behaviour. For example, an important finding to emerge from the Epidemiologic Catchment Area Program in the USA was that most individuals identified as psychiatric 'cases' were not in receipt of mental health care. Conversely, many mental health care visits were made by persons who were *not* identified as cases (Shapiro *et al*, 1985). In the UK, Commander *et al* (1997) found that approximately one-third of people in a UK inner-city health district with mental health problems did not consult a GP. Goldberg & Huxley (1980) also found that only about 1 3% of the population are in contact with psychiatric services, despite there being much higher rates of psychiatric disorder in the community.

It is clear, therefore, that need for services should not be confused with, identified with or measured by help-seeking behaviour alone. Indeed, Rabkin (1986) suggests that it is often the most severely disabled who are the least articulate (or motivated) in their demand for services, while potential users of mental health services may have particular difficulty in articulating demand because of their vulnerability, relative powerlessness (Hostick, 1995) and lack of insight. They may also prefer to avoid rather than seek out what may be perceived by them as a coercive relationship between professional and patient (Hostick, 1995). The potential for stigmatisation may further discourage the mentally ill from demanding services (Wing, 1994). Also, many of those who are likely to have disproportionately high needs for mental health services lack the information or resources to make demands on services (Hostick, 1995). All the foregoing are important considerations in themselves. However, their importance is emphasised by the fact that it is DoH policy that service users *should* be involved in needs assessment, both in terms of their own individual clinical and social needs and in terms of aggregate service development (DoH, 1992*a*, 1993*c*).

Demand by proxy

Proxy demand for health services, expressed most commonly by clinicians on behalf of their patients, may give rise to conflict both among professionals and between professionals and patients. Such conflict arises in a very unusual 'market' since, in health care, it is assumed that professionals, because of their expert knowledge, are best able, or are at least in a more powerful position than is the patient, to determine need and to make appropriate demands (Sheaff, 1996). Hence, in market economic terms, it is argued that, through their greater knowledge and market (clinical) power, unusually the provider is more able to influence demand than is the recipient patient. However, third-party demand may not always be efficient. Professionals who act as agents for their patients, or for society, effect a specific type of demand which may or may not approximate the actual needs or demands of their patients (Stevens & Raftery, 1994). For example, Commander *et al* (1997) found that half of the people with a mental health problem in an inner-city UK health district failed to have their problem recognised by their GP, and that subsequent access to specialist services was highly restricted (albeit partly because of lack of supply).

Proxy demand is especially pertinent in forensic mental health care. Here, demand for services may result not merely from third-party intervention (e.g. psychiatrists or social workers) but sometimes from intervention by third parties who have no explicit health role at all (e.g. the Probation Service, courts or Home Office). Such proxy demand may be particularly contrary to the patient's self-perceived need or demand for services. Some MDOs may, therefore, never have made any demand at all for the services they use and, certainly, many patients are likely to be involuntarily detained or made subject to other compulsory orders (e.g. probation orders with a condition of treatment). Further, proxy demand may also be expressed in the NHS by health authorities on behalf of patients, and sometimes without the patient's consent. This is particularly so in relation to the seriously mentally ill in general and in relation to MDOs in particular. Alternatively, third parties *with* a health role (e.g. psychiatrists) may demand services on behalf of users but demand may then not be translated into utilisation because of over-riding decisions by other, non-health third parties (e.g. by judges or the Home Secretary).

Service utilisation

Service utilisation is usually, but not always, a consequence of articulated demand. It occurs when an individual actually receives care, whether or not she or he needs it (Matthew, 1971, cited in Wing, 1990, p. 4). Some researchers have assumed that measuring the utilisation of health services provides a valid measure of the underlying need for those services (e.g. Warheit *et al*, 1977). However, the relationship between need and utilisation is by no means a direct or exclusive one and, in any event, service utilisation is probably substantially mediated by both the demand for, and supply of, services (Rabkin, 1986). Hence, utilisation is not simply a consequence of need, user demand or even third-party demand (Wing *et al*, 1992). Like both need and demand, it is likely to vary according to the socio-demographic characteristics of the population. For example, inner-city areas are likely to have higher psychiatric morbidity, higher rates of offending by both the mentally normal and disordered populations and to make greater use of MDO services than are rural areas. Utilisation is also likely to vary according to service availability (e.g. availability of medium-security beds) and ease of accessibility (e.g. lack of bed-blocking). Access barriers, whether arising from the patient, mental health services, courts or the Home Office, may hinder or prevent service usage by individuals who satisfy even the most stringent definitions of need. For example, users may refuse access to recommended services or agree access to services which fall short of what a professional recommends (Schinnar *et al*, 1992). Professional attitudes may also serve as access barriers. For example, some psychiatrists may not believe that psychopaths as a class of patients are treatable (Cope, 1993) and, therefore, may never admit them to psychiatric services. The shortfall in medium-security services has also been identified as an access barrier for those MDOs who are over-contained in special hospitals, inappropriately detained in prison or unsafely contained in general mental health services (DoH/Home Office, 1992; Maden *et al*, 1993). Additionally, the Home Office often creates access barriers for restricted patients waiting to move to lesser security, sometimes even when the 'need' for such a move has been reinforced by a mental health review tribunal recommendation.

In summary, need is not necessarily expressed as demand and demand is not necessarily followed by utilisation, while, on the other hand, there can be demand and utilisation without real underlying need for the particular service used (Häfner, 1979; Wing, 1990).

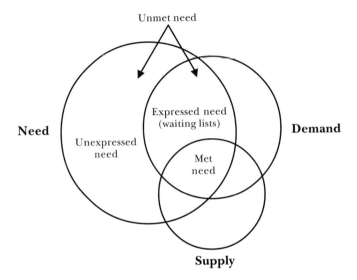

Fig. 1. Need, demand and supply: the present situation. From Crown (1991).

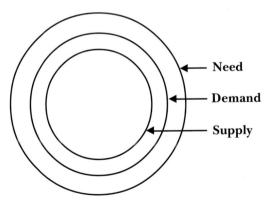

Minimal unexpressed and unmet need
No appropriate supply

Fig. 2. Need, demand and supply: the ideal situation. From Crown (1991).

Supply

Supply refers to available interventions, agents and settings, whether or not they are used (Johnson *et al*, 1996). It is influenced not only by need and demand but also by public, political, economic and professional pressures and constraints. Current supply is also strongly influenced, because of substantial capital investment and other factors determining service inflexibility, by historical patterns of supply, rather than by current need or demand (Stevens & Raftery, 1994). The reader will recall that, in Chapter 1, we outlined how these various factors determining of supply have shaped policy both concerning services for MDOs *per se* and related needs assessment. Over-provision occurs if supply exceeds need or demand, and unmet need may occur either if need is not translated into demand or if there is inadequate supply to respond to demand (Johnson *et al*, 1996).

Stevens & Gabbay (1991) argue that any useful needs assessment will require not only an analysis of the relationship between need, demand and supply for the many (mental) health conditions under consideration, but an attempt to see how the three can be made more congruent. Hence, Crown (1991) provides a useful diagrammatic representation of the relationships between need, demand and supply (which is not equivalent to utilisation) (Fig. 1). She suggests that purchasers aim to bring these three dimensions into as close alignment as possible so that demand is solely a subset of need, and supply is solely a subset of demand (Fig. 2). Both Figs 1 and 2 represent unmet need. However, whereas in Fig. 2 supply is provided only to those who both demand and need it, such that no patients receive unneeded services, in Fig. 1 there is supply of services to patients who do not need it.

Richman & Barry (1985) suggest that the idea of massive unmet need for mental health services is a myth, generated and perpetuated by processes within the systems which provide psychiatric care. They argue that "needs ... [may be] less massive if the boundaries of psychiatry are defined so as to include only those disorders which the profession is best able to treat" (p. 164). This is an argument that may be particularly relevant, on the basis of the current state of scientific knowledge, to patients with a diagnosis of antisocial personality disorder (Dolan & Coid, 1993).

Need

Fryers (1979) provides an approach to defining and conceptualising need. He developed a four-level hierarchical classification of need that also acts as a framework for defining the broad purposes of needs assessment and the types of data that can be used for it at each level. First, 'national needs' are measured for the purpose of resource allocation by central government and are based primarily on formulas that use national statistics (e.g. standard mortality ratios). Second, 'area/district needs' are measured for the purpose of provision of large health care institutions and agencies (e.g. large district general hospitals) and may use local planning information such as existing epidemiological data. Third, 'group needs' are measured for the purpose of planning and providing smaller health care services concerned directly with the care of specific patient groups (e.g. the elderly, MDOs, people with learning disabilities or schizophrenia). A wide range of data may be used to assist the planning process at this level, including socio-demographic and epidemiological data on specific sub-populations (such as people with specific clinical syndromes). Fourth, 'individual needs' are measured for the purpose of determining the type and effectiveness of health care as experienced by the patient and these may be measured using "clinical, psychological and sociological understanding", as well as via standardised needs assessment instruments. Fryer's approach offers a very useful conceptual framework for understanding the different levels at which needs may be assessed. Levels 3 and 4 are of particular relevance in terms of current needs assessment policy, although needs assessment methods for commissioning purposes are not well developed at these levels.

Wing (1994) argues in favour of a multi-factorial, or 'case-mix', approach to formulating need. Such an approach takes account of the social disabilities resulting from mental disorder,[14] and at the same time addresses the methods of treatment and the services required to alleviate the identified problems. According to Wing *et al* (1992) "social disablement is ... associated with an amalgam of factors that produce a pattern, level and persistence of malfunctioning that is not diagnosis-specific. It is this pattern, level and duration that principally determines need for care and services" (p. 3). The severity of social disablement, they claim, may result from the severity and duration of psychological and physiological dysfunctions, from adverse circumstances and disadvantages that can affect social functioning independently of illness (e.g. poverty), and

---

[14] Social disabilities include subjective symptoms, associated behavioural problems, suicide attempts, socially embarrassing or unacceptable behaviours, slowness and lack of motivation, poor self-care (negative impairments), lack of insight into problems, and overall social disablement.

from personal reactions to the first two factors (e.g. loss of self-esteem; stigmatisation). Wing *et al* define services as the organisational structures which facilitate the identification of people in need, as well as the delivery of appropriate methods of treatment and care, including agents (e.g. nurses, formal and informal carers), settings (e.g. day units) and aspects of organisation, management and economy. In this context, methods of treatment or care may include medication, training, treatment programmes and various kinds of support and shelter.

Wing (1994) argues that such a case-mix approach allows patients to be assigned to recognisable groups that reflect the nature and cost of the care they need. In general, the more severe or persistent the problem, the more service filters (Goldberg & Huxley, 1980) are passed and the greater the short-term and long-term costs (albeit that the number of likely cases decreases). Problems and settings which are currently typical are outlined as follows (Wing, 1994):

(1) self-limiting problems, common in general populations, that largely do not give rise to needs for care from the NHS;
(2) problems seen and treated in primary care without specialist referral;
(3) more severe problems that can be treated after referral for specialist advice or ambulatory care (and which may be from a health centre or out-patient department) or casualty or liaison referrals from secondary NHS sources;
(4) short-term intensive care (e.g. hospitals, acute day hospitals, domiciliary nursing);
(5) medium-term intensive care (or 'new long stay');
(6) longer-term care (or 'old long stay'), with persistent, high dependency needs.

Levels 4–6 may consist of hospital or community alternatives. Further, one individual may, at different times, experience quite different sets of symptoms or disabilities and may therefore present at different case-mix levels. Clearly, MDOs may fall into any of the six categories, although the more severe cases are likely to fall into the latter three groups.

The application of this framework to the problems of MDOs, and the services they require, highlights some of the complexities involved in formulating MDO needs. Diagnostically, MDOs are a heterogeneous group, since they may fall into any organic or functional diagnostic category. Many have multiple problems and/ or dual diagnoses, often including severe personality problems and substance misuse. Many are chronically disabled, both mentally and socially, and have multiple behavioural difficulties. The most prominent of their 'social disabilities' is, of course, their antisocial or violent behaviour, which leads to both personal and social difficulties and which tends to define their needs for specific services and interventions. Yet, MDOs may have a very wide range of treatment and care needs, some of which are present regardless of their antisocial behaviour and which are similar to those of general psychiatric patients. These needs can be addressed by general psychiatric services if the severity of their antisocial behaviour permits it. Other MDOs may require specialist intervention from forensic services. They may thus require treatment and care across the full range of psychiatric settings described above, including high-security special hospitals, medium-secure units, minimum-security wards, open wards or community and out-patient care. They may also be in contact with a wide range of agencies, each of which may be best placed to meet particular aspects of their needs. This implies that the settings described above by Wing should be expanded to include input from non-health services such as the Probation Service or therapeutic communities contained in prisons such as at HMP Grendon Underwood. MDOs may also have a complex array of needs for treatment and care within the settings themselves. They share many of these with other, general psychiatric patients (e.g. medication, behaviour therapy, social skills development, recreation, education), but some are specific to them as MDOs (e.g. perimeter and internal ward security, or anger management courses aimed at preventing violence).

The Department of Health's definition of need

The DoH provides its own definition of need in order to assist commissioners in their needs assessment task. Thus, the NHS Management Executive (1991) stated that

"the 'need' for services for a population depends on that population's ability to benefit in terms of health gain from the service (including preventive through to rehabilitative services). The total ability of a population to benefit depends on how much of a problem there is (prevalence/incidence), and on what can be done about it (effectiveness)." (p. 16)

Sheaff (1996) accepts that this definition of need is more specific than previous official definitions but questions whether it is any clearer. However, the definition does provide a policy framework which narrows the definition of need from the (broader) 'need for

health' *per se* to the (narrower) 'need for health care' (Crown, 1991).
According to the NHS Management Executive (1991):

> "The *need for health* is a broad term measured in health surveys,
> surrogate measures such as deprivation indices and relative
> measures such as standardised mortality ratios – all measures which
> do not easily translate into what can or should be done to improve
> health." (p. 4)

On the other hand:

> "The *need for health care* is much more specific. It is dependent on
> the availability or potential availability of health care and prevention
> services to respond to the disease or risk factors – *and* to secure an
> improvement in health, i.e. *the ability to benefit* from effective health
> care or prevention services." (p. 4)

The NHS Management Executive model grounds needs assessment in an epidemiological framework and requires that the size
of the 'health problem' be established (Stevens & Raftery, 1992).
Any such health problem may arise from risk factors for disease,
diseases *per se*, disabilities or handicaps (Stevens & Raftery, 1994). The
epidemiological approach also incorporates an added dimension
of 'effectiveness', which requires that need should not be defined
solely on the basis of the size of the health problem in a population
but also on the basis of the population's ability to benefit from
health care. Such 'health care' may include prevention, diagnosis,
continuing care, rehabilitation and palliative care (Stevens &
Raftery, 1994). The greater the ability to benefit, the greater is
the need (Robinson & Elkan, 1996). The 'effectiveness' dimension
arises not only from the 'efficacy' of health care (i.e. a particular
intervention's potential to bring about benefit in ideal research-
based circumstances), but is defined in terms of 'real-world'
outcome (i.e. the likely achieved benefit in a local setting) (Stevens
& Raftery, 1992). Also, 'ability to benefit' does not imply that every
outcome is guaranteed to be favourable (or even likely to be so in
terms of efficacy) but rather that, on average, there is potential
benefit (Stevens & Raftery, 1992, 1994). This definition forces
planners and commissioners to examine the health outcomes that
are wanted and to define what they mean by the term 'benefit'
(Robinson & Elkan, 1996). It is not sufficient to identify a health
problem as amenable to some kind of treatment or intervention;
it is also necessary to specify what sort of outcome or benefit
the intervention is intended to bring about (Robinson & Elkan,

1996). This binds the concept of need profoundly to that of 'outcome'.[15]

In summary, if people do not have the ability to benefit from the treatments and services currently potentially available then they are not in need (Robinson & Elkan, 1996) *and* if there is no effective intervention, treatment or care setting, then there is also no need for health care (Crown, 1991). That is, ineffective services are not needed, and effective services with no takers are also not required (Stevens & Raftery, 1994). However, Wing *et al* (1992) suggest that 'state of the art' interventions that exist but are not locally available should be included in the definition. They consider it important "not to define need in terms of the care, agent or setting already in place, thus automatically perpetuating the present allocation and priorities on unwilling people" (Wing *et al*, 1992, p. 6).

Ability to benefit

There are many possible clinical and non-clinical benefits arising from health care, including physical, psychological and social benefits (Robinson & Elkan, 1996), *and* many potential recipients of such benefits, including patients, carers and society in general. Hence, many health problems (e.g. infectious diseases) have a social dimension and, consequently, the list of beneficiaries of health care can extend well beyond the patient suffering from the condition (Stevens & Raftery, 1994). Benefits *per se* may, as already described, include those which extend life, adding 'years to life', and those which enhance the quality of life, adding 'life to years' (Robinson & Elkan, 1996). In practice, however, benefits tend to be defined narrowly in terms of quantifiable outcomes rather than by reference to more qualitative outcomes, simply because the former are easier to measure (Robinson & Elkan, 1996). The NHS Management Executive (1991) attempted to provide clarification. It stated that 'health benefits' should be measured not only in terms of clinical health status (i.e. outcome) but also in terms of other factors which constitute the process of health care (e.g. reassurance, prevention, rehabilitation, palliative care, social and psychological support to patients and carers) (Robinson & Elkan, 1996).

---

[15] Outcome is considered separately from need in this text (see Chapter 7). According to the Department of Health's definition of need, such separation is unjustified. However, the lack of outcome data linked to specific inputs (or processes) makes any other approach impractical. Hence, Chapters 3–6 are written largely on the assumption that any MDO 'needs' defined could, in therapeutic terms, be 'met'.

Specifically as regards MDOs, there are further difficulties concerning their 'ability to benefit'. There is a dearth of empirical evidence regarding their ability to benefit from health care interventions beyond evidence of the benefits that would accrue to non-offender patients. Also, one of the main concerns about this group of patients is their potential risk to the public, and there is an expectation that treatment will (and should) substantially reduce (or even remove) this risk. Therefore, it is common for the 'outcome' of treatment for MDOs to focus narrowly on recidivism, and for this aspect of 'ability to benefit' to overshadow other clinical and social benefits (again, see Chapter 7). However, as already suggested, 'ability to benefit' defined in terms of reoffending refers not only to the individual's ability to benefit from treatment and care but also to the powerful benefit to society of detaining and treating individuals who pose a threat to public safety. Indeed, some might argue that the provision of secure settings is mainly a response to *society's* need, or demand, for protection against potentially dangerous MDOs rather than a response to the *patient's* need for a secure environment for treatment.

'Ability to benefit' for MDOs is also constrained by legal rules. The inability to detain certain patients under the Mental Health Act 1983 may preclude psychiatric treatment, even though they may have an identified mental health need. This may be either because the disorder is not severe enough (or its consequences are not severe enough) to warrant sectioning (and they are non-consenting) or, in the case of 'psychopathic disorder' and 'mental impairment', because the disorder is considered 'untreatable' for the purposes of the Act.[16] More generally, the coincidence of any mental disorder and offending may indicate a need for mental health treatment but, unless the individual is sectionable under the Mental Health Act, the need may remain unmet because the person is unwilling to receive treatment.

The NHS Management Executive's definition of need is clearly based on the presumption that not all health problems can be successfully treated or cured, and that some conditions respond better than others to health care interventions (Mooney, 1994). However, although it acknowledges that the assessment of need involves decisions about effectiveness, priorities and costs, it provides little guidance about how to balance priorities in the real world. It also leaves unresolved fundamental and controversial

---

[16] Once detained under the 1983 Act, being 'untreatable' has not, until recently, been sufficient, legally, to determine discharge (*R* v. *Cannons Park, Mental Health Review Tribunal, ex parte A* [1994] 2 All ER 306, reported in *The Times*, 24 August 1983). The Scottish case of *Reid* v. *Secretary of State for Scotland* (1998) has, however, altered this situation.

questions about what constitutes a 'health gain' and what it means to benefit from health care. It also leaves sub-questions about how these factors should be defined and measured, who in society should ultimately decide what are desirable benefits and outcomes, and on what grounds (Stevens & Raftery, 1994; Robinson & Elkan, 1996). These are not politically neutral or value-free questions and they take us back to the political and ethical issues discussed earlier in the chapter. Indeed, lack of empirical evidence about specific health gains achieved by MDOs (see Chapter 7) is noteworthy, given the recent substantial allocation of resources to MDO services by the government. Such a lack of empirical evidence suggests that resource allocation may have been based on a definition of need (including 'ability to benefit') that is heavily weighted in favour of *public* benefit, the latter arising essentially from the detention and control of MDOs.[17] It is debatable whether such a definition implies a *health* need, so that it is properly the concern of the DoH, or whether, by contrast, it better implies a *criminal justice* need, so that it is more properly the concern of the Home Office. Such questions go, of course, to the heart of public and jurisprudential policy relating to MDOs (see Chapter 8).

Defining 'mentally disordered offenders'

It is clear from the above discussion that the assessment of need is a complex and problematic activity, and that there are many philo-sophical, political, theoretical and methodological difficulties involved in the process. However, there is yet one further problem involved in the assessment of MDO needs which warrants discussion. That is, what does the term 'mentally disordered offender' mean? Regardless of the way in which need is defined, or the methods adopt-ed to assess it, it is essential that the target population is adequately and properly defined. This is important for methodological research purposes and because of the pejorative nature of the label 'MDO' itself, and the stigma attached to it both in society and within health and related services. It is to that definition to which we now turn.

There is no generally agreed operational definition of the term 'mentally disordered offender'. The Reed report (DoH/Home Office, 1992) defined the MDO as "a mentally disordered person who has broken the law", adding that "in identifying broad service

---

[17] See also below in more detail, including suggestions that problems of prediction of future offending make even this 'ability to benefit' definition of 'need' a far from uncontroversial one (in terms of the Department of Health's definition).

needs [the] term is sometimes loosely used to include mentally disordered people who are alleged to have broken the law" (p. 115). This definition implies a necessary combination of mental disorder and criminal convictions or charges, while also implying that the combination might arise merely as a coincidence (there need not be a chronological or causal link between the (alleged) offence and the mental disorder). However, such a strictly 'legal' definition of MDOs is inadequate for a number of reasons. First, it is well recognised that some mentally disordered individuals behave in ways which seriously violate the law and yet they do not come into contact with the criminal justice system at all. This may be a consequence of diversion from the criminal justice system before any contact with it (e.g. where a patient is violent in hospital but is not charged with, or even interviewed about, an offence). Conversely, some mentally disordered individuals who do come into contact with the criminal justice system do so only for minor offences (Home Office, 1994). Many of these individuals do not show serious behavioural problems beyond petty offending, and may not require interventions going beyond those needed by 'ordinary' psychiatric patients (e.g. they may not need treatment for specialised pathology or behaviour predictive of serious violence). It is therefore debatable whether, from the perspective of planning or securing services, a 'legal' definition of 'MDO' is helpful, particularly given the tendency for general psychiatric services to reject offender-patients (Coid, 1991*a*). Indeed, James & Hamilton (1991) have pointed out that it is, to some extent, arbitrary whether a minor offender with a mental disorder enters the criminal justice system or the mental health system, and that this is often dependent upon local or idiosyncratic factors. Cripps *et al* (1995) also note that it is not uncommon for somebody to be a 'community catchment area' admission on one occasion and an 'MDO' admission on another, with arrest sometimes acting as a final safety net for individuals who are out of contact with community services. Further, just as some mentally disordered people have special needs, despite a lack of legal charges or convictions, some defendants who *are* in the criminal justice system may have mental health needs which do not warrant diversion to either general or forensic psychiatric services, regardless of the seriousness of their offending. The needs of such individuals may be adequately addressed through primary care within the prison health care system, or even by strictly non-health agencies (e.g. probation). It is as important to avoid 'over-psychiatrisation' (or 'over-specialisation' of treatment) of defendants and offenders as it is to avoid 'criminalisation' of the mentally disordered.

From a different perspective, the mental health charity MIND (1997) has criticised the label 'mentally disordered offender' and *per se* would like to see an end to its use. It argues that "[t]he label 'mentally disordered offender' itself confuses criminality and mental distress and is applied loosely and damagingly to people who may be neither offenders nor mentally disordered" (p. 2). Examples of its concern are that the term may be extended to cover some offenders who are (merely) addicted to substances or to include some mentally ill people who are (merely) disruptive of mental health services. MIND (1997) has also argued that defendants should be given the choice about whether or not they wish to be diverted from the criminal justice system to the mental health system, and that this choice is an important aspect of assessing the needs of the individual.

The Reed report attempted to overcome these various definitional problems by providing further definitions of individuals with 'special needs' who are 'difficult to place' or 'challenging'. Hence, 'difficult to place' individuals were defined as "those with a mental disorder which results in their displaying at times unacceptable and/or disturbed behaviour which requires specialised assessment, treatment, rehabilitation and care in a flexible (not permanently) secure environment" (p. 114). The term 'challenging behaviour' was applied to individuals "with either learning disabilities or mental disorder" and was defined as "behavioural disturbance through assaultive, aggressive or destructive behaviour and/or irresponsible conduct" (p. 113). 'Aggressive behaviour' was further defined as "verbal and/or physical actions or serious intentions that are outside the usually acceptable range of harmful or confrontational behaviour, the consequences of which are likely to cause actual damage and/or real distress occurring either recently, persistently or with excessive severity" (p. 113).

Although these definitions, taken together, do provide a conceptual framework for understanding the types of behaviour which logically place patients in a group according to some commonality of service need, they also have their own practical and ethical problems. Particular problems arise from the terms 'MDO', 'difficult to place', 'challenging' or 'aggressive', since each of these labels may result in stigma attaching to, and service rejection of, the individual so labelled. Indeed, recent approaches to service delivery have tended explicitly to separate out MDOs from other psychiatric patients (Gallwey, 1990). This split between forensic and general psychiatry services has then been reflected, not surprisingly, in a separation between MDO needs assessment and needs assessment within general psychiatry. The latter has tended to be reinforced naturally by the much greater problems there are in conducting needs assessment within general mental health contexts, as we describe in Chapter 7. Hence, ironically, the fact that MDOs have been subject to their own, separate report – the Reed report – has itself tended to reinforce the very separation of forensic and general services which, in its core philosophy, that report argues against. It is questionable, therefore, whether such terms are uniformly helpful towards developing seamless services for MDOs, particularly for those MDOs who *can* be managed within general psychiatric services. Further, the broad definitions we have described allow, as MIND criticises, for the inclusion of extremely diverse groups of patients under the general rubric 'MDO', and this may be both stigmatising and unhelpful in research terms, including in needs assessment research terms. Overall, therefore, it is extremely important when conducting needs assessment to adopt tight operational definitions of the term 'MDO', and it is also important to be conscious of the indirect service effects which even use of the term (and other related terms) can have.

Risk to others and the 'needs' of MDOs

We have already alluded to the need of society for protection from MDOs and clearly the concept of 'risk of harm to others' is one of the core defining characteristics of MDOs. This substantially shapes public opinion, public policy and service responses with regard to MDOs (Lagos *et al*, 1977; Steadman & Cocozza, 1978) albeit that it represents only one of the needs – others relate directly to the MDO him/herself – that have to be weighted in arriving at the MDO's composite need. Yet, the risk to others is notoriously difficult to define and to predict (Rennie, 1978; Monahan, 1981; Prins, 1990). It is not a constant trait of an individual but may change over time in relation to a range of factors, including both the presence of psychiatric symptoms and environmental influences (Mullen, 1997).[18]

The presumed necessary link between dangerousness and service response is clearly illustrated in the Reed report (DoH/Home Office, 1992) itself. For example, the report describes special hospitals as providing:

> "a similar range of therapeutic services as ordinary psychiatric hospitals but in a level of utmost security to enable the treatment

---

[18] The reader is referred to a standard textbook of forensic psychiatry, such as Bluglass & Bowden (1990) or Gunn & Taylor (1993), for detailed consideration of the concept of 'dangerousness' and of the related process of clinical risk assessment. The former is now commonly eschewed because it suggests that the risk of violence lies solely in the patient, rather than arising by way of interaction with external circumstances.

of patients ... who ... require this because of their dangerousness, violent or criminal propensities ... and [where] a lesser degree of security would not provide a reasonable safeguard to the public." (p. 117)

Similarly, 'medium security', claims the Reed report, "care[s] for patients who are too difficult or dangerous for local hospitals but who do not require the higher security available at Special Hospitals" (p. 117).

'Low security' is defined as "local hospitals [which] have wards coping with 'difficult' patients which provide a degree of physical security by being locked or having an above average staff ratio" (p. 117).[19]

The perceived nature and degree of risk to others is thus primarily responsible for determining whether intervention is thought to be required at the general psychiatry or specialist forensic psychiatry level of mental health care. However, how this secondary–tertiary care distinction should, or will, operate is far from clear, particularly because general psychiatric services vary in the extent to which they are able or prepared to respond to different levels and types of dangerous or violent behaviour. Indeed, it is noteworthy that Reed defines high security in terms of patient characteristics ("patients ... who ... require this *because of* their dangerousness" – emphasis added) but defines medium security in terms of the inability of lower-level services to cope ("care for patients who are too difficult or dangerous for local hospitals"). At another level, the public protection imperative may also operate outside of secure settings, in circumstances where the risk to the public is perceived to be relatively small. This may arise where an MDO who no longer requires security still receives support within a specialist out-patient setting, with the aim of preventing relapse of the mental disorder, and consequent increased risk to others, and/or more general preventative supervision. Such community care may also be 'needed' where, by contrast, there is a perceived high risk to public safety but where it is not possible to detain the individual under the Mental Health Act, albeit the person is (at least partially) willing to accept out-patient treatment.[20]

---

[19] Utilisation, even within this major government report, of 'patient characteristics' (e.g. 'dangerous') and also 'lower-level service inability to cope' in order to determine where patients should be placed, *or* to define levels of secure services, is unlikely to bring about a coherent and seamless service system. This disparity is dealt with later in the chapter, as well as in Chapters 7 and 8.

[20] In either circumstance there will be a need to decide whether the relevant community care should be provided by a (parallel) tertiary specialist service or by an (integrated) secondary service.

The central place of both dangerousness and the related need for security in defining MDOs as a distinct 'service group' means that the rhetoric of individual patient need must be carefully disentangled, both practically and ethically, from the public protection imperative. Hence, it can be argued that the involuntary containment of patients in secure settings may be a response not so much to the needs of the individuals so detained but to the needs of society for protection. Indeed, it is undeniable that many MDOs do not perceive themselves as needing psychiatric intervention at all, albeit that this is also true of other psychiatric patients. Taken to extremes, this could suggest that it is misleading to apply the concept 'assessment of need' to such circumstances. That is, the public protective aspects and coercive qualities of psychiatric treatment are incompatible with assessing 'true need' (meaning need solely of the individual patient).

However, there are at least two responses to this argument. First, while it is undoubtedly correct that public protection is a key central purpose of secure mental health services, it can also be argued that detention not only protects the public but also benefits the patient. It may do so by preventing the negative consequences for the individual of offending, through removing the individual from society (and from the opportunities for offending). It may also do so by providing treatment which aims to ameliorate the psychiatric disorder, *and* reduce the future risk of antisocial behaviour.[21] Indeed, it may be considered unethical to fail to provide such treatment and care for individuals whose mental disorder renders them 'not fully responsible' for their actions (implying that there is not only a public protection imperative but also an individual duty of care imperative). It may also be considered unethical to allow a mentally disordered individual to remain within the prison system, where compulsory psychiatric treatment cannot be delivered (other than briefly under common law 'necessity'), merely because the Home Office will only allow admission to a secure psychiatric facility. Ultimately, therefore, it may be beneficial for patients to have their security needs assessed explicitly. This is further emphasised by evidence both of the 'over-containment' of many special hospital patients (Maden *et al*, 1993) and of the inappropriate placement of many of the mentally disordered in prisons (Gunn *et al*, 1991*a*; Brooke *et al*, 1996). It is also important to recognise that MDOs have a range of clinical and social needs,

---

[21] There is not, of course, necessarily a substantial causal connection between an MDO's offending and his/her mental disorder, so that reduced risk of harm to others *may* not arise from treatment of the mental disorder *per se*.

regardless of where they are contained. However, some of these needs will be specific to the secure environment. It may only be via secure containment that such primary individual needs can, or will, be met. Turning the coin over, it follows of course that, even within a single level of security, patients will not be homogeneous across variables and will present with a range of clinical and social needs (Maden *et al*, 1993; Taylor *et al*, 1996). Second, it can be cogently argued that the boundary of needs assessment can, in any event, be validly drawn so as to include the need for public protection. The potential justification of this can be demonstrated by way of reference to a methodological analogy. Cost-benefit analysis is, like needs assessment, a tool used in public policy decision-making and, specifically, in resource allocation. Like needs assessment, 'cost-benefit' addresses, and attempts to measure, 'benefit', albeit cost-benefit analysis also measures cost.[22]

Within cost-benefit analysis, a primary decision which has to be taken in applying the tool to any particular resource allocation problem is, in fact, the decision about what boundary will be drawn around benefit (and also cost); that is, *whose* benefit will be included in the benefit calculation. Hence, intrinsic to the methodology is the need to *choose* who will be included as valid 'beneficiaries' of any potential new public policy intervention. Since needs assessment attempts, albeit in a different way, to allocate benefit (by way of reversal of disbenefit arising from disorder), it follows that there is nothing intrinsically inappropriate in defining the boundaries of a given needs assessment exercise so as to include public benefit. However, if public benefit and individual patient benefit were to be mutually inconsistent, rather than congruent with one another, the needs calculation would have to balance the one against the other.[23]

In summary, the preceding discussion illustrates that MDO needs assessment is profoundly complicated by issues of public protection and patient coercion, which draw one ultimately to questions concerning whose needs it is that are being met – those of the MDO or the public? These issues and questions cannot be ignored. However, MDOs do have a range of clinical and social needs which they share with general psychiatric patients, irrespective of any conceptual complexity arising out of uncertainty about whether security is a need of society or of the individual MDO. Also, security can be a

---

[22] The distinction between, and relationship between, 'economic' approaches to resource allocation and 'needs assessment' approaches is dealt with in detail earlier in the chapter.
[23] This raises profound issues concerning potential patient disbenefit arising from detention, or secure detention, *per se* which are philosophically beyond the scope of this book.

'need' of the individual MDO or/and be validly included as a public need within MDO needs assessment.

Defining services for MDOs

There is a further major class of difficulties in conducting MDO needs assessment that concerns the definition of the services that are expected to respond to MDO need. Such services are inconsistently and commonly poorly defined. Indeed, this is a logical consequence of poor operational definition of the term 'MDO'. However, even services aimed unequivocally at MDOs (e.g. medium-secure units) are poorly defined, and admission criteria are often inadequate or undefined (Taylor *et al*, 1996; Eastman & Bellamy, 1998). Further problems arise from the policy of pursuing a multi-agency approach to assessing and meeting the needs of MDOs (DoH/Home Office, 1992). Although this multi-agency approach is entirely rational, given the variety of agencies with which MDOs come into contact, it creates its own needs assessment difficulties. Different agencies inherently have different general purposes (or balances between different purposes) and different specific roles in relation to MDOs. They therefore tend to adopt varying constructs about, and attitudes to, MDOs, as well as different views about their professional responsibilities to them. They may also *disagree with one another* about what the primary focus of needs assessment should be. Such disagreement will reflect their varying and different philosophies of care (or sometimes non-care in the case of the criminal justice system), as well as the conflicting pressures imposed upon them by policy makers. The different geographical boundaries and catchment areas of the agencies involved may also make a coordinated approach and shared responsibility for needs assessment difficult. Similarly, diverse methods of data collection across agencies make information sharing additionally problematic. More generally, information sharing between agencies, especially between 'caring' and criminal justice agencies, is complicated by proper concerns about confidentiality (Fryers & Greatorex, 1992).

Finally, difficulties can arise from any system that tends to split provision from commissioning of services, be they health or social services. Although commissioners have the primary responsibility for needs assessment, it necessarily involves providers, and the two bodies may well have different approaches to needs assessment and different motivations for conducting it. This can create tensions between what information providers can, or may wish, to make available to commissioners and what commissioners may wish to obtain. Limited financial resources within both provider units and commissioning authorities also substantially restrict the scope and methodological rigour of needs assessment projects, sometimes even disallowing such projects altogether (Cohen & Eastman, 1996).

Defining 'needs assessment'

A final and even more fundamental definitional issue than those already considered relates to the term 'needs assessment' itself. Here, Warheit *et al* (1977) offer a useful approach; in fact, we have taken this in order to underpin the structure of the rest of this book. These researchers have used their extensive research experience in the field in the USA to divide needs assessment into five broad categories, defined according to method. This provides a useful summary framework for understanding and conducting needs assessment. They categorise needs assessment according to whether it is conducted by means of (1) survey, (2) rates under treatment, (3) social indicators, (4) key informants or (5) community forum/ opinion methods. These five categories are presented in Table 1, and under each we list some questions that appear commonly to be asked specifically about MDOs within that method. Indeed, subsequent chapters of this book describe the five needs assessment approaches in turn, evaluating the applicability of each method specifically to MDO needs assessment and placing previous known research relevant to MDO need into each approach and into the overall framework.

'Direct' and 'indirect' methods of needs assessment have been distinguished. Direct needs assessment involves research activities that are designed specifically for the purpose of assessing mental health needs. By contrast, indirect methods employ existing data collected for a variety of purposes unrelated to mental health (e.g. census statistics). Alternatively, they use mental health statistics and research findings but where the data were not collected specifically for the purposes of assessing need (e.g. statistics about psychiatric service utilisation or data from existing epidemiological surveys) (Holzer *et al*, 1988).

A more fundamental needs assessment distinction which has been drawn is that between assessment which is 'population based' and that which is 'individually based'. Aggregate needs assessment, for example in relation to a geographical population (district), is usually used as a tool for planning services and allocating resources within or between geographical areas. By contrast, needs assessment on an individual basis is commonly used, and sometimes

TABLE 1

Needs assessment methods and common questions about MDOs
which may be addressed by each method

Needs assessment method	Common questions which can be addressed by the method
(1) Survey	How many MDOs are there in a district? How many MDOs in a district require medium-security/special hospital/ intensive care/hostel accommodation? How many MDOs from a district are in prison? How many MDOs need a local court diversion scheme? What are the psychological and social needs of MDOs in special hospital? What are the treatment and security needs of MDOs with personality disorder?
(2) Rates under treatment	How many people from a district used medium-security/special hospital beds in the past year? How many MDOs are on the local probation service case-load? How many MDOs used general psychiatry beds in the past year?
(3) Social indicators	What socio-demographic variables predict the number of MDO cases in a geographical area? What socio-demographic variables predict utilisation of medium-security/special hospital beds?
(4) Key informants	What do local stakeholders in a district think are the needs of MDOs?
(5) Community forum/opinion	What does the local community think are the needs of MDOs?

procedurally required in the UK, as a clinical tool with which to identify the individual clinical and social needs of specific patients and with which to identify the appropriate forms of treatment and care that must be offered. However, the population–individual distinction must be seen as operating not dichotomously but rather on a continuum. For example, it would be possible to assess the individual needs of all people with mental disorder within a geographical area and then to aggregate the data in order to produce a measure of population need (i.e. 'bottom-up' population needs assessment) (Strathdee & Thornicroft, 1992). However, it is unlikely that this ideal-world scenario would ever be feasible in such a pure and comprehensive form, for both practical and methodological reasons.

Yet another important needs assessment distinction is that between 'quantitative' and 'qualitative' needs assessment (Hayward *et al*, 1993). The former refers to incidence and prevalence data, as well as data on the effectiveness of services, on service provision and utilisation, and data concerning local factors (e.g. sociodemographic characteristics of a population) which reflect 'need'. By contrast, the qualitative approach refers to (often detailed) information obtained from key informants (e.g. mental health professionals, service users and their relatives and informal carers), and from community members, regarding their perceptions of the needs of particular communities or patient groups (Warheit *et al*, 1977). The two approaches are properly seen as complementary to one another, and it has been suggested that, in combination, they provide better perspectives on 'need' than does either alone (Hayward *et al*, 1993).

Of course, the various needs assessment approaches which we have briefly considered here produce greatly varying types of information, resulting from the particular theoretical framework upon which they are built, their methodology and the level at which the analysis of their data takes place. Even *within* one particular approach, the type and complexity of information obtained, as well as the level of analysis of it, may vary widely between applications, according to the sampling frame and the methodology used.

Returning to Warheit *et al*'s (1977) five approaches, these should *not* be seen as mutually exclusive. Indeed, limitations associated with each technique have led many experts within the field to recommend multiple approaches to needs assessment, so as to work towards a 'convergent' analysis (Warheit *et al*, 1977; Rabkin, 1986; Hall & Royse, 1987). Indeed, the NHS Management Executive (1991) recommended just such a 'hybrid' approach to needs assessment, and we will describe this in more detail in Chapter 3. However, it has to be acknowledged that the adoption of multiple approaches may not always be practical, particularly given the financial resources available for needs assessment (Hall & Royse, 1987; Cohen & Eastman, 1996). Even if multiple approaches are used, it is still possible for planners then to be faced with several sets of data that do not obviously and unambiguously translate into a clearly defined and quantified need for services. Indeed, various data types may be in conflict with one another and, even though this may be confusing, it is a predictable result of the broad boundaries which characterise the state of the art of needs assessment (Royse & Drude, 1982).

In summary as regards methods, selection of the most appropriate needs assessment approach(es) for a particular policy field will occur only if there is clarity about the appropriate level at which the assessment is intended to take place. This, in turn, will determine the type and complexity of information that is required sensibly to inform the planning and commissioning activities that must follow. For example, planners will need to adopt a very different approach if they are attempting to predict the need for in-patient psychiatric beds across several districts than if they are planning services which address the psychological and social care needs of psychotic out-patients in their districts.

Conclusions

This chapter has been concerned with the problems of defining needs, the need for health care, the need for mental health care and the need specifically for MDO mental health care, as well as the complications which arise from inclusion of the public's 'need' for protection. It has also addressed various approaches to needs assessment, including using various 'proxies' for need. Necessarily, the chapter has been written broadly, in terms of both general health needs and general mental health needs, although clearly the latter are directly relevant to all MDOs. However, MDOs have additional needs (as well as potential benefits and costs) and we have attempted also to include these, as well as placing them within the more general frameworks that we have described and discussed. We have sometimes been somewhat drawn away from problems of *definition* towards problems relating to methodology and measurement. However, we have tried to restrict ourselves as much as possible in this chapter to definitional and general matters, so as to provide a theoretical grounding for the rest of the book. Where we *have* strayed away from these strict confines, this reflects a degree of artificiality in drawing distinctions between definitions, method-ology and and measurement. Indeed, many papers and texts which we reviewed in the process of preparing the book do, in fact, weave the two together, sometimes almost without making (or perhaps even recognising) the distinction. Hopefully, where we have ourselves strayed into specific method and practice, this will have provided insights and trailers for the main body of the book.

As described at the end of Chapter 1, Chapters 3–6 will now describe each of the needs assessment approaches listed in Table 1 and will address their applicability specifically to needs assessment for MDOs. They will also provide a review of research relating to needs assessment for MDOs, categorised according to the five empirical approaches.[24] Chapter 7 will then address 'outcome' and 'ability to benefit' in relation to MDOs.

---

[24] For the purposes of the research review, aside from reviewing published material, we carried out a national survey of projects relating to needs assessment for MDOs. We contacted public health departments in all DHAs in England and Wales and key informants whom we identified from the published literature. We asked for information about any previous or current needs assessment projects in relation to MDOs. Some of the responses are reported in the following chapters. However, much of this work cannot be helpfully summarised because of diverse methodologies and the variable quality of the information provided. In summary, it is clear that many DHAs have conducted needs assessments for MDOs. However, the methodological sophistication and breadth of the work varied considerably and it is unclear to what extent even the very local needs assessment projects have affected the planning and commissioning of services.

3 The survey approach

Introduction

The survey approach to needs assessment uses surveys of community samples or of samples of population subgroups, in order to establish estimates of need. This approach to needs assessment is most frequently associated with the concept of the epidemiological survey. In its favour, Warheit *et al* (1977) argue that the epidemiological survey is the most direct and powerful method for determining the size and nature of mental health problems in a community. It commonly measures the prevalence and incidence of psychiatric disorder using standardised diagnostic instruments. Samples may be drawn from specific geographic areas (or even whole countries) or from selected sub-populations defined not by geography but by some pre-selected status (e.g. prisoners). The epidemiological survey may also focus on one disorder (e.g. schizophrenia), adopting a case-finding strategy which most effectively seeks out that condition (Mann, 1990). Such a strategy is appropriate when the disorder is rare and, therefore, likely to be detected in the general population only if very large (and expensive) samples are drawn.

The NHS Management Executive (1991) specifically recommended an epidemiological approach to needs assessment. This requires measurement of both the incidence and prevalence of 'the problem' within the population, along with a measure of the population's ability to benefit from health care interventions (see Chapter 2). However, there are several fundamental problems in adopting this approach to needs assessment, in relation both to mental health care in general and to care for MDOs in particular. Existing local epidemiological data are often lacking or deficient and it is seldom feasible to conduct epidemiological studies specifically for the task of needs assessment, in particular, because of the cost, expertise and time required to complete them (Rabkin, 1986). Hence, Hirsch & Jarman (1993) argue that "using direct surveys of mental health

66

service needs for every community would be a highly impractical way of determining how resources for health care should be distributed" (p. 519). Additionally, information about the effectiveness of interventions and the outcomes of treatment is rarely available, especially at the local levels required by purchasers, and economic evaluations are also frequently inadequate (Stevens & Gabbay, 1991; Donaldson & Mooney, 1991; Stevens & Raftery, 1992; Robinson & Elkan, 1996). However, Stevens & Raftery (1992) suggest that, for most diseases, national estimates of incidence and prevalence can, in fact, be applied locally if they are interpreted in the light of knowledge of factors accounting for local variations in morbidity. This assumes, of course, that the factors accounting for local variation are clearly elucidated. However, this may not always be the case, particularly for disorders with complex and poorly understood aetiologies, and such disorders include many types of mental disorder.

The most fundamental problem with the epidemiological approach, however, is that measurement of the prevalence and incidence of psychiatric disorder alone is insufficient to establish the needs of a population. Hence, although the results of epidemiological studies using standardised measures of morbidity can be useful for estimating the likely burden of psychiatric disorders in the population, and thus for providing indirect evidence of needs for treatment (Rabkin, 1986), they cannot be directly translated into estimates of service need. As Bebbington (1992, p. 103) has concluded, "We cannot assume that subjects in the community need psychiatric treatment merely because they meet symptomatic case criteria". Similarly, according to Wing (1994):

> "although different diagnoses suggest likely contingencies for treatment and care, they do not point at once to specific patterns of need. Part of the reason for this is that most symptoms can occur at all degrees of clinical severity from mild to severe and, independently, at all degrees of chronicity from a brief single episode to life-long disablement. A severe anxiety state can be more devastating than a mild psychosis." (p. 211)

Establishing rates of disorder *per se* is, therefore, only a first step in the assessment of the need for services and treatment in the general population. In order for an epidemiological study to measure need directly, it is necessary that it be extended so that prevalence and incidence are measured in conjunction with measures of need for specific services or specific types of treatment and care. However, direct measurement of need has not traditionally been a component of epidemiological studies (Lehtinen *et al*, 1989).

A number of epidemiological studies have included measures of service utilisation as additional proxy measures of need. Others have gone beyond simply measuring psychiatric diagnoses by also including dimensions of social performance or impairment (Leighton *et al*, 1963; Shapiro *et al*, 1985; Ciarlo *et al*, 1992*a*; Meltzer & Jenkins, 1994). However, as Bebbington (1992) has stated, although these studies are superior to other epidemiological studies that only measure the prevalence and incidence of mental disorder, their implications for health planning are unclear. He has argued, therefore, that a fourth generation of epidemiological surveys is required, focusing on the evaluation of need for specific treatments and for the services within which they are most appropriately provided. This recommendation has been echoed by Wing *et al* (1992) (see Chapter 2).

The national survey of psychiatric morbidity (Metzler *et al*, 1995*a*, 1995*b*, 1995*c*, 1996*a*, 1996*b*; Gill *et al*, 1996; Foster *et al*, 1996) represents the latest (and largest) community survey of psychiatric morbidity in the UK. It estimated the prevalence of adult psychiatric morbidity in private households and institutions. It also examined physical complaints, service utilisation and treatment of adults with psychiatric disorders, as well as surveying the social functioning, and service usage by, adults with psychotic disorders living in the community and in institutions. Further, it included a survey of psychiatric disorder among the homeless. Overall prevalence rates were broken down in the survey by RHA boundaries, thus illustrating the variation in psychiatric morbidity across those geographical areas. The survey also provided valuable information about the influence of personal, social and economic factors on rates of morbidity, while the service utilisation data provided useful information about the types of psychiatric morbidity found in various residential care settings and psychiatric hospitals. However, this information is not reported by the survey on a DHA basis and is not broken down according to type of NHS psychiatric hospital or ward. Hence, although this major study provides a valuable new data source for the epidemiological approach to needs assessment, it falls short of Bebbington's (1992) recommendations in that it provides only indirect measures of need, that is, in terms of rates of psychiatric morbidity and of service utilisation.

The NHS Management Executive (1991) recognised the method-ological difficulties and information deficiencies involved in the epidemiological approach to needs assessment and recommended, therefore, that DHAs adopt a 'hybrid approach' to needs assessment (see also Chapter 2). It suggested specifically that local health authorities should combine the 'strict approach' implied by its definition of need with a two-pronged 'pragmatic approach', which recognises that the 'strict approach' is not always possible or desirable in the real world. The first element of the 'pragmatic approach' is described as the 'comparative' method. Hence, if people with the same characteristics in different districts are not receiving the same services, those who are not receiving a service, or receiving a 'lesser' service, can be viewed as in need. This example corresponds specifically with Bradshaw's (1972) notion of 'comparative need' (see Chapter 2). Similarly, if one provider within a district is achieving better outcomes than another, then those served by the latter provider are in need. The second element of the 'pragmatic approach' is described as the 'corporate' method. This requires that commissioners take account of the views and opinions of other agencies and individuals involved in health and social care (e.g. GPs, hospital providers, health care workers, service users, local people, RHAs and the NHS Management Executive itself). However, the NHS Management Executive provided no guidance about how inevitably conflicting views about local 'needs' or 'demands' were to be balanced and prioritised (the discussion in Chapter 2, particularly in relation to 'demand' and 'proxy demand' for services, is pertinent here). In particular, conflicts can arise between perceptions of need on the part of policy makers, professionals, users and lay people. Also, some stakeholders may be better able to articulate their demands than others (Robinson & Elkan, 1996). Such a lack of central direction will now be addressed, however, through the National Service Framework for Mental Health (DoH, 1999).

Finally by way of general introduction to the survey approach, Stevens & Raftery (1994) have stated that, in order to be of practical value, epidemiological data and information about effectiveness and outcome should be complemented by a third component, namely, information about the services currently provided. Changing provision for the better necessitates, they argue, knowledge of existing services, so as both to determine which services ought to be changed and to identify opportunities for release of the resources which will enable the change to occur.

The survey approach and needs assessment for MDOs

The epidemiological approach to needs assessment as applied to MDOs has its own particular and additional problems. These centre on the fact that the establishment of the prevalence and incidence of 'the problem' (i.e. the number of MDOs) and of the ability of this group to benefit from health care is not a simple task. This is because, as has already been discussed at some length in Chapter 2, 'the problem' is itself ill defined.

There are no epidemiological studies which examine the size of the 'MDO problem' in the general population (Jenkins, 1990). Indeed, epidemiological studies of this kind are neither practicable nor sensible. Both serious psychiatric disorder and serious offending are relatively rare and they are rarer still in combination. Therefore, a very large and expensive community study would be required in order to identify cases where both conditions were met. Further, it is uncertain with what reliability the general population would be willing to confess offending behaviour to researchers, so that many cases would be likely to remain unidentified. Ethical considerations regarding what to do about cases actually identified in the community are also pertinent. For example, what do researchers do if they discover a homicidal paedophile at large in the community who requires (indeed needs) immediate treatment in a (perhaps special) hospital? Further, although even an ideal study might provide precise rates of psychiatric disorder coupled with offending, it might not translate validly into need for, or uptake of, services, either nationally or locally. For instance, many individuals identified by this method may have no desire for psychiatric treatment whatsoever, and it could be argued that it would be unethical to identify cases and then coerce them into treatment. Rather, a specific assessment of need for intervention, as well as the individual's attitude to service uptake, would have to be undertaken. Furthermore, addressing the possible causal link between 'caseness for psychiatric disorder' and 'caseness for offending' would be highly problematic, particularly because of the complex chronological and causal relationship between psychiatric disorder and offending. A decision would have to be made about the chronological link between the two variables. For example, MDO caseness might be defined for the purposes of such a study as 'psychiatric caseness in the past six months coupled with offending or equivalent behaviour in the past six months'. However, these two variables may have occurred independently of each other over that time. Also, neither may currently require intervention of any kind. Overall, therefore, even though it may have great advantages in addressing risk factors for violence in mental disorder (Monahan & Steadman, 1983; Swanson *et al*, 1996; Wessely, 1997), the community survey method cannot be recommended for MDO needs assessment.

We turn therefore to survey studies of specific sub-populations.

Needs assessment surveys in the prison population

As emphasised previously, in order for an epidemiological study of the 'MDO problem' truly to address questions about service needs, it is necessary to extend the question beyond prevalence and incidence to 'What do these cases need in terms of treatment, care and security? What psychological and social needs do they have, and how can these be met?' Very few epidemiological studies have extended their remit to include a measure of need in conjunction with psychiatric morbidity.

Several studies designed explicitly to address the remand and sentenced prison population have shown high rates of psychiatric morbidity (Banks, 1978; Gunn *et al*, 1978; Taylor & Gunn, 1984). They have also highlighted the elevated suicide rates among prisoners (Home Office, 1986; McClure, 1987; Dooley, 1990; Her Majesty's Chief Inspector of Prisons for England and Wales, 1990). These studies do not provide a measure of need for specific services, and were never intended so to do. However, they do provide useful information about the existence and size of 'the problem'.

A number of recent epidemiological studies of the national prison population (in England and Wales) have measured both psychiatric morbidity and the need for specific services.

Gunn *et al* (1991*a*) carried out a cross-sectional epidemiological survey of 5% of the male sentenced prisoners in England and Wales (*n* = 1769). They found that 37% of the sample was suffering from some psychiatric disorder. Two per cent were found to suffer from a psychotic illness, representing approximately 730 men in the prison population as a whole. A large proportion (23%) was diagnosed with substance misuse, and 10% were found to have a personality disorder. Gunn *et al* also identified those requiring some form of psychiatric intervention. They allocated prisoners to one of five treatment categories, based on the clinical judgement of an interviewer or of a research panel. They concluded that 52 prisoners (3%) required immediate transfer to NHS hospitals: 17 were thought to require treatment in a special hospital, 21 in an RSU and 14 in district psychiatric services. Of the total 1769, a further 96 (5%) required treatment in a therapeutic community for the personality disordered, 90 (5%) required further assessment and 176 (10%) required treatment in prison.

These findings suggest that nationally, at the time of the study, approximately 1100 prisoners warranted transfer from prison to NHS psychiatric hospitals. However, it is noteworthy that all psychotic prisoners were not thought to need treatment outside prison (albeit that the vast majority did). It is also noteworthy that prisoners who did not want treatment, and who were also thought not to be detainable under the Mental Health Act 1983, were considered by the researchers not to be in need. It is important to note, further, that not all prisoners who were in need of treatment were judged to require it within a secure setting.

Gunn *et al* recommended that provision of (particularly long-term) medium-security facilities should be improved and that services for people with personality disorders and substance misuse (the largest group) should be further developed within both the Prison Service and the NHS. They also recommended that a second therapeutic prison similar to HMP Grendon Underwood should be developed and that specialised assessment and treatment units specifically for sex offenders would be a valuable addition within both the Prison Service and the NHS. They recommended, further, that hospitals should develop special treatment programmes for personality disordered offenders.

Maden *et al* (1994*a*) reported findings specifically regarding the women prisoners (*n* = 258) surveyed by Gunn *et al* (1991*b*) and compared these findings with those in the male sample. A total of 147 women (57%) were given at least one psychiatric diagnosis. The prevalence of psychosis in women prisoners was found to be about 2%, similar to the rate found in the male sample. However, women had higher rates of mental handicap (2% vs. 0.4%), personality disorder (18% vs. 10%), neurotic disorder (16% vs. 6%) and substance misuse (35% vs. 23%) than the male sample. Overall, the number of sentenced women prisoners with a psychiatric disorder in England and Wales was estimated to be 760 (16 with a psychotic illness, 184 with a personality disorder and 364 with substance misuse or dependence). Of the total sample, 113 women were considered to require some kind of psychiatric intervention. Twelve (5%) were considered to require transfer to psychiatric hospital and 20 (8%) to a therapeutic community. A further 25 (9%) were judged to need further assessment and 56 (22%) 'out-patient' treatment in prison.

Maden *et al* concluded, therefore, that many sentenced female prisoners have unmet needs for psychiatric treatment within the Prison Service and the NHS. They identified a particular gap in relation to the treatment of personality disorder and substance abuse within the Prison Service and recommended a trial of a prison wing run on therapeutic community principles. This recommendation was reiterated in a later paper related specifically to the needs of sentenced prisoners for therapeutic community treatment within both the Prison Service and the NHS (Maden *et al*, 1994*b*). The findings also suggest that male and female prisoners should not be seen as a homogeneous group and that their needs for treatment may differ substantially.

Maden *et al* (1995) subsequently conducted a cross-sectional survey of psychiatric morbidity and need in male and female remand prisoners in England and Wales; the results relating to female prisoners are described here and those relating to male prisoners, reported by Brooke *et al* (1996), are discussed below. Among the female remand prisoners (n = 245), at least one psychiatric disorder was found in 77% of cases. Psychotic disorders were detected in 5%, personality disorder in 16%, neurotic disorder in 44% and substance misuse/dependence in 42%. Sixty-eight per cent of women were considered to require some kind of treatment or intervention, 32 (13%) in an NHS psychiatric bed – 13 a medium-security bed and 19 a local psychiatric bed. A further 14% of the sample were thought to require treatment in a therapeutic community, 3% within the prison health care system and 27% as out-patients in the community or prison. Nine per cent were adjudged to need motivational interviewing and 2% were thought to require monitoring.

Brooke *et al* (1996) conducted a cross-sectional, point prevalence study of psychiatric morbidity in the male remand prison population (n = 750). They detected psychiatric disorder in 63% of prisoners. The main diagnoses were substance misuse (38%), neurotic disorder (26%), personality disorder (11%) and psychosis (5%). A total of 414 (55%) prisoners were adjudged, on clinical grounds, to have an immediate need for psychiatric treatment of some kind. Of these, 64 (9%) were adjudged to require transfer to a NHS bed (30 to a local hospital, 32 to a medium-secure unit and 2 to a special hospital). A further 131 (17%) were thought to require psychiatric treatment within the prison health care service, and 115 (15%) were adjudged to need motivational interviewing in order to address their substance misuse problems. A further 104 (14%) were adjudged suitable for treatment within a therapeutic community. Extrapolation to the remand population as a whole suggested that approximately 680 male prisoners required transfer to hospital for psychiatric treatment, including about 380 men with serious mental illness, and half of the beds required were at the medium-security level. It is particularly noteworthy that psychotic disorder was present at four to five times the level found in the general population. As with the Gunn *et al* (1991*a*) study, cases who both refused treatment and did not qualify for admission under the Mental Health Act were considered not to be in need and, again, not all prisoners who did require transfer to hospital needed secure psychiatric facilities. The high proportion of cases with substance misuse problems was also of note.

Aside from the obvious implications for NHS and private sector psychiatric service development, both Brooke *et al* and Maden *et al* recommended that prison staff should be better trained to deal with mental disorder in the prison population and that additional specialist psychiatric input within the Prison Service should be encouraged. They also suggested that improvements should be made in the links between the Prison Service and psychiatric services in order to facilitate the speedy diversion of remand prisoners, and guidelines should be established within prison for the management of mentally disordered prisoners.

The most recent and largest study of psychiatric morbidity in prisons was carried out by the Office of National Statistics in 1997 (Singleton *et al*, 1998). This survey, which was commissioned by the DoH, examined psychiatric morbidity among male and female remand and sentenced prisoners in England and Wales. It also examined use of services and receipt of care in relation to mental disorder, and attempted to establish current and lifetime factors associated with mental disorders of prisoners (e.g. child abuse and unemployment). Table 2 illustrates the main findings regarding psychiatric morbidity. The study also described the socio-demographic characteristics of the sample, and reported on intellectual functioning, self-harm, comorbidity, use of medication and services, daily living and social functioning and risk factors for mental disorder.

These major prison studies provide valuable data on rates of psychiatric morbidity and need in sentenced and remand prisoners. However, they do so only on a national level. It is extremely difficult to extrapolate the findings to local NHS districts or even regions. This is because all the studies failed to report the geographical origins of the prisoners sampled, and because there are no available statistics about the number of prisoners from specific geographical locations, let alone by health district or region. Indeed, other prison studies have shown how poorly recorded is this type of information within the prison system (Mitchison *et al*, 1994). Hence, findings can only be extrapolated over several stages, and this is likely to reduce substantially the validity of the information obtained.

There are other studies of psychiatric morbidity and need in remand prisoners (see Table 3), but these have only examined rates of morbidity and need within single remand prisons. Their general value is even more limited, therefore, than the national studies already reviewed, although the results may, paradoxically, be of more direct use at a local level than data extrapolated from national studies (albeit that prisoners are not necessarily detained in their local NHS catchment areas).

TABLE 2

Main findings of the Office of National Statistics survey of psychiatric morbidity in prisoners (data adapted from Singleton et al, 1998). Initial (lay) interviews were conducted with 3142 prisoners, and follow-up clinical interviews with a one-in-five subsample (n=505)

% Psychiatric problem	% Male remand prisoners	% Male sentenced prisoners	Female remand prisoners
Functional psychosis in past year[1]	10 (184)	7 (210)	14 (109)
Personality disorder[1]	78 (181)	64 (210)	50 (105)
Neurotic disorder in past week before interview	59 (1250)	40 (1121)	Remand: 76 (187)
			Sentenced: 63 (584)
Alcohol misuse (i.e. harmful or hazardous drinking in the year before imprisonment)	58 (1250)	63 (1120)	Remand: 36 (187)
			Sentenced: 39 (581)
Drug dependence in the year before imprisonment	51 (1241)	43 (1119)	Remand: 54 (185)
			Sentenced: 41 (583)
Drug use in the year before imprisonment	73 (1244)	66 (1121)	Remand: 66 (186)
			Sentenced: 55 (583)

1. Obtained from clinical interviews on the one-in-five subsample.

TABLE 3
Surveys of psychiatric morbidity and need in sentenced and remand prisoners in England and Wales

Authors	Sample	Rates of psychiatric disorder	Need

Gunn *et al* (1991*a*)	5% cross-section of male sentenced prisoners in England and Wales	Psychiatric disorder = 37%
		• psychotic = 2%
		• personality disorder = 10%
		• neurotic disorder = 6%
		• substance misuse = 23%
		• organic disorder = 0.8%
			In need of psychiatric intervention = 23%
			• transfer to NHS hospital = 3% (*n* = 52)
			  – special hospital = 1% (*n* = 17)
			  – regional secure unit = 1% (*n* = 21)
			  – district psychiatric hospitals = 1% (*n* = 14)
			• therapeutic community = 5%
			• further assessment = 5%
			• treatment in prison = 10%

Maden *et al* (1994*a*)	25% cross-section of female sentenced prisoners in England and Wales (*n* = 258)	Psychiatric disorder = 57% • psychotic = 2% • personality disorder = 18% • neurotic disorder = 16% • substance misuse = 35% • mental handicap = 2%	In need of psychiatric intervention = 44% • transfer to NHS psychiatric hospital = 5% • therapeutic community = 8% • further assessment = 9% • treatment in prison = 22%

Maden *et al* (1995)	82% cross-section of female remand prisoners in England and Wales (*n* = 245)	Psychiatric disorder = 77%
		• psychosis = 5%
		• personality disorder = 16%
		• neurotic disorder = 44%
		• substance misuse = 42%
			In need of treatment = 68%
			• transfer to NHS psychiatric bed = 13% (*n* = 32)
			  – medium-secure unit = 5% (*n* = 13)
			  – local district psychiatric bed = 8% (*n* = 19)
			• therapeutic community = 14%
			• treatment in prison = 3%
			• out-patient treatment in community/prison = 27%
			• motivational interviewing = 9%
			• monitoring = 2%

contd....

TABLE 3 (contd...)

Authors	Sample	Rates of psychiatric disorder	Need
Brooke *et al* (1996)	9.4% cross-section of male remand prisoners in England and Wales ($n = 750$)	Psychiatric disorder = 63% • psychosis = 5% • personality disorder = 11% • neurotic disorder = 26% • substance misuse = 38%	Immediate need for treatment = 55% • transfer to NHS psychiatric bed = 9% ($n = 64$) – special hospital = 0.3% ($n = 2$) – medium-secure unit = 4% ($n = 32$) – local district psychiatric bed = 4% ($n = 30$) • therapeutic community = 14% • treatment in prison = 17% • motivational interviewing for substance misuse problems = 15%
Watt *et al* (1993)	20% sample of male remand prisoners in HMP Bristol ($n = 31$)	Psychiatric disorder = 13% Personality disorder = 13% Past/current substance misuse = 54%	In need of involuntary in-patient treatment = 3%
Birmingham *et al* (1996)	Consecutive male remands to HMP Durham ($n = 569$)	One or more current mental disorder (excluding substance misuse) = 26% Acute psychosis = 5%	In need of psychiatric treatment = 30% • urgent treatment = 9% • immediate transfer to NHS psychiatric bed = 3%

See Table 2 for a summary of the findings of the ONS survey of psychiatric morbidity in male and female sentenced and remand prisoners (Singleton *et al*, 1998).

Watt *et al* (1993) conducted a pilot study to assess the feasibility of mounting a full-scale prevalence study of psychiatric morbidity in the male remand population of Bristol Prison. They drew a 20% sample over a three-month period of all males remanded for the first time on current charges (*n* = 31). Rates of past and current substance misuse were high (up to 54%). Thirteen per cent of subjects satisfied diagnostic criteria for psychiatric disorder and a further 13% satisfied criteria for personality disorder. However, only one subject was thought to require involuntary psychiatric treatment. The authors concluded that a national morbidity study would be feasible.

A study by Birmingham *et al* (1996) revealed deficiencies in the prison screening system. Over seven months, they screened consecutive male remands to Durham Prison (*n* = 569) for psychiatric disorder using standardised diagnostic instruments. They found that 148 (26%) had one or more current mental disorders (excluding substance misuse), including 24 (5%) with an acute psychotic illness. However, routine reception screening identified only 34 cases with a mental disorder and six with an acute psychosis. Birmingham *et al* identified 168 (30%) of their sample as requiring psychiatric treatment and 50 (9%) as needing it urgently. Of these 50, 16 were judged to need immediate transfer to a NHS bed, and only 17 were placed in the prison hospital wing at the time of the study. The authors concluded that routine prison screening for psychiatric disorder is neither sensitive nor specific enough in detecting mental disorder and they recommended that screening should be improved, although bed availability would have to be increased in order to meet the demand that would follow.

All of the studies so far described – with the exception of Singleton *et al* (1998) (see Table 2) – are summarised, so as to assist comparison, in Table 3.

Needs assessment surveys in the special hospital population[25]

Several aspects of the functioning of special hospitals have caused concern in recent years (Mental Health Act Commission, 1989, 1991, 1993; DoH/Home Office, 1992) and have been widely

---

[25] Surveys in this section of the chapter are all focused on patients who are currently using services. It could therefore be argued that they belong more properly within Chapter 4, which describes the 'rates-under-treatment' approach to needs assessment. However, we believe that they fit more appropriately into this chapter because they aim to measure 'need' directly,

discussed in the public domain (Bynoe, 1990, 1992; Bluglass, 1992; Dillner, 1992). Indeed, as we write, Ashworth Hospital has recently undergone its second major inquiry in the space of five years (Fallon *et al*, 1999). Not only are there moral concerns about the very existence of the special hospitals as 'total institutions' (Goffman, 1961), but there are also concerns about the proportion of patients who appear to be over-contained in special hospitals, and about the organisational and bureaucratic obstacles to transfer (Dell, 1980; Dell & Robertson, 1988; Dolan & Shetty, 1995; Brown *et al*, 1996). The Fallon inquiry into Ashworth Hospital arose because there was evidence not of abuse of patients, as reflected in the earlier Blom-Cooper inquiry (Blom-Copper *et al*, 1992), but because there was inadequate control of patients. The range of concerns tends, itself, somewhat to validate Blom-Cooper's letter to the then Secretary of State for Health accompanying the first Ashworth report, which argued that English special hospitals are too large and problematic to be capable of sustained effective management.

A number of recent surveys have examined specifically the treatment and security needs of special hospital patients (Table 4).

Dell & Robertson (1988) asked responsible medical officers (RMOs) at Broadmoor special hospital to provide information about the number of men who were, at the time of the study, being processed for transfer and the number they considered not to require maximum security. Of the psychotic men ($n = 127$), 24% were already within the discharge or transfer process. A further 37% were described as not needing maximum security and yet a further 10% were described as probably not needing it (i.e. only 28% were judged definitely to need maximum security). Of the non-psychotic men, 39% were already being processed for discharge or transfer. A further 29% were considered not to require maximum security and, again, yet a further 10% were described as probably not requiring maximum security (i.e. only 23% were judged definitely to need maximum security). Dell & Robertson also identified considerable delays in transfer, consistent with the earlier findings of Dell (1980). They noted the shortfall of medium-secure units and recommended that smaller, regionally based facilities would best meet the needs of those adjudged to require long-term care.

Taylor *et al* (1991) carried out a survey of the security needs of all special hospital patients on a census date ($n = 1708$). Patients' RMOs

---

whereas the rates-under-treatment approach attempts to assess 'need' indirectly. The RUT approach does this by measuring service utilisation without directly addressing whether the individuals using the services are appropriately placed (see Chapter 8 for a more detailed discussion of categorical overlap between methods of needs assessment).

TABLE 4
Surveys of security needs in special hospitals

Authors and date	Sample	Raters	% found not to require maximum security
Dell & Robertson (1988)	All men with psychopathic disorder (n = 106) matched with psychotic men (n = 127)	RMOs	Psychotic men: • subject to discharge proceedings = 24% • probably do not need maximum security = 10% • do not need maximum security = 37% Non-psychotic men: • subject to discharge proceedings = 39% • probably do not need maximum security = 10% • do not need maximum security = 29%
Taylor et al (1991)	All patients on a census day (n = 1708)	RMOs	59%
Courtney et al (1992)	All special hospital patients from a Leeds catchment area (n = 21)	RMOs	43%
Maden et al (1993)	20% cross-section of all patients (excluding those admitted for < 1 year) (n = 296)	Research team Clinical team	63% 50%
Shaw et al (1994a)	Patients from North Western Region (n = 119)	RMOs Panel	45% 67%
Murray et al (1994)	Patients from North West Thames Region (n = 75)	Research panel	48%
Bartlett et al (1996)	Patients from South West Thames Region 1992 (n = 92) 1993 (n = 87)	RMOs	47% 40%

were asked to rate each patient's need for maximum, medium or minimum security on three dimensions: perimeter security, internal security and dependency needs. A total of 23 patients (1.4%) were identified as having no maximum security needs (i.e. for perimeter or internal security) and no maximum dependency needs. Only 87 (5%) were described as having both maximum security and maximum dependency needs. A wide range of intermediate need was also identified. A total of 597 (35%) patients were thought to need maximum perimeter security and 287 (17%) were thought to require maximum internal security. A total of 182 cases (11%) were thought to require both maximum internal and perimeter security. Additionally, 263 (15%) cases were adjudged to have maximum dependency needs, and nearly two-thirds of these were thought to require at least one other dimension of maximum security. Overall, only 41% of the special hospital population were rated as needing one or more dimensions of maximum security.

The majority of patients who were adjudged not to require maximum security were thought to require at least one aspect of medium security (n = 755). Of the total sample, 644 (38%) were thought to need medium perimeter security and 359 (21%) were thought to require both a medium-security perimeter and internal security.

Of the special hospital patients, 248 (15%) were considered to require minimal or no security, mostly within general psychiatry services or equivalent (non-secure) mental handicap facilities. The 23 cases evaluated as having no maximum security or maximum dependency needs at all were more likely to be female, older and to have been in hospital for longer than the rest of the sample. Nearly of all of them were not subject to any discharge or transfer plan. A total of 634 cases were considered as 'probably ready for transfer', although more than half were experiencing transfer delays, the majority for longer than six months. The most frequently cited reason for delays was lack of an appropriate alternative facility.

Hence, Taylor *et al* (1991) highlighted the shortfall in medium-security beds, including long-stay beds, and also identified deficiencies in secure facilities for patients with mental impairment in the south-east of England. Further, they identified a need for more specialist treatment facilities for personality disorder within the special hospital system.

Courtney *et al* (1992) surveyed RMO opinion about the readiness to move of all special hospital patients originating from a Leeds catchment area. RMOs rated only 12 of the 21 (57%) special hospital patients from the catchment area as unfit for transfer to lesser security. The researchers also recorded referrals for transfer made by special hospital consultants to RSUs and special care units (SCUs), and noted any obstacles to transfer. Four patients were awaiting transfer to an appropriate placement outside special hospital and one was waiting for Home Office approval for transfer to an SCU or RSU. Three patients with a diagnosis of learning disability and psychotic disorder required transfer to an SCU for patients with learning disability, but no such facility was available. Another patient was considered ready for transfer to a lower level of security but RSU staff had judged this patient as too dangerous for their unit.

Maden *et al* (1993) examined the treatment and security needs of a 20% cross-section of patients in the special hospitals (*n* = 296). The treatment and security needs of the sample were judged by a research panel and by the patients' clinical teams. Both the research and clinical teams rated over 80% of cases as needing medium or higher security, with the research team identifying maximum security needs in 37% of the sample and clinical teams identifying 50%. The research team and clinical team estimated that 63% and 50% of patients, respectively, did not have an immediate need for maximum security. Estimated immediate security needs as rated by the research and clinical teams are shown in Table 5.

Between one-third and two-thirds of those who were considered to have a need for medium security were thought to require long-term care (i.e. over two years).

Maden *et al* extrapolated their data so as to identify a need nationally for between 460 and 675 additional medium-security beds arising from the special hospital population. They also identified a need for 'new long-stay' beds at all levels of security, from open wards to medium security. They further emphasised the need for treatment and rehabilitation within the special hospital system in order to improve the quality of life of patients there and to increase the chances of transfer. They suggested specifically the need for an increased range of environments and treatments more closely tailored to the individual needs of special hospital patients

TABLE 5
Estimated immediate security needs of a 20% cross-section of the special hospital population
(n = 296) (Maden et al, 1993)

Security need	Ratings of research team (%)		Ratings of clinical team (%)	
Maximum	108	(37)	149	(50)
Medium	135	(46)	92	(31)
Locked general ward	28	(10)	12	(4)
Open general ward	15	(5)	27	(9)
Non-hospital care	10	(3)	16	(5)

(e.g. mixed-gender wards and psychotherapy). They also encouraged the making of better links between the special hospitals and district psychiatric services, including appropriate financial links. They noted further that most special hospital patients were expected to show little significant clinical improvement over the next five years, and that even those thought to be suitable for non-hospital treatment would require specialised, high-dependency facilities which would be difficult and expensive to develop. In spite of their findings of large numbers of misplaced special hospital patients, the authors saw little scope for decreasing the number of special hospital beds, because they envisaged that demand from the prison system would fill any beds emptied of over-contained patients.

A number of other studies have examined the security needs of special hospital patients from specific RHAs (Table 4).

Shaw *et al* (1994*a*) used a research panel and RMO opinion to rate the current and future placement needs of all special hospital patients from the North West Region (*n* = 119). RMOs stated that 45% of patients did not currently require maximum security and that 33% required medium security (with a 1:3 ratio of long-term to short-term medium security). The research panel assessed 67% of patients as inappropriately placed in a special hospital and adjudged 60% to need medium security (with a ratio of long-term to short-term medium security of 2:1). As in the Maden *et al* (1993) study, there was a trend for RMOs to recommend higher levels of security than the research panel. However, they agreed that 26% of cases were appropriately placed in special hospital and that 40% of patients should be in lesser security. RMOs and the research panel predicted that 52% and 84% of patients, respectively, would not require special hospital in two years' time. The disagreement between RMOs and the research panel may reflect a number of factors. RMOs may be more familiar with the needs of their patients, and may have a better understanding of transfer difficulties than the research panel. Disagreements may also reflect RMOs' pessimism about the availability of beds outside the special hospitals into which patients could be transferred. The findings overall were consistent with those of both Taylor *et al* (1991) and Maden *et al* (1993) and were considered by the authors as representative of the special hospital population as a whole. Shaw *et al* (1994*b*) recommended an increase in short-term medium-security bed numbers, particularly at a local level, and a corresponding decrease in special hospital beds (while bearing in mind the effect of potential unmet need within the Prison Service).

Murray *et al* (1994) conducted an audit of the security needs of all special hospital patients from North West Thames Region (*n* =

111), again by using a research panel. Of the 75 cases who were finally assessed, 39 (52%) were considered to be appropriately placed in a special hospital (although in 16 cases there was some doubt expressed about this). Of the 36 (48%) inappropriately placed cases, 15 were judged suitable for short-term medium security, 16 for long-term medium security, four for a long-stay locked general psychiatry ward and one (a prisoner on remand) was not considered to be mentally disordered at all. Murray *et al* extrapolated their findings and suggested a national demand for 750 maximum-security beds, adjusted for regional variations in morbidity and for unmet need within the prison population. They also suggested that smaller regional units may be preferable to the larger special hospitals currently in existence. They further recommended that a reliable information system should be introduced as a matter of urgency in order to provide comprehensive information about regional and district responsibility for individual patients in special hospitals.

Bartlett *et al* (1996) carried out two audits in 1992 and 1993 of the security needs of special hospital patients from South West Thames Region (n = 92 and n = 87, respectively), using a survey solely of RMO opinion. They found that 47% and 40% of patients were considered ready to move in 1992 and 1993, respectively. Approximately 60% of both samples were considered suitable for medium-security facilities, and approximately 76% of both samples were considered suitable for long-term medium security, should such a facility ever exist. The authors recommended that urgent consideration be given to the further provision of medium security, including long-term provision. They also recommended that providers could use similar audits to prioritise the clinical review of special hospital patients. Finally, they suggested that needs assessments of this kind could be carried out regularly, bearing in mind the low costs involved in such research exercises.

Needs assessment surveys in other in-patient populations

There are few studies of the security needs of MDOs detained and treated outside the special hospital system.

Coid (1991*b*) assessed all patients from five district catchment areas who were in private secure facilities over a four-month period (n = 30) and then followed them up two years later. Twenty of the 30 patients had mental illness or psychopathic disorder, and only four of these were thought to require ongoing treatment in a secure unit. Eight were considered ready to move to their catchment area and the remaining eight were judged to be 'difficult to place' and to require long-term structured care. Seven of the 30 patients were mentally impaired. Four of these required admission to a specialist unit for mentally impaired offenders, two were assessed as 'difficult to place' and to require long-term structured care and one was considered 'difficult to place' because of her age and unique behavioural problems. Three of the 30 cases were brain-damaged patients who appeared to be appropriately placed in secure care, although usually owing to a lack of local alternative facilities.

Coid also identified a need for structured, long-term in-patient provision to accommodate the 'difficult to place' cases he identified, including:

(a) locked, intensive-care wards for short-stay patients during acute periods of disturbed behaviour, consequent upon their underlying mental disorder;

(b) long-stay, highly structured in-patient settings for chronically disturbed, treatment-resistant patients whose conditions do not appear amenable to rehabilitation in the foreseeable future;

(c) RSUs for patients requiring conditions of security that cannot be offered in district facilities, but at a level below that offered by the special hospitals;

(d) special units with a level of security and specialist staff appropriate for dealing with mentally impaired patients who pose deviant, challenging and criminal behaviour, and who have little prospect of rehabilitation;

(e) special units for brain-damaged patients with additional psychiatric and behavioural problems who require long-term, highly structured, in-patient care.

Another comprehensive study of unmet needs was carried out in Leeds (Courtney *et al*, 1992). Researchers contacted a wide range of professionals involved in the provision of psychiatric services for the catchment population and asked them to identify those individuals on their case-loads who required secure care but were not receiving it. A 100% response rate was received, except from probation officers (60% response rate). A researcher interviewed the respondents in order to obtain further information about the individuals identified and to determine the need (or not) for a secure bed. Information about the clients' background character-istics, history and previous utilisation of secure services was collected.

Additionally, members of clinical teams at each secure facility serving the catchment area were asked to indicate the appropriateness of placement for each patient in the facility, and to indicate the suitability of alternative placements. All patients currently resident in the special hospitals, RSUs and SCUs were included (results relating to special hospital patients are reported earlier in this chapter). Clinical teams identified four patients in the SCU and two patients in the RSU as inappropriately placed; these patients were thought to require long-stay SCU or RSU beds. Local hospital services nominated two patients for transfer to either the SCU or the RSU and community services nominated 69 individuals for possible admission to a secure unit. Twenty of these 69 cases were judged to have no unmet needs by the research team, based on research criteria. The remaining 49 cases were followed up by the research team, who interviewed the referring agent. Perceived problems within this group were identified as difficulty in gaining access to statutory agencies and lack of stable, structured, residential accommodation in the community. This group were mostly disruptive and potentially violent individuals, many of whom were recidivists. A large proportion of these patients were resistant to involvement with psychiatric services and the services themselves did not welcome them. The authors suggested that such individuals are likely to require considerable inter-agency cooperation to provide for their needs, being likely also to need a specialist inter-agency team which could be backed up by a local SCU or RSU forensic psychiatric service.

Reed (1994) carried out a national telephone survey of the requirements for long-stay care among patients occupying private and NHS medium-security beds during one week. Consultant psychiatrists identified 461 patients as requiring longer-term secure care (i.e. over two years). This group was predominantly male, aged between 16 and 35 years and suffering from mental illness. Most had been admitted from NHS hospitals (25%), special hospitals (24%) or prisons (21%) and were detained under Part III of the Mental Health Act. Of the 461, 278 (60%) were thought to need long-term low-security care and 183 (40%) to need long-term medium security. The former group contained more women, patients admitted from NHS facilities, patients with mental impairment and those on civil sections. Reed acknowledged that the study was 'quick and dirty' but expressed reasonable confidence in the estimates. He concluded that there was a need for the development of longer-term low- and medium-security facilities and that local planners and commissioners should undertake a more comprehensive assessment of need in this regard, as well as considering whether current services were operating efficiently.

Surveys of the individual clinical and social needs of MDOs

All of the surveys described so far addressed the actual service needs of specific patient groups. Some needs assessment surveys, by contrast, select existing psychiatric sub-populations (e.g. attenders at a day hospital) within a small geographical area and then use standardised needs assessment schedules to measure individual needs for treatment and care. These standardised instruments are typically very detailed, cover a wide range of symptoms, behaviours (e.g. positive psychotic symptoms, violence or threats to self or others) and personal and social skills (e.g. social interaction skills, personal cleanliness) and are applied to general psychiatric populations. They usually attempt to establish met and unmet needs within different domains, and attempt also to identify over-provision and appropriate future interventions. Examples developed in the UK include the Needs for Care Assessment (NFCA; Brewin & Wing, 1989) and the Community Placement Questionnaire (CPQ; Clifford *et al*, 1991*a*, 1991*b*) (see also below). Many of these approaches gather information not only from the individual whose needs are in question but also ask the opinions of mental health professionals, formal and informal carers and family members about the needs of the patient.

A large number of studies in the general psychiatric population using the above needs assessment schedules have been carried out over the past ten years.[26] For example, the NFCA has been used to assess the needs of the users of day centres and sheltered residential accommodation (Brugha *et al*, 1988) and their relatives (MacCarthy *et al*, 1989), psychotic in- and out-patients (Lesage *et al*, 1991*a*) and non-psychotic out-patients (Lesage *et al*, 1991*b*), long-stay psychiatric in-patients (Pryce *et al*, 1991, 1993), severely mentally ill patients split into short-term, long-term, in-patient and out-patient groups (van Haaster *et al*, 1994*b*), hostel residents with long-term mental illness (O'Leary & Webb, 1996) and mentally ill hostel residents (Hogg & Marshall, 1992). The CPQ has been used to assess the needs of 'new long-stay' psychiatric in-patients in five hospitals (Clifford *et al*, 1991*a*, 1991*b*). Marshall modified the NFCA to produce the Cardinal Needs Schedule (Marshall, 1994; Marshall *et*

---

[26] Discussion of the psychometric properties of these instruments is beyond the scope of this chapter. Critical analyses are provided by Brewin & Wing (1993), Marshall (1994), Marshall *et al* (1995), Phelan *et al* (1995), Slade *et al* (1996), Clifford *et al* (1991*a*, 1991*b*) and van Haaster *et al* (1994*b*).

al, 1995), and this was used in Scotland to assess the needs of adults with a history of psychotic illness (Murray *et al*, 1996). Phelan *et al* (1995) developed a research and clinical version of the Camberwell Assessment of Need (CAN), and used it to assess the needs of mentally ill patients using in-, out- or day patient services (Slade *et al*, 1996). Hansson *et al* (1995) successfully modified the CAN for use on a Swedish in-patient and out-patient population. Similar instruments have also been developed and used in the USA (Levin *et al*, 1978; Lynch & Kruzich, 1986; Holcomb & Ahr, 1986; Solomon & Beck, 1989; Waismann & Rowland, 1989; Moxley & Freddolino, 1991; Ford *et al*, 1992; Richman & Britton, 1992).

Most of the standardised instruments mentioned above could be used to assess some of the individual needs specifically of MDOs, since they cover generic needs which are common to all psychiatric patients and also include measures of violence/dangerousness to self and others. However, it is likely that they would require some modification for use with particular MDO groups (e.g. some patients currently within special hospitals) in order to cover their 'special' needs, particularly in relation to the risk of severe harm to others and deliberate self-harm. This is an area for future research.

Gillespie *et al* (further details available from the authors on request) used the NFCA to assess the extent to which the forensic part of a privately run hospital (St Andrew's Hospital) was meeting the needs of a sample of its long-term mentally ill residents (*n* = 60). The forensic population was different from other groups on which the NFCA had been used in that they were younger, showed higher levels of personal and social skills, higher rates of drug side-effects and an increased risk of violence to self and others. Gillespie *et al* found a surprising absence of rated unmet needs and concluded that the NFCA was adequate for application to a forensic setting in terms of rating general clinical needs. However, an independent assessor suggested that the NFCA should properly be expanded in order to identify specific forensic needs, especially in relation to risk assessment – although there was some debate about the extent to which 'risk to others' could be conceived of as a need of the patient rather than as a need of society. The independent assessor also suggested that, in constructing a measure of deliberate self-harm and management of violence to others, the two should be disentangled from one another.

McMurran *et al* (1996) assessed directly the problems experienced by female patients in Rampton Special Hospital (*n* = 30) using the Behavioural Coding System (BCS), a measure developed to identify a range of maladaptive behaviours and to provide a profile of problem areas. The BCS was scored by a researcher (using patients' case notes), the patient's keyworker or the patient herself. The results suggested that emotional problems, auditory hallucinations, antisocial behaviour and deliberate self-harm were primary concerns in this group and that, therefore, interventions should be directed at these problems. Perhaps of even greater significance was the finding that staff and patients differed in terms of the problem areas they identified. The authors also found problems in the use of the BCS on female special hospital patients. They therefore redesigned it so as better to suit the specific problems of the group. They also recommended that appropriate needs assessment instruments for use with women patients in secure settings should be developed.

At another special hospital, Horne *et al* (personal communication, 28 April 1997) are developing a specialist MDO measure of need, the Broadmoor Hospital Checklist to Assess Needs. This is designed to describe patient needs in a standardised form in accordance with CPA guidelines. It is intended for use by clinical teams as a prompt for the identification of aspects of functioning which are particularly problematic (e.g. basic self-care, health and safety, emotional security, relationships, therapeutic achievement, self-actualisation) and for the appropriate interventions and resources required to address identified problems. It relates only to needs arising specifically out of the patient's mental disorder. The check-list has been piloted on a limited number of patients but still requires psychometric validation.

Related surveys within the criminal justice system

A number of surveys have examined various aspects of 'need' directly within the criminal justice system. Many of these studies can be described neither as 'needs assessment' studies *per se* nor as true epidemiological studies, because they do not select representative samples from the population of interest and/or do not use standardised measures of psychiatric morbidity. Essentially they represent diverse attempts at (highly limited) surveys of MDOs within individual segments of the criminal justice system, often conducted in conjunction with a particular service intervention. Nevertheless, they provide very useful information about innovative services for MDOs, the characteristics of some mentally disordered individuals passing through the criminal justice system, the nature of both service gaps and inter-agency communication gaps and the outcomes and effectiveness of services designed to facilitate diversion from custody. Such studies have taken place within remand prisons, court diversion schemes and police stations.

Prison-based surveys

During a six-month study period, Courtney *et al* (1992) found that 23 patients in the Leeds catchment area were remanded to prison for medical reports. Two were subsequently transferred to an RSU or SCU. Four were assessed as having a learning disability, but were deemed not to be detainable under the Mental Health Act 1983, and five were noted to have a psychiatric disorder but with no treatment recommendations being made. A review of recommendations made by visiting forensic psychiatrists during the six-month study period suggested that there were no cases of unmet need for transfer to a NHS bed. Similarly, a two-year retrospective study of the same service found no unmet need for transfer from prison to hospital (O'Grady, 1990). This finding contrasts with the difficulties experienced in services without adequate available secure beds (e.g. Coid, 1988), and illustrates the wide scope for local variation in need, demand and utilisation.

Dell *et al* (1993*a*) studied a group of psychotic and non-psychotic female remand prisoners (*n* = 196). They found that custodial remands were an ineffective way of obtaining psychiatric help for the psychotic women in their sample (*n* = 95) who were not initially offered beds. Rather, they found that most of these women were remanded in custody for extended periods of time while awaiting a bed and were then often refused one, being discharged back into the community without any input from either health or social services. This usually resulted in a cycle of petty reoffending and repeated remands in custody. Dell *et al* recommended that effective liaison between the police and health and social services, based on appropriate financial structures and revenue flows, should be encouraged in order to facilitate the appropriate diversion of these women. They also recommended a range of appropriate community accommodation, particularly for homeless women charged with minor offences (who tend to be remanded in custody unnecessarily). They further identified a need for better access to hospital, again based on appropriate financial structures, and a need for outside psychiatrists to visit prisons more quickly and to use informal and civil admissions to hospital more often. They also recommended that Section 48 of the Mental Health Act be used more frequently (there is good evidence that, in the last few years, this has been pursued to good effect).

Dell *et al* (1993*b*) also identified a number of placement difficulties for the non-psychotic women remand prisoners they followed up (*n* = 101). They particularly identified as problematic one group of mentally unstable women charged with arson who were referred to outside psychiatrists for assessment and treatment of needs arising from personality disorder or mental handicap. These women often remained on remand for considerable periods of time while professionals argued about their treatability, appropriate security and length of treatment required. A second group of disturbed young women was also identified as presenting particular problems. These women were often homeless and were remanded in custody for minor offences either because of extremely bizarre behaviour or because their need for help was otherwise obvious. Like the first group, they were often referred to outside psychiatrists because of their personality disorder or mental handicap and were also usually rejected because they were not considered amenable to help by in-patient treatment. However, this group still presented major problems to health and social services. They spent considerable periods remanded in custody, were subsequently rejected by services and then sent back to conditions in the community similar to those in which they were living before their arrest, and where they would again be likely to present to services.

Mitchison *et al* (1994) examined the medical reception and screening procedures in a male remand prison. They found that routine medical screening for psychiatric disorder missed a considerable number of cases and failed to follow up a large proportion of those who reported previous psychiatric treatment. They recommended that screening should be improved and audited, and that prison medical staff should always routinely request information from outside agencies about prisoners who report a psychiatric history.

Robertson *et al* (1994) followed up 101 men remanded to Brixton Prison and subsequently given hospital orders by the courts. In the great majority of cases (93%), hospitals acknowledged that the admission had been appropriate. Yet the authors found that the process of referral and admission of these men resulted in them spending, on average, between two to three times longer in custody than other (non-mentally disordered) men charged with similar offences. They recommended that specialist psychiatric remand facilities be established in London in order to provide an in-patient assessment service to the police and to the London courts, so that overtly ill defendants could be diverted from custody as soon as possible.

Anderson & Parrott (1995) carried out a retrospective study of all remand prisoners transferred from another London prison,

HMP Belmarsh, to psychiatric hospital specifically under Section 48 of the Mental Health Act over one year (n = 22). The majority (n = 15) were suffering from a paranoid psychotic illness (68%) and most (n = 14) were transferred to a locked general psychiatric ward (63%). Five (22%) were transferred to a medium-secure unit and 3 (14%) went to special hospital. Anderson & Parrott identified a significant increase in Section 48 prison referrals on a regional and national level and pointed out the resource implications of this, especially the need for increased numbers of general psychiatry locked wards.

At the same prison, Banerjee *et al* (1995) investigated the characteristics of a six-month cohort of male remand prisoners who required formal transfer from prison to hospital. The aim of this study was to evaluate the effectiveness of the Belmarsh Prison 'contracted in' NHS psychiatric service (the service that gave rise to the Anderson & Parrott study just described). Fifty-three of the 1229 new remands during the study period were transferred to psychiatric units under the Mental Health Act. The majority of the transfer group suffered from schizophrenia (79%) and had a history of in-patient treatment (77%). However, only 34% were in psychiatric care at the time of their arrest. Thirty (57%) were transferred under Section 37 and 16 (30%) under Section 48. The remainder were transferred under Section 2 (n = 1, 2%) or Section 35 (n = 6, 11%). The majority of cases (40%) were transferred to an open ward and 34% to a general psychiatric locked ward. RSUs accepted 21% of patients and special hospitals accepted 2%. Four per cent were transferred to learning difficulty units. None of the prisoners recommended for transfer was refused a bed or was missed by prison reception screening. The average length of time spent in prison by the transfer group was 32.6 days. Black people were over-represented in the transfer group compared with the total remand population, while the group also had significantly more offences categorised as 'other' (e.g. criminal damage, threatening behaviour) and fewer acquisitive offences than the overall remand population. Banerjee *et al* recommended that pathways to custody should be further examined specifically in relation to ethnicity. They also supported recommendations for beds at all levels of security, especially in light of the high proportion of cases transferred to open or locked general psychiatric beds. They argued further that the psychiatric skills required to deal with the remand population are not confined to the forensic psychiatrist but are, to a large extent, found in general units. Ultimately, the authors were cautious in their comments on the effectiveness of the Belmarsh scheme, but suggested that transfers to hospital appeared to be more rapid from the scheme than from a traditional system operating in a neighbouring prison.

Court-based surveys

One of the most pioneering surveys linked to a court is the study by James & Hamilton (1991). They carried out a nine-month prospective survey of all referrals to a court liaison scheme in central London. The authors compared the amount of time spent in custody of cases seen by the scheme ($n = 80$) with that of cases placed on hospital orders after being remanded to Brixton Prison for psychiatric reports ($n = 50$). The 50 remand prisoners assessed in prison spent an average of 33.7 days from the time of arrest to their appearance in court with a psychiatric report and an average of 50.8 days from arrest to hospital admission. By contrast, those prisoners seen by the liaison scheme spent significantly less time on remand in custody (5.4 days and 8.7 days, respectively). The number of hospital orders made by the court also increased fourfold after the liaison scheme began. James & Hamilton concluded that such liaison schemes could greatly reduce the amount of time that MDOs spend in custody and that they were thus superior to the traditional model of carrying out psychiatric reports in prisons. A further effect could clearly be the achievement of substantial savings in remand costs (albeit with costs being absorbed by the health service).

Hillis (1992) has described a diversion scheme with a somewhat (but not very) different service model, in the West Midlands. This scheme assessed a total of 519 defendants over a year. The vast majority were male ($n = 455$, 88%) and many were charged with minor offences ($n = 177$). On assessment, 258 had an identifiable mental health problem. The most common diagnoses were schizophrenia ($n = 94$, 36%) and alcohol dependence ($n = 66$, 13%). Seventy of the 258 (27%) were recommended for in-patient assessment or treatment and 47 (18%) were admitted to hospital. Of those admitted to hospital, six went to an RSU and 41 to local psychiatric hospitals. Eighteen were compulsorily detained. Out-patient treatment or assessment was recommended in 159 cases (62%) and in 124 (48%) this was followed through. Twenty-nine defendants (11%) were remanded in custody for the purpose of a medical report or psychiatric assessment.

Exworthy & Parrott (1993) reported on the first 150 defendants referred to yet another court psychiatric assessment and diversion scheme. Overall, 64% of cases were diverted from custody, including 23 admissions to psychiatric hospital. The majority subsequently received psychiatric treatment on a voluntary basis in the community. The authors argued that such an assessment service could successfully serve a number of courts within a local area. They pointed out that large numbers of MDOs were diverted and that the duration of psychiatric remands in custody was substantially reduced. They also demonstrated that the scheme had a minimal impact on the overall number of admissions to hospital. This suggested that the added costs to the NHS were limited to the remand period not spent in prison.

One of the most comprehensive diversion scheme evaluations is that carried out by Joseph & Potter (1993a). They described a psychiatric diversion scheme based at two inner-London magistrates' courts. Over 18 months, 201 referrals of 185 individuals were made to the scheme. Defendants were predominantly single male recidivists charged with minor offences and of no fixed abode. Of the 185 assessed, 163 individuals received a psychiatric diagnosis, the most common primary diagnoses being schizophrenia (39%) and neurosis/personality disorder (15%). The most common multiple diagnoses were combinations of schizophrenia, alcohol dependence and personality disorder. However, only a quarter of these defendants were currently in contact with psychiatric services. Overall, 62 referrals (31%) were recommended for hospital admission and 25% ($n = 51$) were admitted following the assessment order. A further 50% ($n = 101$) were released and 25% ($n = 49$) were returned to custody. Of those returned to custody, 14 eventually received hospital orders. In total, 24 cases (12%) were admitted under criminal sections of the Mental Health Act (Joseph & Potter, 1993b). For cases admitted to hospital, the average time from arrest to hospital admission was significantly more rapid than for prison-based assessments.

Joseph & Potter (1993a) suggested that their diversion scheme facilitated admission to hospital from the point of arrest, and that this occurred more rapidly than prison-based assessments. They also argued that the overall effect of early diversion on hospital and prison resources was small, and this appears to confirm the findings of Exworthy & Parrot (1993). They also pointed out a need for acute beds on locked psychiatric wards for defendants requiring remand in custody for medical reports and recommended increased use of Section 35 of the Mental Health Act in order to facilitate this. Joseph & Potter recommended the establishment of specialist community-based bail hostels managed by the Probation Service that could accommodate those MDOs who do not require remand in custody.

It is noteworthy that the majority of cases identified by this and other court diversion schemes were referred to general psychiatric services and often charged with minor offences. This suggests that many individuals referred to such schemes may be on the less severe end of the 'MDO spectrum'.

Unlike most other studies, Joseph & Potter (1993*b*) then followed up the 201 referrals to their scheme. Fifty of the diverted cases (77%) were judged to have benefited from psychiatric admission, 29 markedly so. Those who did badly were more likely to be of no fixed abode and to have had higher rates of both previous criminality and compulsory admissions to hospital. Absconding was the largest management problem and 30 (46%) of those who were admitted subsequently absconded. Violence to people or property was reported in nine (14%) cases. Twelve months after admission, all patients except one had been discharged. Ten (15%) had been readmitted to hospital. The outcome component of this study highlights the gap in many previous studies of diversion schemes. Other studies tend to concentrate on diversion *per se*, presumably based on the assumption that a positive psychiatric outcome would follow and that, once in care, any patient (MDO or not) would experience the same, or at least some, positive outcome. Of course, that is far from clear and, indeed, Joseph & Potter's study emphasises that the health outcome for MDOs may be, for various reasons, different from that for non-offender patients with similar illnesses.

Brabbins & Travers (1994) have further emphasised the relative diversity of court diversion experience. They describe a court diversion scheme at a Liverpool magistrates' court. They interviewed 13 defendants detained by the police before their first appearance in court and found very little mental illness but high levels of substance misuse. The latter defendants were found to be neglected by current diversion and liaison initiatives, and the authors recommended that outreach workers from drug and alcohol services would be more effective in serving this group than a psychiatric liaison scheme. They also showed that the demographic profile of their group differed substantially from that reported by Joseph & Potter (1993*a*) in central London. This finding, albeit from a very small sample, probably demonstrates the advantages of local needs assessment initiatives for local solutions (see later).

By contrast with the small numbers in the Liverpool study, Hudson *et al* (1995*a*) described the operation of a psychiatric assessment and liaison scheme at Horseferry Magistrates' Court, which serves all the magistrates' courts in three central London boroughs. Over one year the scheme assessed 264 cases, making up just under 0.5% of all custody cases from the police stations in the catchment area. Cases were primarily socially deprived young men ($n = 229$, 87%). The majority of cases had a history of both psychiatric illness (76%)

and defaulting from care (44%). Many were charged with violent offences (n = 152, 57%) and 40% had previous violent convictions. The majority were psychotic (n = 185, 70%) and a significant number reported alcohol misuse (30%) and use of illicit drugs (35%). Of all those assessed, 158 (60%) were admitted to hospital, 55% of these to locked or secure wards. Forty-four per cent of cases (n = 115) were admitted under Part III sections of the Mental Health Act and 16% (n = 41) were admitted on Part II sections. There were only two informal admissions. Sixty per cent of the men admitted to hospital after assessment by the scheme had been identified as suffering from mental disorder by the remand prison. Because of bed shortages, over half of the Section 37 cases spent more than 22 days in prison waiting for a bed, and the length of time spent on remand in custody was positively correlated with the level of hospital security required. Nevertheless, it was estimated that the court assessment and liaison scheme saved approximately 5298 days on remand in prison over the year. Another important finding was that the people assessed were significantly more serious offenders than those reported by other court diversion schemes (including in London). It was also noted that the group was particularly difficult to treat and follow up because of their degree of illness, the presence of dual pathologies, and the high levels of disturbed backgrounds, homelessness and rootlessness.

Hudson *et al* (1995*a*, 1995*b*) concluded that the system of cross-remand to Horseferry Magistrates' Court had proved successful in terms of efficiency, quality and economy of scale. They therefore recommended similar systems for other London courts. They stated that it was possible to make assessment at court, rather than prison, the focus of a local forensic service, also noting that a major advantage of the scheme was its location within mainstream local services. This, they argued, quickened assessment, improved access to information and beds, increased identification of illness, facilitated close working relationships with local community agencies and improved overall efficiency. They recommended that court diversion schemes be planned as part of comprehensive local community psychiatric provision rather than as a parallel service, and that local commissioners should be encouraged to specify such schemes in their contracts so as, eventually, to take over from central Home Office funding. They also identified a need for community outreach services to deal with the difficult group of individuals they had identified. They recommended that diversion schemes located at police stations be developed in order to identify and divert less serious offenders who appeared no longer to be passing through the court-based scheme (such a scheme is described below).

However, whether the inherent culture conflicts between the criminal justice system and the NHS, as well as budgetary systems, can be overcome in order for NHS commissioners to specify court diversion schemes in their contracts with psychiatric providers is far from clear. Rowlands *et al* (1996) described the first year of a court diversion scheme in Rotherham and follow-up of the cases an average of 12 months after diversion (*n* = 82). The majority of cases were male (*n* = 69, 84%) and most (*n* = 47, 57%) had no prior contact with psychiatric services. The most common diagnoses at initial assessment were substance dependence (*n* = 28, 34%), psychotic disorder (*n* = 19, 23%) and depressive disorder (*n* = 17, 21%). More than half had previous convictions for violent offences (*n* = 49, 60%) and current charges of violence (*n* = 51, 62%). A total of 21 cases (26%) were admitted to hospital either directly or following remand in custody; only five received hospital orders (three with restrictions). Overall, 31 cases (38%) were not considered to have benefited from the court intervention, and 15 (18%) were thought to have received a substantial, sustained benefit. The majority of those with psychotic disorders remained in contact with services at follow-up and also showed greater symptomatic benefit than other diagnostic groups. At follow-up, most cases were in the community, although the reoffending rate was 17%. Rowlands *et al* concluded that a court diversion scheme could be run successfully with a community psychiatric nurse as the pivot. They highlighted the need for more secure beds for those requiring remand in custody for medical reports, and pointed out that some cases were thought clinically to be suitable for community or open beds but that the court would not agree.

Greenhalgh *et al* (1996) described a three-month pilot mental health assessment and diversion scheme in Leeds. They found that 77% of the 57 cases in police custody who were assessed before their court appearance were mentally disordered. Almost half (*n* = 27) had substance misuse problems and the number with psychotic disorders (*n* = 8, 14%) was small in comparison with rates found in London. Psychiatric recommendations were made in 37 (61%) of cases, although lack of local medium-security beds resulted in four cases being remanded in custody. Twenty-five cases were recommended for out-patient psychiatric treatment, but attendance was poor. Greenhalgh *et al* recommended that bail hostels specialising in psychiatric problems be established to facilitate diversion.

More radically, James *et al* (1997) examined the feasibility of amending or abolishing court powers to remand defendants in custody for psychiatric reports. They studied all admissions from three London boroughs to any NHS or private hospital from courts or prisons in the UK during a one-year period. The rate of compulsory admission to hospital for non-serving prisoners was 24.5 per 100 000 population, which reflected a total of 106 admissions, 85% of which were after assessment at court. Fifty-three per cent ($n = 56$) were admitted to secure facilities, 34% ($n = 36$) to an open ward and 13% ($n = 14$) to an open ward with an intensive care component. Half the patients were subject to Section 37 of the Mental Health Act (two with restriction orders) and a quarter each were admitted on remand orders (Sections 35, 36 and 48/49) and civil orders (Sections 2, 3 and 4). One case was admitted under the Criminal Procedure (Insanity and Unfitness to Plead) Act 1991.

The authors found that the three boroughs involved in the study generated seven times the national average of unrestricted Section 37 admissions and 3.27 times the national average for Section 48 admissions. They concluded that a mainstream court assessment service with local service flexibility and ease of access to beds at different levels of security had proved successful in central London. They argued, therefore, that the widespread availability of similar schemes would permit a change in legislation limiting remand in custody for reports to a maximum of one week (albeit that some serious offenders would always be remanded in custody). Such a legal change would, they argued, not only reduce remands in custody but also encourage rapid development of court assessment services *per se*. This represents an interesting alternative to merely encouraging the NHS and other agencies to develop court diversion schemes, based on the proposition that 'sticks' are more effective in achieving MDO services than 'carrots'.

Police-based surveys

The Revolving Doors Agency (1994) carried out a survey of custody records at Paddington Police Station and showed that 79 people with mental health problems were encountered by Paddington Division between May and October 1993 (1.6% of the custody records). This included 29 removals to a place of safety under Section 136 of the Mental Health Act and 41 cases where a mental health problem was suspected. For the other nine people in the sample, there were incidents recorded which also suggested a mental health problem (e.g. attempted suicide) but they were excluded from the main analysis. Another 17 either had been taken by police to St Charles' Emergency Mental Health Unit but did not appear in custody records, or were identified from records of the local court diversion scheme and probation office at Marylebone Magistrates' Court. This brought the total figure of Paddington Police contacts during the study period to 96, equivalent to 200 cases per year. Cases were predominantly male minor offenders, and half were homeless or in temporary accommodation. Almost half (46%) of the 70 cases were taken to Paddington Police Station as a 'place of safety', contrary to local agreements drawn up by the police, social services and mental health services, which stipulated a local hospital as the appropriate place of safety. Only 3% of those arrested were referred to Marylebone Magistrates' Court. However, 37% of arrests resulted in the person being released without any attempt by the police to establish a connection with local psychiatric services.

The Revolving Doors Agency recommended that improved liaison between the police and other agencies should be encouraged so as to facilitate more referrals from the police, and that Section 136 arrangements should be monitored more closely.

Lyall *et al* (1995) conducted a prospective study specifically to identify the number of people with a possible learning disability taken into police custody at a Cambridge police station over two months. This study showed that out of the 255 cases screened, at least 4% had an educational history indicative of some level of learning disability.

Hudson *et al* (1995*b*) described the first six months of a pilot assessment and diversion scheme at three central London police stations. The police scheme was developed because the local court assessment and liaison scheme at Horseferry Magistrates' Court was receiving referrals of increasingly serious offenders (who would have previously been assessed in prison) rather than the relatively minor offenders it had assessed in past years (Hudson *et al*, 1995*a*). The fate of these minor offenders had thus become uncertain, and it was suspected that they were remaining unrecognised at the police station. During the six months, the new scheme saw 115 cases (82% male), which represented between 0.35% and 1.04% of the total number of cases passing through custody during that time. Just under half the group had been involved in violence of some kind, and a large proportion had a history of seeing a psychiatrist (79%) or of being a psychiatric in-patient (72%). Half were diagnosed with schizophrenia and related disorders and half admitted to regular substance misuse. Twenty-nine cases were recommended for an assessment under a section of the Mental Health Act; 26 (23%) of these were subsequently detained under a civil section and two (2%) under a forensic section. Another eight cases (7%) were recommended for voluntary admission and a further 68 (59%) were referred to local services such as the homelessness mental health team, community mental health teams, a drug/alcohol team, social services, out-patient departments and GPs. In eight cases (7%), no psychiatric outcomes occurred. Outcome was unspecified in three cases. In terms of legal disposal, 42 (37%) were charged with an offence, 27 (24%) were cautioned or given a formal warning and 46 (40%) were not charged.

The characteristics of those seen by the police scheme were similar to those seen at the Horseferry Magistrates' Court assessment and liaison scheme in terms of age, residential stability, diagnostic profile, psychiatric history and substance misuse. However, the court group were charged with significantly more serious violence than the police group, and had higher previous psychiatric admission rates, higher rates of compulsory detention and longer criminal records. It was also found that black people were over-represented in the court group. Hudson *et al* noted that the police group were similar in profile to cases previously reported by court diversion schemes in other London locations (e.g. Joseph & Potter, 1993*a*). They concluded that the pilot scheme at the police station had been a success in effectively assessing and diverting relatively minor offenders from the criminal justice system, and they suggested that similar schemes should be established in order to ensure the appropriate diversion of minor offenders.

Finally, Robertson *et al* (1996) observed all detainees arrested in seven London police stations to determine the presence of mental illness, and then followed those identified through the criminal justice system to court disposal. They found just over 1% of cases (*n* = 33) to be acutely ill and also that diversion was common. The factor most strongly associated with entry into the criminal justice system was the presence of violence at the time of arrest, followed by a history of persistent petty offending and failure to appear at court. They also found that petty offenders often moved from the street to the police station and then to the courts without the benefit of either health or social care. They recommended that a dedicated facility for this group of MDOs should be established in central London.

Conclusions

There are several fairly clear conclusions from all the studies described in this chapter. First, there is strong and consistent evidence of high levels of psychiatric morbidity in both the remand and sentenced prison populations. Further, substantial numbers of these prisoners require psychiatric intervention either from the Prison Health Care Service or from the NHS (or equivalent services in the independent sector). Second, there are particular groups of MDOs who are especially difficult to divert to mental health care from remand in custody. These include female petty offenders with personality disorders and both men and women with learning disabilities. Third, significant numbers of MDOs are still caught in the cycle of arrest, remand and re-arrest. Finally, substance misuse has been identified as a large problem in several studies. These findings suggest that the effects of the Reed report and of Home Office circular 66/90 have been limited. Related to this is the conclusion from the studies identified that court diversion schemes appear to have had a fairly slight effect on NHS and justice resources. This, in turn, implies the need for still more effective means of MDO identification within the various segments of the criminal justice system, as well as more integrated court and police station diversion schemes and more specialist remand facilities, such as bail hostels and low-security NHS facilities. Identification could be increased by improved screening protocols within prisons. This would be facilitated by any substantial transfer of responsibility for prison mental health care to the NHS. The latter would also improve liaison between prison staff and NHS mental health care teams, which would, in turn, effect transfer more reliably and promptly. Such liaison, together with any improvement in diversion at the court stage, should be directed at general mental health care services, since the studies demonstrate that this is the part of the NHS which should mainly be responsible for the relevant MDO care. The high need for intervention in relation to offenders with drug and alcohol addiction also implies closer relationships between the criminal justice system and the NHS (and independent) addiction services. However, this raises important questions concerning whether the strictly consensual model of addiction treatment is sustainable for MDOs, particularly given the importance of substance misuse in the context of dual diagnosis and the significance of substance use in increasing the risk to others from MDOs. Finally, ideally there should be more effective community outreach services aimed at preventive care.

Alongside, or perhaps driving, some improvement in diversion, there has been a very substantial proportionate increase in the number of Section 48 transfer orders. Both these and, especially, Section 35 orders should be used more. However, the latter would be more problematic to achieve than the former, given that courts cannot *require* the NHS to provide remand beds.

Finally, as regards diversion and prison studies, there is little information on the cost implications of further improvement, either for the criminal justice system or the NHS. Central to this issue is the relationship between Home Office and NHS budgets. There is still no resolution of the problem of arranging 'money going with the

MDO' (who is diverted). To the NHS, diversion seems to imply that such a transfer of revenue should occur, or indeed must occur for diversion to be effected on a wide scale. For the Home Office, NHS districts have already received their *per capita* allocation and should be grateful that the Home Office already funds its own prison health service for NHS patients who happen to be in prison. One solution would be to transfer not only the responsibility for prison health care itself to the NHS but also to transfer the responsibility for *commissioning* such care to the NHS. However, there is no sign of the latter 'radical' solution being adopted by government.

Turning to surveys of need of patients already in the mental health care system, there is a clear picture given by the studies reviewed of over-containment in high security. This holds true across assessments by high-security hospital teams, RMOs and research panels – although research panels consistently judge more patients to be over-contained than clinical teams or RMOs. These studies are important in terms of service planning. However, most have been conducted on the apparent assumption that security need alone determines the need to be in a particular service facility. As currently provided, this is a false assumption. If, by contrast, we define a matrix of service needs of which security is one dimension and if, for example, the need for very substantial intramural occupational facilities represents another valid dimension then a different interpretation is possible. Hence, if only high-security hospitals *provide* the high level of occupational facilities that some patients require, then, even if their risk to others infers that they only require medium security, their 'proper' placement within *existing* service types is high security. However, this leads naturally to the conclusion of many of the special hospital studies that there is a great need for long-term medium-security facilities. Such facilities, particularly if they were joined with generic (medium-term) medium-security services, would be sufficient as regards critical mass to provide the combination of the 'correct' level of security and the necessary level of occupational (or other) services.

The special hospital studies, as well as some other studies, also imply the need for many more low-security units within general mental health care services. There is, similarly, a need for high-dependency community placements, sufficient to unblock in-patient facilities of a number of types. Also, within all secure facilities there needs to be much greater attention paid to 'quality of life' measures. This reflects a general tendency for there to be much greater concern with the provision of secure services *per se* than with what goes on in those services and what is their outcome, beyond mere containment and the provision of general mental health care (see Chapter 7). This complaint relates also to the importance of paying particular attention to the assessment of individual patient need[27] and to 'care planning' based on systematic repetition of individual needs assessment throughout the period of care and containment.

This requirement is particularly important in the case of patients with 'special needs', such as those with learning disability, personality disorder or even women.[28] Finally, there should be established an agreed range of valid and reliable individual needs assessment tools for MDOs requiring security (and perhaps others too) in order better to systematise their care (see Chapter 8).

[27] There is currently a major research project under way in all three high-security hospitals to carry out a comprehensive assessment of all major categories of need (including the need for security) of all patients, under the direction of Professor G. Thornicroft.

[28] The special hospital population with learning disability and the women in the special hospitals will be assessed somewhat differently and in advance of other patients in the study by Thornicroft.

4 The rates-under-treatment approach

Introduction

The rates-under-treatment (RUT) approach to assessing need involves a descriptive enumeration of those who have utilised health services, social services or voluntary agencies within a specific geographical area. The underlying assumption is that rates of service utilisation can be used to estimate both demand and need for services (Warheit et al, 1977). However, the complex relationship between need, demand, supply and utilisation (see Chapter 2) makes it problematic to assume a direct link between rates of treated disorder and need (Holzer et al, 1988). Not all people who need services necessarily receive them, and not all people who receive services necessarily need them (Baldwin, 1986). According to Fryers & Greatorex (1992), "Data on service use cannot tell us directly about demand, even less need" (p. 84), and judging the volume of services needed from the volume of services used is inherently circular (Glover, 1990). Hence, "it is important not to define need in terms of the care, agent or setting already in place, thus automatically perpetuating the present allocation and priorities" (Wing et al, 1992, p. 6).

A major criticism levelled at the RUT approach is that, by focusing only on individuals who are actually using services, it fails to provide information about unmet need (Häfner, 1979; Goodman & Haugland, 1994). Another criticism is that the RUT approach fails to uncover the inappropriate use of services (Häfner, 1979). Hence, the use of this approach in relation to secure forensic psychiatric services (e.g. special hospitals and medium-secure units) will fail to identify significant unmet need for NHS psychiatric care within the prison system (Gunn et al, 1991a; Maden et al, 1994a, 1995; Brooke *et al,* 1996). It must also fail to identify unmet need for lesser security within the special hospital system (Dell & Robertson, 1988; Taylor *et al,* 1991; Maden *et al,* 1993; Shaw *et al,* 1994*a*; Murray *et al,* 1994; Bartlett *et al,* 1996), unless a survey of individual security needs is also carried out.[29]

However, the RUT approach can provide not only a measure (potentially) of met need, but also, by way of some indication of the pressures on services, indirect evidence of unmet need/demand. For example, Goldberg (1990) has argued that optimal general psychiatric bed occupancy should be approximately 85%, and that higher rates suggest that there are insufficient beds to run a service properly. Hence, occupancy rates that exceed this indicate high pressure on services and potential unmet need.[30] Short durations of stay with high readmission rates can also serve as similar indicators of high pressure on services (and possible undersupply) (MILMIS Project Group, 1995). However, although indicators of this kind can illustrate pressures on services, they cannot on their own provide information about the reasons for those pressures, or the organisational or attitudinal barriers to treatment (Bloom *et al,* 1988). For example, high occupancy rates may reflect blockages elsewhere in the system rather than actual unmet 'need' for the particular service under consideration.

Despite these criticisms of the RUT approach, it has been identified as an extremely valuable source of information about the configuration of past and present services and about patterns of service utilisation (Rabkin, 1986). Hence, it has been argued that

---

[29] Surveys of this kind were discussed in Chapter 3. However, they may be confused with RUT studies. This is because they focus only on patients in receipt of services. For the purposes of this book, studies have been distinguished into the 'survey' and 'RUT' approaches according to whether or not they explicitly address the needs of patients (i.e. whether they are 'direct' or 'indirect' needs assessments) and also in terms of the location in which they occurred. For example, some of the surveys described in Chapter 3 are neither strictly epidemiological nor strictly needs assessment studies (e.g. court diversion scheme studies). Therefore, they cannot rightly be classified within the RUT approach because the individuals concerned are not receiving treatment within the health service (albeit that one could describe a court diversion scheme itself as a form of treatment or intervention and then classify these studies under the RUT approach). This type of somewhat fine distinction reflects the generally overlapping nature of the needs assessment approaches, as well as the fact that, in the real world, 'pure' approaches are seldom practicable. There is also an obvious overlap between the RUT approach and the social indicator approach (Chapter 5), in that the latter has frequently been pursued by using RUT data as a criterion measure within social indicator models.

[30] Of course, the 'threshold' suggesting service inadequacy will vary according to the average length of stay and, in the case of secure services, the latter will be longer than within general mental health care, thus implying a 'threshold' of more than 85%.

information about service usage is essential for planning and developing future services and that "a starting point ... for needs assessment ... is knowledge of the existing 'cases' and of their relationship to services already provided" (Stevens & Raftery, 1992, p. 44). Thus, careful analysis of RUT data should be a component of any needs assessment (Warheit *et al*, 1977; Bloom *et al*, 1988). Indeed, the NHS and Community Care Act 1990 states that data on both past and present service utilisation are essential components of the health care planning process. RUT information is thus also an important component of the contracting process (Fryers & Greatorex, 1992) and is likely to be a significant part of contract monitoring requirements. It is, perhaps, the approach to needs assessment that is most grounded in practicality and in practically available data.

The NHS Management Executive (1991) recommended that RUT data should be used as part of its 'hybrid' approach to needs assessment. In particular, it recommended the 'comparative method', involving the comparison of service receipt across different geographical areas on the assumption that similar populations should receive similar services. However, once a discrepancy between areas has been established, it may be difficult to determine in which direction the shift in service delivery should occur. In other words, should population A receive more services or should population B receive fewer? Such decisions require adequate knowledge of the profiles of local populations and their needs, as well as of the efficacy and outcomes of particular local services, and this information may often be lacking (Stevens & Raftery, 1994).

Sources and types of RUT information

It is possible to obtain RUT data from central sources (e.g. DoH hospital episode statistics) or from local mental health information systems, including case registers. Of course, in order for such statistics to be useful, it is necessary that central and local mental health information systems produce valid and reliable data at the required level of detail. However, there is evidence that mental health services data are often incomplete and inaccurate (Glover, 1990). According to Lelliott (1995), the current national data set for mental health is "an anachronism ... that cannot meet even the most basic requirement of community-oriented services for information. Aggregated data derived from it have little relevance to service planning or to measuring the effectiveness of care delivery" (p. 91).

The UK government has introduced initiatives to facilitate the development of nationally standardised local mental health information systems (NHS Executive, 1994*b*; Wing, 1995). In that context, Wing *et al* (1992) have argued that each local area should have an information infrastructure which is both able to cope with the multi-agency nature of psychiatric services and capable of providing data of value to clinical teams, commissioners and providers. According to Wing (1995), such an information system would facilitate rational decision-making at the level of the individual patient, the local population and national strategy. It would also underpin a needs assessment and planning strategy by basing it on "the well-accepted principles of clinical audit, as amplified and quantified in needs assessment systems informed by consensus guidelines for good practice" (p. 1). According to Wing (1995), such a comprehensive information system would incorporate information ranging from face-to-face assessment of need, followed by intervention and then reassessment (as in the classic audit cycle) (i.e. 'bottom-up'), to the epidemiologically based equivalents required to plan and rationally manage a geographically designated area (i.e. 'top-down'). Wing (1995) outlined the components of such a system:

(a) local history, topography and communications;
(b) sociodemographic indices and epidemiology;
(c) local services (agents and settings), and their functioning and efficiency;
(d) clinical data about the needs of people in contact with services and how far they are being met;
(e) opinions of local users and carers;
(f) local guidelines and research; other databases.

However, in contrast to Wing's counsel of perfection, local information systems of this kind are still only developing, and current systems vary considerably in terms of quality and detail across local provider units and commissioning authorities. They also frequently differ even within hospitals (Lelliott, 1995; Nemitz & Bean, 1995; Cohen & Eastman, 1996). This tendency towards the separate development of information systems has, of course, often resulted in incompatible and incomparable information within and across districts. Hence, Nemitz & Bean (1995) found considerable discrepancies and inaccuracies in statistics for detained hospital patients within the four RHAs covering London. Such inaccuracies and discrepancies were found between statistics held by different hospitals *and* between local statistics and those held centrally. This led the authors to question the value of such statistics for planning purposes.

As regards MDO service data, a number of studies have shown that some data about special hospital utilisation are inaccurate, with cases being allocated to incorrect RHAs and DHAs (Bartlett *et al*, 1996; Murray *et al*, 1996). A study in South Thames Region (Cohen & Eastman, 1996) showed that purchasers' data requirements regarding forensic psychiatric services varied considerably across DHAs and between the east and west of the region. Hence, it also found, perhaps partly as a consequence of varying commissioner requirements, that routine data collection by forensic providers varied considerably and that each provider also had a different capacity to produce contract monitoring and needs assessment information. Interestingly, commissioners were wary of obtaining more information from providers because they were uncertain both about how they would manage additional data technologically and about how they would interpret it for planning purposes. Similarly, providers were wary of increasing the information they produced for commissioners (and for their own purposes), because of the extra time and resources it would require.[31] Some of these discrepancies in information were thought to reflect differences in local priorities rather than a haphazard approach to information collection and contract monitoring. However, whatever the cause, incompatible data hinder comparison across districts and prevent the aggregation of information across neighbouring districts. This makes the DoH's 'comparative approach' extremely difficult to undertake. It also has obvious implications for the planning of supra-district or supra-regional services (e.g. long-stay medium-secure units).

A further difficulty is that (general and forensic) mental health information systems may not contain comprehensive RUT information. Warheit *et al* (1977) suggest that at least the following should be part of RUT information:

(a) socio-demographic characteristics;
(b) presenting problems;
(c) characteristics of care/services provided;
(d) frequency and duration of the care/treatment process;
(e) sources of referral;
(f) outcome of treatment/services provided.

---

[31] It cannot be ruled out, of course, that providers had other, more strategic or tactical, motives for not wishing to produce additional data that would more explicitly, and in greater detail, describe the service they were providing to commissioners.

However, information systems may not contain even this level of data. For example, the Special Hospitals Research Unit database contains a large amount of demographic information but very little about the treatment and progress of the patients (Bartlett, 1993). Similarly, a survey of forensic service databases in South Thames Region showed that some providers held very limited RUT data and even less information about treatment outcomes (Cohen & Eastman, 1996). Further, RUT information may not be available at the geographic level required and, unless recently collected, may be invalidated by changing regional or district boundaries (Mann, 1993). For example, the Home Office provides statistics about the use of Part III of the Mental Health Act 1983 (Home Office, 1994) but fails to provide information about the type of hospital or unit to which the patient was admitted (other than if it was a special hospital) or its geographical location. If those two pieces of information were included, then the statistics would be very much more useful for local planning purposes. Another point related to the recency of RUT information (or indeed any other type of needs assessment data) is that there is often a considerable delay between the time when a study takes place and its publication. Hence, studies of utilisation which are published several years after taking place may be of little use to planners other than as an historical account.

Aside from data incompatibilities within individual service types (e.g. mental health), information from different agencies (e.g. health and social services) may also be difficult to interpret as a whole. This is both because of different health and local authority boundaries and because the type of data about MDOs which are of particular interest to one agency may well be very different from the type of data which interests another. The experience of one of the authors in advising multi-agency, geographically defined policy steering groups (see Chapter 6) was that the primary purpose and culture of the particular agency so drove its generic data collection that even the most simple level of commonality of data was almost impossible to achieve. This was particularly so where a mental health agency (with a 'care' ethos) was set alongside a criminal justice agency (with a 'justice' or 'punishment' ethos), even if it was the Probation Service.

Other difficulties may arise from the necessity for information sharing between both agencies and services (Fryers & Greatorex, 1992). There may be problems about the confidentiality of patient information, as well as of 'business/commercial' information. However, according to Warheit *et al* (1977), the focus of the RUT approach is on broad socio-demographic, geographical and service information, not on individual cases. Hence, if cases are to be

tracked across different agencies, then methods can be developed
for protecting the identity of cases, and without the risk of double
counting (e.g. by assigning each case with a unique identity number). Also, Bloom *et al* (1988) have suggested that the RUT approach
may, by increasing competition between agencies that are sharing
information, result in improved understanding of the service
delivery system as a whole and in the improvement of programme
coordination and integration. Conversely, any competition between
providers may discourage information sharing, and the types of
information collected and produced may be influenced more by
market concerns than by patient 'needs'. According to Murray
(1996), "Conflict between a commercially favourable description
of a service and the academic requirement for frank reporting, warts
and all, may prove to be an area of some controversy in the new
model NHS" (p. 520). Such concerns may be particularly appropriate in the field of forensic mental health care, where there has
been a burgeoning of private and NHS provider interest and much
evidence of quite stark competition and empire building (and
defending).

There is an alternative approach to collecting RUT data from
established information systems, and that is to conduct a survey of
the records of the agencies which have contact with the population
of interest (Warheit *et al*, 1977). The quality and detail of the
information collected in this way will depend, of course, upon the
quality of the record keeping of the agencies concerned, and issues
of patient/client confidentiality may also be difficult to overcome.
Such an approach is also more expensive than using existing
information systems. However, it may be the only alternative where
there is no established information system or where vital pieces of
information are missing. This method has an obvious overlap with
the survey approach described in Chapter 3, but the chief distinction
is that the RUT approach simply measures utilisation of services
rather than the needs of those within the service.

The RUT approach and needs assessment for MDOs

Some studies of the special hospital population have examined
patient profiles (e.g. age, gender, psychiatric diagnosis, status under
the Mental Health Act, criminal behaviour), admission rates, referral
sources and length of stay (Tennent *et al*, 1980; Hamilton, 1990;
Naismith & Coldwell, 1990; Special Hospital Services Authority,
1991). However, these studies were primarily concerned with describing the operation of the special hospitals and the characteristics

of their populations rather than the 'needs' of the patients them-selves. Other studies have examined various characteristics of medium-secure units, again without specific reference to patient 'need'. This includes the physical characteristics of the units (e.g. location, physical structure), staffing, ward policy, admission rates and criteria, patient profiles (e.g. socio-demographic, clinical and criminal characteristics), referral sources/procedures and discharge details (Higgins, 1981; Reid *et al*, 1982; Gudjonsson & MacKeith, 1983; Treasaden, 1985; Faulk & Taylor, 1986). Also, these studies were primarily conducted as descriptions of the first generation of medium-secure units, which began to appear in the early 1980s. Many of the survey studies described in Chapter 3 are also useful sources of descriptive information about patient populations.

A number of recent studies have explicitly examined the utilisa-tion of secure services. Many of these involve surveys of simply the use of services, either on a census date or over a given time. However, some of the studies do attempt to tap unmet need, through an examination of waiting lists for admission. What distinguishes these studies from the surveys reported in Chapter 3 is that they do not explicitly and directly address the 'needs' of the patients using the services. Rather, they provide an overall picture of the pressures on services (e.g. in terms of high bed occupancy rates), without taking into account whether the individuals occupying the beds are actually in need of the service. For example, high rates of bed occupancy and long waiting lists for medium-security facilities may not mean that there is actually a 'need' for more of them. Individuals in beds may be inappropriately placed and those waiting for admission may actually need a lesser (or higher) level of security, but medium security may be the only secure service available.

Studies of RUT in secure services

Coid (1993*a*) carried out a point prevalence survey of all private ($n = 5$) and NHS medium-secure units ($n = 25$), as well as all special hospitals ($n = 4$), in England and Wales in 1993. He found that NHS medium-security services, with 721 usable beds, were functioning at 96% capacity and that private medium-security facilities, with 340 usable beds, were operating at 99% capacity. The special hospitals reported 92% occupancy of 1651 available beds. However, when beds which were being kept open for trial leave patients and beds which were about to be filled were taken into account, true occu-pancy for NHS medium-secure units and special hospitals was closer to 98% and 99%, respectively. Only two of the NHS facilities reported having beds available on the census date, and private facilities had no vacancies. Further, only five NHS medium-secure units kept (or perhaps were able to keep) an emergency bed open as a matter of policy. Special hospitals reported that 12 people were waiting to be admitted from prisons and other NHS facilities. Medium-secure units reported considerable pressure from the criminal justice system and from within the NHS, with 99 people waiting for admission. Of these, 43% were in prison, 17% were in other NHS facilities and 40% were in special hospitals. Coid concluded, therefore, that NHS and private medium-security facilities were no longer coping with demand on the census date (albeit that further point prevalence studies would be required to confirm this conclusion generally), in part because of an increase in transfers from prison.[32] He therefore questioned whether medium-security facilities could continue to fulfil their original intended purpose. He further questioned the effects on the demand for medium-security beds of possibly inadequate local locked and 'new long-stay' provision. He recommended additional medium-security provision to alleviate the pressures (as well as additional staff training). He also suggested that the quality of NHS and private medium-security provision should be explicitly compared, particularly given that private facilities often suffered the disadvantage of being geographically far from the patient's district of residence, with implications for lack of 'seamless' service provision out into lower security and community care.

Murray (1996) also conducted a national survey of bed utilisation in NHS medium-secure units in England. On a census day in 1991, he found that 555 patients were occupying beds. They were predominantly young psychotic men with a history of contact with psychiatric services. Afro-Caribbean patients were over-represented, which confirmed the findings of an earlier study of a single medium-secure unit (Cope & Ndegwa, 1991). Murray also found that the majority of admissions were of remand prisoners (56%) charged with serious offences, and that fewer than 30% of admissions were from special hospitals or other parts of the NHS. Most patients were currently on sections under Part III of the Mental Health Act 1983 (approximately 80%), although there were 17 (3%) informal patients. The average duration of stay (including for those patients still occupying beds) was 332 days. Twelve per cent of patients had

[32] In recent years the Home Office has actively and effectively pursued 'diversion' from prison to hospital by way of its power to direct patients into hospital by means of transfer orders under Sections 48/49 and 47 of the Mental Health Act 1983.

been in a bed for longer than two years. Nearly half the sample were expected by their RMOs to be discharged within one to six months. It was expected that a similar proportion would be discharged into the community. RMOs expected that a further 27% would be discharged to a NHS hospital.

Murray acknowledged that his study did not provide a comprehensive account of aggregate demand for medium-security services because it did not measure demand from prisons, special hospitals or the private sector. Nevertheless, he argued that it did provide a valuable account of the in-patient workload of medium-security forensic services on a specific day, and he considered it reasonable to assume that the day chosen was representative of others.

Murray also argued, perhaps somewhat surprisingly, that there was no evidence of significant accumulation of long-stay medium-security patients. However, he recognised that this did not necessarily imply negligible unmet demand for long-stay medium-security care in other locations (e.g. special hospitals), and he accepted that later evidence from Reed (1994) suggested an increase in the average length of stay since 1991. Murray concluded that medium-secure units were predominantly accommodating remand prisoners and, as a consequence, current bed numbers were inadequate to satisfy demand from the special hospitals and for 'difficult to place' patients from within the NHS. However, he suggested that this failure arose from under-provision rather than inappropriate use of medium security, and that the restricted availability of non-forensic services and the effects of this on medium-security demand should be examined. He also recommended that attention should be paid to the over-representation of Afro-Caribbean patients within secure services.

Kennedy *et al* (1995) examined length of stay among medium-security in-patients. Studying the Reaside RSU they found that 6.7% of those admitted stayed for longer than two years. When compared with a control group of patients who stayed less than two years, the long-stay group were significantly more likely to have been of no fixed abode and unemployed on admission or arrest and to have been admitted from a special hospital. They were also more likely to be detained subject to restrictions, to have a longer history of contact with psychiatric services and to have committed a serious index offence of violence. An audit of the case notes of the long-stay patients also revealed three main factors that had contributed to longer stays: first, the seriousness of the offence and the uncertainty about the risk posed by the patient; second, discharge problems resulting from disagreement between forensic and local psychiatric services about the patient's security and treatment needs, as well as lack of rehabilitation beds in general psychiatry or appropriate community services; and third, specific clinical problems (e.g. treatment-resistant psychopathology coupled with disturbed behaviour). The authors provided illustrative vignettes of a selection of the individual long-stay patients. They concluded that there was a group of long-stay patients accumulating within medium-security services and that they had much in common with general psychiatric long-stay patients, in that they were chronically ill, socially disadvantaged, isolated and suffering from multiple disabilities. They recommended that long-stay medium-security facilities be developed to meet this demand and that failure to do so could render the existing medium-security system ineffective, with consequent negative effects for MDOs entangled in the criminal justice system and the health service. This need, they claimed, was reinforced and made more urgent by the clear evidence of unmet need for long-term medium-security care present in both the special hospital and medium-security populations.

Cripps *et al* (1995) described the first 15 months of operation of the Rollin Unit, a 40-bed local 'hybrid' forensic and intensive-care unit set up to fill an identified gap between local intensive-care units and the related regional medium-secure unit. The Rollin Unit was intended to have a different function from both local intensive-care units and RSUs, but also to overlap with each. Specifically, it was intended to deal with some both serious and minor offenders, to act as a remand facility, to have a high admission and turnover rate and to operate in a fluid system capable of allowing quick and easy transfer of patients between different tiers of security. It was not intended that it should admit as large a proportion of special hospital cases as RSUs. The unit therefore fulfilled a 'transit' and 'gap-filling' role in relation to other services, being, in some regards, analogous with some (rather heterogeneous) private secure facilities.

The Rollin Unit admitted 219 patients on 255 occasions during the study period. Men and black people were over-represented. Most admissions were suffering from schizophrenia or similar states (66%); drug or alcohol misuse was noted in 25% of admissions. The vast majority (84%) had had previous psychiatric admissions. Just over half the patients (51%) were admitted from open psychiatric wards, followed by those admitted from a local court diversion scheme (18%), from prison (17%) and from the community (13%). Only two patients were admitted from locked facilities (an RSU and a special hospital). The majority of admissions were under Part II sections (158, 62%) and the remainder (38%) were under Part III of the Mental Health Act (22% remand orders and 17% restricted) and many of these had committed serious offences. Many of the Mental Health Act Part II patients were also admitted because of violent or antisocial behaviour. Eighty per cent and 50% of those subject to sections under Part III and Part II, respectively, had had previous convictions. It is noteworthy that 13 of the Part III patients were admitted from open intensive-care wards and five of the Part II patients were admitted from a court diversion scheme that related specifically to the unit. The average length of stay for those admitted on Part III and Part II sections was 78 and 51 days, respectively. Within two months, 71% of admissions were discharged, the majority (78%) to open psychiatric beds.

Cripps *et al* noted that the intensive-care group and the narrowly defined 'MDO' group were similar in many ways (and, indeed, overlapped on occasion). They highlighted that many cases from the courts required only brief periods within a secure setting and were then successfully integrated into local psychiatric services, thus allowing for treatment closer to their homes and with less stigmatisation. However, the authors expressed uncertainty about the appropriateness of accommodating civil patients alongside individuals convicted of serious offences, and questioned whether less overtly disturbed patients would receive less attention in such an environment. They also questioned whether the level of security was becoming too high for civil intensive-care patients and were aware that the pressure to refer to such local services could result in the sacrifice of quality to volume.

Cripps *et al* concluded that the Rollin Unit was successful in providing a service for both acute intensive-care patients and MDOs, and that many of the patients would probably have been admitted to a medium-secure unit had the Rollin Unit not existed. They argued that the unit fulfilled a different function from other secure facilities, in having higher admission rates, shorter lengths of stay, a lower percentage of admissions under Part III sections, a higher proportion of referrals from NHS hospitals and in offering a minimal service to the special hospitals. They also suggested that the Rollin Unit performed an important function in terms of remand assessments and diversion from the criminal justice system. They concluded that units such as theirs could have an important part to play in the seamless provision of services to MDOs, because they can respond quickly to demand and are well integrated with local psychiatric services. Development of more of these 'hybrid' units might thus reduce the need for medium-security places, and would not require fully trained forensic psychiatrists in order to function properly. The integration of such units into the spectrum of secure care could allow RSUs to focus more closely on the rehabilitation of more serious offenders and could also reduce the likelihood of violent patients being inappropriately placed on open wards. The authors also recommended that the outcomes for patients discharged from such units should be examined, and that the overall over-representation of black patients, albeit with a lower proportion of referrals of black people from prisons and courts, should be examined.

Murray *et al* (1997) evaluated the first year of operation of a pilot service somewhat similar to the Rollin Unit but more narrowly defined (funded by the DoH and North West Thames Regional Health Authority). This service aims to provide rapid assessment and admission of remand prisoners (from the North West Thames catchment area). The service, located at the Bentham Unit, is dedicated exclusively to the assessment and treatment of remand prisoners, and has exclusive use of 14 beds in locked wards. In its first year, the unit assessed 150 remand prisoners, the vast majority of which (83%) came from the local prison. The most frequent psychiatric diagnosis was psychosis and the majority had a history of psychiatric contacts. Twenty-eight (17%) had been psychiatric in-patients in the previous year. However, only half of the referrals were currently in contact with psychiatric services. Black people and those charged with violent or sexual offences were over-represented in comparison with the overall remand population. More than half the referrals were made to the Bentham Unit within two weeks of remand, and more than two-thirds of assessments were undertaken within five days of referral. One-fifth of cases were transferred to a bed within five days, and more than half within two weeks of assessment. The authors pointed out that these delays fell within government targets. A total of 62 (42%) cases were admitted, 55% on Section 48, 29% on Section 35 and 10% on Section 38. Most subsequent transfers were to a medium-secure unit or locked ward (*n* = 24, 39%), with less than 31% (*n* = 19) going to an open ward (mostly under Section 37). Ten cases (16%) were referred for out-patient care, including probation, and eight (13%) were sent back to prison. Three months after transfer, 35 (56%) were still in-patients, although five were on extended leave. Thirteen (21%) were subject to community supervision through the Probation Service, psychiatric services or both, and six had absconded or were lost to follow-up.

Murray *et al* concluded that, with resources like the Bentham Unit, delays in transfer from prisons to the NHS can be decreased, and that improved screening of new prison receptions can further reduce the delay before referral to psychiatric services. They identified the narrow remit of the Bentham Unit as a crucial factor in its success. Personnel did not have other service commitments (e.g. out-patient appointments) beyond dealing with remand prisoners, and the service had exclusive use of properly staffed secure beds. Murray *et al* pointed out that the reduced time spent in custody resulted in reduced costs to the Home Office but increased costs to the NHS, particularly as the majority of cases admitted to the Bentham Unit were more serious offenders and were destined for the crown court. The authors pointed out the significance of these extra costs for NHS purchasers, who would be expected to fund the scheme after its pilot period ended. However, they suggested that the Home Office should recognise the substantial cost transfers resulting from such schemes, and consider joint funding of similar initiatives. The high proportion of cases destined for the crown court also led the authors to identify an artificial ceiling on therapeutic gain during the time spent waiting for trial, which they attributed to uncertainty about the eventual outcome of the court case. They recommended that pilot schemes like the Bentham Unit should be established elsewhere, and that similar services specifically for women and young offenders should be considered, but with a wider geographical catchment area.

Weaver *et al* (1997) subsequently carried out an independent evaluation of the service provided by the Bentham Unit. They compared the number, rate and speed of referrals, assessments and transfers of remand prisoners before and after the introduction of the pilot service. They noted that, before the establishment of the Bentham Unit, remand prisoners were seen by an NHS psychiatrist from the patient's catchment service or RSU. They found that the number of referrals and admissions of remand prisoners increased significantly after the Bentham Unit was established, although they pointed out that this could be accounted for by the higher number of violent offenders referred, particularly sex offenders. There was also a significant decrease in the interval between remand and first assessment after establishment of the Bentham Unit (from 27 days to ten days), in particular for patients subsequently transferred to NHS in-patient care. There was also a significant decrease in the interval between remand and transfer to an NHS hospital (122 days versus 46 days). A significant reduction in the number of prison assessments by catchment area psychiatrists was also found, which suggested that the Bentham Unit was now assessing these cases.

Weaver *et al* concluded that the Bentham Unit had achieved its aims, albeit that the changes they identified could have resulted from factors other than the new service, and that statistical problems could have produced spurious effects. They suggested that the regular presence in the prison of a psychiatrist from the Bentham

Unit had clearly coincided with significant reductions in the intervals between remand, assessment and transfer to NHS care, and that the outreach component of the service had had an important impact on case identification. They also noted the ability of the Bentham Unit to achieve speedy transfer onwards to local services. They recommended that units with remand beds should incorporate a similar outreach component into the prison system, although they recognised that, in order to justify the retention of such a service in terms of demand, it might be necessary to have a large (at least a sub-regional) catchment area. However, they noted that, as a regional service, the Bentham Unit appeared to reverse the principle of local provision promoted by government policy. However, they argued that this needed to be weighed against both the difficulties of developing local services of this kind for MDOs and the demonstrated benefits of the service.

Mohan *et al* (1997) examined all admissions to the RSU in North West Thames Region over 12 years (*n* = 282). They found that the majority of cases were psychotic men. Afro-Caribbean patients were over-represented and Asians under-represented. Demand for beds was found to be four times greater in urban than in rural areas. These characteristics remained constant over the 12 years, as did source of admission, length of stay and discharge location. However, they found that the type and severity of offences of those admitted had changed over time, with patients recently admitted having committed more violent and sexual offences than patients in previous years. They also found that a higher proportion of cases were being diverted from the criminal justice system at an earlier stage than before, and that approximately half those admitted had stayed in the RSU for longer than two years. They recommended that the consistently greater demand for medium-security beds from urban areas should be recognised in terms of resource allocation between areas and, like other authors, they identified a considerable unmet need for long-term medium-security provision.

James *et al* (1998) examined admissions over one year from prisons and courts (but not from police stations or via Section 136 of the Mental Health Act) to open, local secure and specialist forensic psychiatric facilities in part of inner London. This included transfers between hospitals and bed usage by patients who were present in hospital at the start of the study period. In the study year, a total of 80 beds were used by cases admitted from the criminal justice system. This was equivalent to 17.3 beds per 100 000 population, with an approximate annual cost of £1.4 million per 100 000 population. Of all bed usage by patients admitted from the criminal justice system, 45% was in local services (21% open beds and 24%

local secure beds), 30% in maximum security and 26% in medium security. A further 5.5 secure beds per 100 000 population were used by patients who had not originated in the criminal justice system. In total, 45% of all bed usage by patients from the criminal justice system took place in local services, and these cases were responsible for 36% of total bed costs. Seven per cent of all open bed usage was by patients admitted from the criminal justice system. James *et al* found that the local secure facility admitted 23 times the number of cases from the criminal justice system than did the RSU. The level of usage of local secure beds and medium- and maximum-security beds for cases from the criminal justice system and elsewhere was between two and three times higher than the average for England and Wales. Levels of local secure bed usage were 30% higher than the inner London average, while medium-security usage was only 56% of the inner London average. These figures reflected the configuration of local secure services, with more admissions from the criminal justice system to local secure services than to the RSU. Such variations could be the result of local morbidity, deprivation and social factors.

James *et al* argued that these bed usage figures were likely to provide a better estimate of actual need than other similar studies, because of the characteristics of the service model in central London. The model is based on an integrated forensic/general service with freedom of flow between different levels of security, rapid access to assessment at court and easy access to beds. This, the authors claimed, should have minimised both under-identification of cases and failure to admit patients due to lack of adequate provision. However, they pointed out that open units may have been forced to admit cases with higher levels of disturbed behaviour than they were designed to cope with, owing to difficulties experienced in finding extra-contractual places. The authors argued for the expansion of forensic services at a local level, and emphasised the importance of developing local secure provision and of expanding community forensic psychiatric services, with a focus on comprehensive after-care.

Studies of RUT in general psychiatric services

The number of NHS psychiatric beds was reduced by approximately 50% in the ten years leading up to the early 1990s (Renshaw, 1994), and between 1986 and 1991 the number of psychiatric beds in locked wards fell from 1163 to 639 (DoH/Home Office,

1992).[33] Consequently, concerns have been expressed about the effects of the closure of open and locked general psychiatric beds on secure provision. Pressure on general psychiatric beds may lead to patients being discharged prematurely and becoming 'revolving-door' cases. It may also be difficult to move patients from higher security levels because of a lack of beds within general psychiatric services. General psychiatric services may also refer 'difficult' cases to higher levels of security because the pressure on their services makes it difficult to deal with such cases. Hence, the close and inter-dependent relationship between general and forensic psychiatric services and the (already demonstrated) close overlap of many MDOs with other groups of general psychiatric patients make a brief foray into RUT studies within general psychiatry relevant.

The following studies of service utilisation within general psychiatric acute and rehabilitation services illustrate some of the points just made. This review is not intended to be comprehensive but, rather, to provide a summary of some recent studies which are particularly illustrative of important points, or which refer specifically to MDOs (although studies of the utilisation of general psychiatric services by MDOs are extremely rare).

Powell *et al* (1995) carried out a series of point prevalence surveys of bed occupancy in Greater London's acute psychiatric units (n = 54) over a four-year period. The average level of bed occupancy was 97.5% and was significantly higher in inner London than in outer London. They found that bed occupancy in inner London exceeded 100% on more than 49% of occasions. Further, a steady and significant decline in bed numbers was illustrated over the four years. They also showed a clear correlation between Jarman UPA8 scores and both bed occupancy and bed provision. Powell *et al* emphasised that the overloading of acute admission wards had resulted in premature discharges, unplanned leave and an inability to admit urgent cases, and that this had inevitably had negative consequences for community care. Further, a high proportion of extra-contractual referrals implied not only that resources had flowed out of the NHS into the private sector, but also that some patients were often moved far from home, with consequences for continuity of care after discharge. Powell *et al* also identified an upward pressure on more secure beds and suggested that the closure of former long-stay wards may also have exerted pressure on acute services. They expressed

---

[33] It seems likely that this decline continued until the mid-1990s, although the high media profile of challenging and offending psychiatric patients and recognised 'over-occupancy' of general psychiatric urban beds (see later) may have stemmed the reduction.

concern that the primary determinant of admission may, therefore, not be patient need, and that the lack of supra-regional monitoring of the hospital closure programme was extremely problematic. They concluded that occupancy rates had become unacceptably high, that careful monitoring of the situation should occur and that remedial action should be taken to prevent a breakdown of services. They recommended that similar studies should be carried out in other parts of the country, and that further research should be conducted to quantify community resources and the number of patients remaining on wards for over six months.

The MILMIS Project Group (1995) aimed to establish a mechanism for monitoring the 'health' of inner London mental health services. The main health indicators they selected were bed occupancy, the proportion of patients detained under the Mental Health Act, the number of assaults committed by in-patients, the number of emergency assessments carried out and the case-loads of community psychiatric nurses. Psychiatrists from 12 inner London services provided service information on a census date, and information relating to one week before and after that date. Services had a combined normal complement of 1109 admission beds, representing a mean of 42 beds per 100 000 population. There were 1236 patients on admission wards on the census day, and half of these were subject to a section of the Mental Health Act. A total of 339 cases (27%) had been in a bed for three to six months, 101 (8%) for six to twelve months and 43 (4%) for over a year. There were 204 patients who were thought appropriate for admission beds but who were accommodated elsewhere (e.g. on non-admission psychiatric wards, medical wards, in the community, in private psychiatric hospitals, or in other NHS hospitals). Significantly, 14 cases were identified as appropriate for the admission wards but, because of a lack of beds, were in prison or police cells. When these cases were added to those actually in beds, the mean 'true bed occupancy' was 130%. Additionally, nine services reported that they were unable to admit a further 84 appropriate cases because of a lack of beds and that 24 cases were discharged prematurely to accommodate new patients. When these were added to the mean true bed occupancy, it increased to 140%. This represented a requirement for 426 additional admission beds (16 per 100 000 population) to meet the demand in the census week.

During the census week, 105 assaults were reported, although only one resulted in major physical injury. There were also 61 reports of sexual assault or harassment and 34 incidents of self-harm. Services reported carrying out 619 emergency assessments during the census week, with a mean of 23 per 100 000 population, although the range was wide. The average reported case-load of community psychiatric nurses was 37, but this indicator was thought to be unreliable.

The MILMIS Project Group concluded that there was significant unmet demand for admission beds during the census week. Because of this, patients were accommodated in inappropriate facilities (including prisons and police cells), were refused admission (despite clinical opinion that they required it) or were prematurely discharged to allow more urgent new admissions. They also found a significant amount of violent behaviour and self-harm on admission wards and a high number of emergency assessments. They suggested that "admission wards are not places of haven but disturbed and dangerous environments for both patients and staff, in which half the patients are legally detained and assault and sexual harassment are daily occurrences" (p. 280). The Project Group noted that their findings highlighted the extent of the problems facing London's mental health services, but did not identify the causes. They stated that "the identification of causes for these disturbing findings, and for provision of the remedies, is the responsibility of local clinicians through clinical audit, service managers through service activity monitoring, commissioning agencies through needs assessment and the government through resource allocation" (p. 280). The MILMIS Project Group intended to re-evaluate the same services at six-monthly intervals to evaluate improvements.

Lelliott *et al* (1994) carried out a national audit of new long-stay psychiatric patients (n = 905) from 59 UK mental health services. New long-stay patients were defined as those who had been hospitalised for between six months and three years. Approximately one-third of these patients had a history of dangerousness or criminality before the index admission. Of these, 163 (18%) had committed a serious violent act, 102 (11%) had exhibited other dangerous or criminal behaviour and 3% had experienced at least one prior admission to a special hospital. In the three months before assessment, 176 (19%) had been violent towards others and a further 20 (2%) had shown a similar degree of sexual assaultiveness. Clinicians judged 115 (13%) to be at high risk of committing a violent or dangerous act if they were discharged, and a further 157 (17%) were identified as a moderate risk. Clinicians considered 383 (42%) of their patients to be at moderate or severe risk of non-deliberate self-harm or self-neeglect and 181(20%) at moderate or severe risk of deliberate self-harm. Patients also showed high levels of deficit in personal and interpersonal functioning, which indicated a need for rehabilitation or care, as well as a need for treatment of positive mental symptoms.

Although the group as a whole was heterogeneous, the authors identified two main subgroups. The first consisted of younger (18–34 years), single schizophrenic men, nearly half of whom (43%) had a history of serious violence, dangerous behaviour or admission to a special hospital and over one-third of whom were formally detained. The second subgroup consisted of older female patients (55–67 years), who were mostly married, or previously married, were diagnosed as having an affective disorder or dementia and were characterised by poor social functioning. More than half were considered to be at moderate or severe risk of non-deliberate self-harm. Lelliott *et al* concluded that, despite the policy of bed closure and the focus on community care, there still remains a group of relatively recently admitted patients who require long-term admission.

Lelliott & Wing (1994) described the effect on services of the new long-stay sample referred to above. They examined the prevalence of these patients, the beds and other residential resources available to services, the distribution of patients within services and clinicians' views as to the appropriateness of their placement.[34] Services varied considerably in terms of the availability of local residential and non-residential provision. England had fewer total residential places (both hospital and non-hospital) than the other UK countries, in particular fewer non-acute beds. The point prevalence of new long-stay psychiatric patients on the census day was 6.1 per 100 000 total population, although the range was very wide. There were substantial differences in point prevalence between countries, with England and Wales having significantly lower rates than Scotland and Northern Ireland. On the census day, new long-stay patients (*n* = 879) were occupying 9% of all beds available, and more than 25% were in 'acute' psychiatric beds.

Clinicians believed that 61% of patients would be more appropriately placed in a non-hospital setting – living independently, with family or in some form of non-hospital residential provision. For just over half the patients who would be best placed in a community setting, a suitable placement was unavailable. Patients who needed continuing hospitalisation had been in hospital longer than those more appropriately placed outside hospital. They were also slightly older and more likely to be formally detained, at moderate or severe risk of non-deliberate self-harm or at moderate to severe risk of acting violently or dangerously if discharged.

---

[34] This study rightly belongs in Chapter 3 (as it adopted a survey approach) but, for simplicity, we report it here.

Lelliott & Wing concluded that their results could be generalised and that many new long-stay patients remain in hospital because their residential needs are not met by existing services.

Conclusions

The studies described above provide a valuable account of the characteristics of secure services and of the patients they accommodate. They highlight the considerable pressures on secure and general psychiatric services and the impact that these pressures have on other parts of the mental health system. Taken together, they also clearly indicate a substantial lack of both secure and non-secure provision for MDOs (and other patients). They also make it clear that this crisis in relation to secure accommodation cannot be seen in isolation from that which is observed in general psychiatric services. It must surely be rational, therefore, for the mental health system to be viewed as a whole, particularly if a seamless service for MDOs is to be developed. Some studies have also provided valuable information about new service models for MDOs (e.g. those of the Rollin and Bentham Units) which aim directly to 'stitch the seams' between traditional medium-security and low-security services.

Several of the studies highlight specifically the over-representation of black people within secure services. The Reed report (DoH/Home Office, 1992) was explicit that the needs of ethnic minorities should be carefully examined, and this clearly should be a focus for future research. Similarly, the needs of women, who are a minority within secure services, should be addressed more explicitly. Indeed, this was addressed by the then High Security Psychiatric Services Commissioning Board through several proposed 'model schemes' for women.[35]

Finally, as regards community psychiatric services for MDOs, there is a dearth of published material by specialist forensic services. Needs assessment for MDOs has clearly focused on the need for

---

[35] In December 1997, a private member's Bill sponsored by Dr J. Lewis was considered by Parliament. It proposed that a duty be placed on each health authority to provide single-gender ward areas in all psychiatric units. If passed into law, it would have required each authority to have a strategy for separate treatment facilities for patients with acute episodes "within separate and therapeutic environments". It would have also placed a duty on authorities to fit security devices to all room and ward doors of existing psychiatric units "to prevent unauthorised intrusion". Although the Bill was not passed into law, the DoH has made some commitment to recognising the special needs of women.

security, but it is equally important that the needs of those MDOs who are in the community (but who may nevertheless have needs for specialist intervention) be addressed. Indeed, as experienced within general psychiatric services, there is an interlocking relationship between community and in-patient services that determines that any failure to respond to need in one context will rebound, in its effects, into the other. The weak spot in needs assessment (and perhaps existing services) for general psychiatric patients is in the provision of in-patient care (with recent concentration on the development of community care). By contrast, the MDO weak spot, certainly in needs assessment terms and, to some extent, in service development terms, is in relation to specialist community care. 'Separation' of forensic and general services, practically, philosophically or culturally, can only reinforce their individual and different weaknesses.

5 The social indicator approach

Introduction

Ill health has long been associated with adverse socio-economic conditions and with social deprivation (Robinson & Elkan, 1996). Research on mental health has also found relationships between both psychiatric morbidity and utilisation of psychiatric services and a wide range of socio-demographic variables. These include age, gender, ethnicity, marital status, social class, poverty, educational level, employment status, social isolation and rural/urban living (Odegard, 1932; Faris & Dunham, 1939; Shepherd, 1957; Dohrenwend & Dohrenwend, 1969; Zautra & Simons, 1978; Goodman *et al*, 1983; Richman *et al*, 1984; Shapiro *et al*, 1985; Hirsch, 1988; Thornicroft, 1991; Jarman *et al*, 1992; Meltzer *et al*, 1995*a*). Because more socially deprived geographical areas tend to have higher rates of psychiatric morbidity and service utilisation, the planning of mental health services and the allocation of resources should reflect this, otherwise service delivery will be inequitable across geographical areas (Hirsch, 1988; Glover *et al*, 1994). However, the development of formulae to quantify the geographical distribution of resources has been slow (Glover *et al*, 1994). Indeed, the uneven distribution of mental illness in the population was not itself addressed explicitly in UK service planning up until the mid-1970s (Glover *et al*, 1994).

The social indicator approach to needs assessment attempts to quantify and take account of geographical disparities in morbidity and in related disabilities and needs for intervention. It estimates need, therefore, in an aggregate, 'top-down' fashion and, as such, is contrasted with the other approaches so far discussed, which adopt counting methods, which are largely 'bottom-up' in nature, albeit with aggregation of what has been thus counted. So, the social indicator approach uses existing data about the socio-demographic characteristics of a population (e.g. census statistics) to develop statistical models or indices of social deprivation (e.g. Jarman, 1983, 1984) which predict morbidity and/or service utilisation and thus, indirectly, establish the level of need for services. The aim is to compare geographical areas in terms of social deprivation (and, by virtue of social deprivation being a proxy for it, ill health) as a guide to resource allocation and service development between those areas. It is, therefore, in the tradition of the approach taken by the 1970s Resource Allocation Working Party (RAWP) to use a morbidity-modified *per capita* approach to resource or revenue allocation (see below). The advantage of this approach is that existing statistics can be used. However, clearly, a requirement is that allocation is based on valid social indicators; that is, indicators that validly predict the need for services for which resources are thus allocated.

A large number of variables have been shown to be associated with psychiatric morbidity and with service utilisation, and many of these have been used to develop social indicator models. These include:

(a) population characteristics, such as population density and mobility;
(b) socio-demographic and socio-economic variables, such as age, gender, marital status, ethnicity, income, occupation, education, social class;
(c) housing characteristics such as type of dwelling, owner- or renter-occupied accommodation, persons per dwelling and indices of substandard accommodation such as overcrowding;
(d) rates of mortality and morbidity, such as infant mortality and suicide rates;
(e) crime patterns and arrest records (Warheit *et al*, 1977).

Individual social indicator models have tended to use either fairly simple designs that incorporate only one or two indicators or very complex designs, incorporating as many as 60 variables; the latter require highly sophisticated statistical analyses (Warheit *et al*, 1977).

Since a very large number of variables have been associated with psychiatric morbidity and service utilisation, choosing which to include in a social indicator model is a complex task. Selection may be determined by research experience, theoretical relevance, intuition or preliminary statistical investigation of the variables within specific categories (Rabkin, 1986). Indeed, according to Cagle & Banks (1986), "The plethora of accessible social indicators may be as much a curse as a blessing for the mental health planner ... how does one decide how many and which ones to use to assess need?" (p. 127). Less despairingly, Holzer *et al* (1988) suggest that the ideal social indicator should be highly correlated with 'true need' regardless of time, place or other circumstances, yet, as this book attests throughout its pages, 'true need' is an elusive concept. The most compelling rationale favours basing the selection of indicators on epidemiological evidence (Cagle & Banks, 1986). We would argue that the social indicator approach is itself merely one *perspective* on 'true need' (see Chapter 8).

Further, even once the 'ideal', or the least optimal, indicators have been selected for inclusion in a model, there may be additional difficulties arising from the fact that relevant variables may not be available at all, *or* may be available but not in the form required for the level of analysis, *or* may be too unreliable to be included. For example, and particularly relevant to MDO need, Jarman (1983) originally intended to include the crime rate in his now highly respected index but, owing to lack of data at the required level, excluded it. However, he did include 'overcrowding of households', which a previous study had shown to be correlated with crime rates. In practice, therefore, the overriding considerations governing indicator selection tend to be data availability, comparability and consistency of the data throughout the geographical area of analysis and the recency of data collection (Rabkin, 1986).

Social indicator analyses may be applied to variously sized geographical areas. However, the population size should be small enough to maximise differentiation and at the same time large enough to ensure reliable observations, albeit these constraints must be satisfied in conjunction with selection of an area that relates naturally to local commissioning authority boundaries. Selection of geographical units that are too large may mask differences between smaller units within it (Robinson & Elkan, 1996), while selection of areas that are too small may provide too few cases to be meaningful (Rabkin, 1986). In general, therefore, social indicator models have been most commonly used at the census tract or enumeration district level.

There are a number of other theoretical issues that must be considered when interpreting information from the social indicator approach. One problem is the risk of failing to recognise what has been termed the 'ecological fallacy' – that it is fallacious to infer that information which holds true at one level of population analysis also holds true for much smaller populations or for individual people (Warheit *et al*, 1977). Hence, it cannot be assumed that all people living in a deprived area are themselves deprived or that non-deprived areas have only non-deprived inhabitants (Robinson & Elkan, 1996). Another type of ecological fallacy is of equal importance, in that the spatial characteristics of a geographical area cannot be presumed to determine the social structures within that area. Hence, while the spatial characteristics of an area influence and limit social conditions and relationships, they do not determine what they must be (Rabkin, 1986).

Leaving aside all such major problems attending the selection of indicators and of interpretation of data for a given geographical area, the social indicator approach does not provide a measure of over-provision. Nor does it 'indicate' the specific types of treatment or care that are required, except in the broadest terms. Different sets of social indicators may well be required to predict different types of service use by different types of patient. Hence, the type of model best suited to predict (for example) specialist forensic service utilisation may be different from that required to predict acute general psychiatric service utilisation (albeit that even this hypothesis is untested). According to Rabkin (1986), therefore, it is preferable to identify indicators for specific sets of criterion variables rather than to develop an indicator model reflective of a generic mental health index. Such a disaggregated approach can provide several health status 'criterion' groups (one of which, for example, might be depressed women) with respect to particular categories of mental health problems, differentiated by type and severity of impairment.

An even more fundamental difficulty with the social indicator approach is that it is difficult to establish the validity of any models that *are* developed and, in particular, the extent to which they measure 'true need' (even though, for us, that question itself has a very restricted meaning). Many models tend to have been developed using service utilisation rates as the criterion measure and, as discussed in previous chapters, measures of utilisation are often poor proxy measures of true need. As a result, the use of such criterion measures may result in the perpetuation of welfare-inefficient and inequitable service provision. Indeed, models frequently use measures of bed utilisation as the criterion and cannot, therefore, provide information about other types of service (e.g. community care), let alone guide their resourcing. This problem will automatically gain some further attention as we turn to those empirical social indicator studies available for us to review.

Studies using social indicators to estimate service utilisation and 'need'

The UK government has, since the mid-1970s, often used the social indicator approach to assist in aggregate health resource allocation to

RHAs. This followed a radical review of the approach of the DoH and Social Security to health resource allocation by the RAWP, an expert working party established by the Department to examine the apparent disparity in crude *per capita* resource allocation between the then 14 health regions. Up until that time NHS funding had been allocated to regions on the basis of the number of hospitals operated within each, a method thought to have resulted in an unfair advantage to regions in the south of England. In addressing the inequity, the RAWP applied the principle that there should be "equal access to resources for equal need" (Glover *et al*, 1994). It therefore devised a general health formula based on the size and age/gender structure of the population, weighted for standard mortality ratios for specific diseases. A separate formula was devised for mental health services; this included weighting for marital status within the population (DoH and Social Security, 1976). The government adopted these formulae and gave RHAs ten years to move towards their RAWP targets, giving rise to regions that lost resources describing themselves as having been 'rawped'. Subsequently, and just before the ten-year period had elapsed, the government called for a review of the RAWP formula in order to improve its sensitivity. The new working party attempted then to develop a formula based on smaller geographical areas of analysis (DoH and Social Security, 1988). However, overall, information was poor. Because of this, and also because the working party felt uncertain about how to take into consideration the effects of community care (Glover *et al*, 1994), no work could be done on mental health services. The RAWP review did recommend, however, the use of not only 'all cause' standard mortality ratios for the under-75s but also an index of social deprivation. But the government failed to adopt an approach that included an index of social deprivation (Carr-Hill *et al*, 1994), thus failing to reflect data directly relevant to mental health care needs (including forensic mental health). The government also decided upon a single funding formula for all services, including mental health, and used this weighted capitation formula to allocate resources to RHAs. They, in turn, used the same or similar formulae to distribute funds to DHAs. As a result, there was a failure to represent differential mental health (including forensic mental health) morbidity across districts in terms of the funds they received. This was significant enough in its own terms, but it also automatically implied that any social (or other) indicators which *did* validly measure local need would determine disparity between need and the financial resources available to meet it. So there was little incentive to carry out valid needs assessment if the money available was not given on a similarly valid basis.

In 1993, the NHS Executive commissioned a study to revise the formula for distributing NHS hospital and community health service funds (approximately £18 billion per annum) to English health authorities (Carr-Hill *et al*, 1994; Smith *et al*, 1994). The study used the underlying principles of previous work but attempted to develop a more sensitive, empirically based model of demand for hospital care for small areas. It also attempted to overcome some of the statistical problems, as well as some other problems related to factoring in supply variables (e.g. access to beds and GPs), which had been identified in the RAWP review (Carr-Hill *et al*, 1994). According to Judge & Mays (1994), this study used more comprehensive data and more sophisticated statistical methods that were better informed by theory than previous approaches. A new weighted capitation formula was developed, based on socio-demographic, health and supply variables. This implied a redistribution of resources in favour of inner-city areas (Smith *et al*, 1994). The new formula was adopted from April 1995 by the government. Its application to psychiatric services is described later in this chapter (Smith *et al*, 1996).

We now turn from DoH and Social Security/DoH initiatives to non-governmental research. Researchers in the UK, USA and Canada have used social indicators and deprivation indices to predict psychiatric service utilisation, in particular psychiatric beds (Hirsch, 1988; Thornicroft, 1991; Jarman *et al*, 1992; Ciarlo *et al*, 1992*a*, 1992*b*; Tweed & Ciarlo, 1992; Ciarlo & Tweed, 1992; Tweed *et al*, 1992; Smith *et al*, 1994; Glover *et al*, 1994). We identified no studies relating specifically to MDO services in our search of the literature. The review that follows focuses, therefore, solely on general psychiatric services. However, the review is, in itself, of substantial direct relevance to MDOs, albeit not to their 'special' needs. We offer, therefore, some speculative comments concerning the use of existing generic indices and the possible development of special indices for MDO services in the section of the chapter that follows.

A Working Party of the Section for Social and Community Psychiatry of the Royal College of Psychiatrists has examined factors influencing psychiatric bed use and service planning, aimed at identifying the reasons why some services report increased (excess) pressure on beds (Hirsch, 1988). The Working Party reviewed a number of studies. It concluded that there was a strong association between psychiatric admission rates and various indices of social deprivation, while there was little evidence to suggest that districts were able to operate with fewer beds per head of population by providing a community-based service. Hence, their study of a stratified sample of psychiatric services based at 20 district general hospitals in all the RHAs in England showed a strong influence of poverty on utilisation and little variation due to differences in the style of service. The Working Party also found that admission rates specifically from South Hammersmith were significantly correlated with Jarman UPA scores, and that this relationship was then borne out in each of the districts of North West Thames Regional Health Authority.

Thornicroft (1991) has developed complex statistical models to examine data for any possible association there may be between a range of socio-demographic variables and mental health service utilisation, specifically in the South Thames (East) Region. He found a significant correlation between psychiatric admission rates and Jarman UPA-8 indices, although the Jarman UPA-8 was out-performed by two other indices, developed by the Department of the Environment (1983). Thornicroft then examined the association between a number of individual census variables and psychiatric admission rates, comparing the performance of such independent variables with that of four derived indices (Jarman, 1983; Department of Environment, 1983; ACORN, 1986). He found that all the individual census variables except those related to age were either strongly or very strongly related to admission rates, and that they outperformed the four derived indices in the majority of cases. He also found that, when single census variables were combined in a regression analysis, they accounted for more of the variance in admission rates than did the derived indices or the single census variables individually. Indeed, nine census variables were found to account for 95% of the variance in admission rates. Thornicroft then tested the data to determine whether a principal components analysis would be better able to predict admission rates than single census variables, derived indices and combined census variables. He identified three components which, when entered into a regression analysis, accounted for approximately two-thirds of the variation in admission rates. This improved on the performance of the derived indices but still fell short of the performance of the individual census variables.

In summary, therefore, in Thornicroft's study each of the derived variables accounted for less of the variance in admission rates than the best individual census variables, taken singly or combined, or the principal components. As a result, Thornicroft (1991) concluded that models of increasing complexity are better at predicting admission rates and that clinical, research and planning applications can, therefore, balance the degree of predictive accuracy desired against the complexity of the analysis required. He argued that this approach may help to identify service needs and target resources at heavy service users, and that it may also allow estimates, at the aggregate level, of unmet need. He recommended that standard data on service utilisation, broken down by district, be made available by the DoH to facilitate this type of analysis. He also suggested that data about receipt of social security benefits on a district and regional basis would be useful for future modelling, and that standard reports of utilisation should be categorised by diagnosis and duration of stay. He further recommended that internationally standardised categories for socio-demographic data would facilitate meaningful comparisons. He suggested that this method could be used by other regions and districts, as well as for smaller-scale analyses, and that it could be extended to other age and patient groups.

Jarman *et al* (1992) examined the association between a large number of social, health status and service provision variables (including the Jarman UPA score) and psychiatric admission rates in England. The aim of the study was to develop a formula to predict admission rates across districts, and thus to assist in the appropriate allocation of resources. They calculated actual and expected admission rates for all districts in England and adjusted these for age, gender and marital status. They then established a 'standardised admission rate' for each district and used a regression analysis to determine which combination of the social, health status and service provision variables best explained the variation between districts in standardised admission rates. They found that the actual number of admissions varied from 79% above to 54% below the expected number of admissions. The variables best able to explain this variation were the rate of notification of drug misusers, standard mortality ratios and levels of illegitimacy. This regression model was able to explain 79% of the district variation in the number of admissions. Jarman *et al* also developed a simpler (but less powerful) model based on the Jarman UPA score which, they argued, had the advantage of being easier to use at the electoral ward level, where some of the variables required by the more complex model were usually not available.

Kammerling & O'Connor (1993) found a strong correlation in Bristol between unemployment rates at the electoral ward level and rates of psychiatric admission. Specifically, they found that 50% of the variation in age-adjusted admission rates for individuals under 65 years of age was explained by unemployment, and that this factor alone outperformed predictions using Jarman UPA scores. Going further, in Bloomsbury and Islington, Cotgrove *et al* (1992) found no association at all between Jarman UPA scores and ward admissions rates.

Glover *et al* (1994) developed an index of need for mental health care using 1991 small-area census statistics for all levels from the

134   *Assessing forensic mental health need*

electoral ward up. They used socio-demographic variables (e.g. poverty, Jarman UPA scores), variables indicative of social isolation (e.g. residents widowed or divorced) and a range of 'other' variables (e.g. ethnicity, economic activity). Data on admission prevalence from the old North East Thames Region were obtained from the DoH's hospital episode statistics and regression models were developed to predict admission rates within each hospital's catchment area. Separate models were derived for the region as a whole, inner London, outer London and Essex. They found that the best predictor variables differed across geographical areas and that prediction was more effective in rural and suburban areas than in inner cities.

On the basis of this earlier work, Glover *et al* then developed a 'mental illness needs index' (MINI) for acute mental health care which is now widely available for use within the NHS and local government. They also developed a computer program which calculates the index for any area definable by its electoral ward composition (Glover, 1996). In addition to calculating the MINI, this program is able to provide the population structure and predicted standardised admission prevalence for people aged 15–64 years, as well as the number of adults likely to be admitted. The MINI program also estimates a range of bed requirements, using two models of comprehensive mental health services developed by Wing (1994) and Strathdee & Thornicroft (1992). These models suggest the range of provision likely to be required for each type of facility, from the most needy to the least needy district. The MINI program locates the selected area within the range of provision for each type of facility and translates this into actual place numbers. However, Glover (1996) has pointed out that the range of secure place numbers suggested by both the Wing and Strathdee & Thornicroft models are substantially lower than the number recommended by the NHS Executive (1995a). It was argued, therefore, that, for secure provision, since local numbers are generally small and since commissioners are usually aware of their 'need' position, a separate calculation could be made.[36]

Glover (1996) states that the MINI provides a simple method of obtaining a first estimate of how a rational allocation of resources might proceed. However, he recognises that it may not take into account local factors which can affect need, such as service availability,

---

[36] It is far from clear from evidence presented in this book, in fact, that local commissioners *are* aware of their need position or are even aware of how to *define* this need position, other than on an 'RUT plus waiting list' basis.

homelessness, staffing levels and local bed management strategies. He notes that the MINI is able to estimate only the number of cases likely to need admission and not the attendant costs, which may vary between districts. He also emphasises that the model offers no estimate of the burden of cases cared for without admission.

Smith *et al* (1996) also developed an index of need for in-patient psychiatric services (the York Psychiatric Index; YPI). This formed part of a much larger project aimed at modifying the weighted capitation formula for resource distribution in the NHS (see above). They analysed variations in all completed in-patient psychiatric episodes in England in 1991/92 across 'synthetic wards' (defined according to the smallest area of residence for which the NHS was able to provide information) with the intention of explaining variations in in-patient psychiatric service utilisation between these small areas. They used population statistics from the Office of Population Censuses and Surveys to explore the relationship between age, gender and service utilisation, and found that the largest users of psychiatric services were young males and the elderly. They were also able to standardise utilisation variables for gender and age. They subsequently used a wide range of census and other data (e.g. mortality, morbidity, housing, unemployment, social class and ethnic origin) to reflect socio-economic and health conditions in the synthetic wards. They then applied sophisticated statistical techniques in an attempt to disentangle the effects of supply from the 'need' determinants of utilisation, although they recognised that their supply measures were necessarily crude. Using multi-level modelling techniques they finally produced an index of need (the YPI) based on six health and socio-economic variables relating to age, lone parenting, social isolation, birthplace, standard mortality ratios and permanent illness.

Since April 1995, Smith *et al*'s YPI has been used by the NHS Executive to distribute £2.2 billion of annual NHS expenditure for psychiatric services between English health authorities. Its developers argue that the YPI is superior to previous indices because it can be used for resource allocation from a national to a regional level, from a regional to a district level or from a district to a locality level, and because it takes account of supply variables. They also point out that use of the YPI implies considerable redistribution towards deprived areas compared with most previous methods of resource allocation. They suggest further that it could prove helpful for locality commissioning, although they note that the use of in-patient episodes as the criterion variable may not take proper account of other types of service need. They also note that there will always be a need for local discretion in the use of this or any other index at the locality level. The only major criticism of the index has come from Lelliott *et al* (1996), who recognise the value of the York model but are critical of the measures of supply used, also arguing that such measures could be a source of distortion.

In the USA, Hall & Royse (1987) designed a study to determine the relationship between measures of socio-economic status (derived from the 1980 census of the US population) and rates of admission to public mental hospitals in the state of Ohio. They found a strong positive correlation between admission rates and five of the nine indicators selected (e.g. median family income, percentage of adults living alone, percentage of high school graduates). The authors suggest that planners could use these predictors locally to identify and rank geographical areas with differential needs for mental health services and that this could form the basis for the allocation of funds, using a formula other than simple *per capita* distribution.

In relation to indices such as the YPI and that of Hall & Royse, Ciarlo *et al* (1992*a*) argue that adopting service utilisation as a criterion measure when developing social indicator models is problematic, because such an approach fails to take into account unmet need. Instead, they recommend that social indicator models be validated against measures of psychiatric morbidity (broadly defined), which they equate with 'true need'. However, as discussed previously, even this approach has its own conceptual difficulties, because of the complex relationships between psychiatric morbidity and the 'need', demand for and use of services (see Chapter 2).

Ciarlo and other researchers in Colorado, USA (Ciarlo *et al* 1992*a*, 1992*b*; Ciarlo & Tweed, 1992; Tweed *et al*, 1992; Tweed & Ciarlo, 1992) conducted a large-scale needs assessment research project over a six-year period. Their primary goal was to test the ability of five social indicator models and one synthetic estimation model to predict the need for alcohol, drug and mental health (ADM) services across the geographical sub-areas of Colorado. A number of these models were, in fact, being used at the time by state public health systems to inform the planning and funding of their mental health services (Ciarlo *et al*, 1992*a*). Five of the models produced quantitative estimates of general population prevalence rates for ADM service needs in different sub-areas and one produced only a ranking of sub-areas with respect to need (Tweed & Ciarlo, 1992). The researchers also evaluated a uniform- or flat-rate model which gave no weight to any existing differences on the social indicators between a region's sub-areas. Instead, it utilised a straight *per capita* allocation of services and/or resources, in which a fixed number of service provider units or dollars per person were multiplied by an area's population in order to obtain its total service or dollar allocation. Each predictive model was validated against epidemiological data obtained from a representative household survey carried out in Colorado specifically for the purposes of the project. This included standardised measures of prevalence of psychiatric disorder, prevalence of dysfunction in everyday living and prevalence of 'demoralisation', thus measuring different types and levels of psychiatric morbidity as proxies of need. These three individual measures were found to be only slightly intercorrelated, suggesting three relatively independent constructs or domains of 'need' (Ciarlo *et al*, 1992*b*). Diagnosable disorders alone were un-related to respondents' use of ADM services. Instead, combinations of two or more need measures were more typically related to service utilisation (Ciarlo *et al*, 1992*b*). Prevalence rates in all three categories varied considerably across geographical sub-areas, which, according to Ciarlo *et al* (1992*b*), challenged the assumption of a flat rate of need for ADM services across sub-areas of the state.

Few of these models as originally constructed performed well in predicting 'need' for ADM services (as measured by the three categories of psychiatric morbidity) across the 48 Colorado sub-areas surveyed (Tweed *et al*, 1992). However, most displayed considerable potential for improving predictive accuracy when compared with the flat-rate approach. A modified two-variable linear regression model was found to be the best all-round predictive model, followed by a synthetic estimation model which ranked sub-areas according to estimates of 'need' (Tweed *et al*, 1992). Two new experimental regression models containing the better predictors found among the original models (namely, poverty and divorce rates) also performed well (Tweed *et al*, 1992). Ciarlo *et al* (1992*a*) recommended that these models be cross-validated on a different survey sample from another geographical area, in order to confirm their generalisability to other states and regions.

A study in Montreal (Lesage *et al*, 1996) compared three different approaches to estimating local catchment area needs for psychiatric services. Lesage *et al* hoped to illustrate the under-supply of psychiatric services that was reported anecdotally by local clinicians and, thereby, to influence future resource allocation towards greater equity. They used Statistics Canada census tract data to predict utilisation of in-patient, out-patient and emergency clinics, as well as overall service utilisation. They also gathered epidemiological data from a random sample of residents from the catchment area (*n* = 496) and informa-tion about service utilisation. They found that the best predictors of overall service utilisation and of utilisation of out-patient services were similar, and that the model that best predicted utilisation of the emergency clinic contained only three variables. Most of the models included variables related to poverty, unemployment, occupational skills, social isolation and ethnic background. Social indicator modelling was found to be highly predictive of overall service utilisation in that it accounted for 73% of the variance. The overall utilisation rate for the sector was 1.5% and the most frequent type of usage was an out-patient visit. Rates of utilisation varied considerably across census tracts, from 0.01% to 0.86% for admissions and from 0.69% to 3.63% for overall utilisation. The epidemiological survey produced estimates comparable to actual service utilisation recorded for the sector, although the confidence intervals were very broad and the authors expressed reservations about the validity of the conclusion. They suggested that the epidemiological data provided too large an estimate of need for the areas under study.

Lesage *et al* concluded, more broadly, that different satisfactory models of specialised service utilisation can be derived, particularly with regard to predicting overall utilisation. However, they pointed out that the social indicator approach is unable to provide information about what is the absolute need for psychiatric services in a sector. Instead, it weighs need against the current balance of existing services. They also noted that the social indicator model under-estimated the need for specialist services in very disadvantaged areas. They concluded, therefore, that while social indicator models are useful, "Sensible allocation must rely on clinicians, planners and users in balancing information from current utilisation, social indicators and suggested national ratios" (p. 5).

The social indicator approach and needs assessment for MDOs

It is, of course, conceivable that the same social indicator models and variables which predict general psychiatric service utilisation will also predict forensic psychiatric service utilisation. Indeed, many of the adverse socio-demographic and socio-economic variables associated with general psychiatric morbidity and service utilisation are also associated with criminality and violence. Certainly, reviews by a number of authors have indicated a relationship between criminality and age, gender, social class, socio-economic status, poverty, previous criminal convictions, unemployment, educational attainment and race/ethnicity (Mulvihill & Tumin, 1969; Toch, 1969; Gulevich & Bourne, 1970; Rubin, 1972; Halleck, 1975; Wolfgang, 1975; Dinitz & Conrad, 1978; Rennie, 1978; Monahan,

1981; Stuart, 1981; Jacobs, 1983; Kroll & MacKenzie, 1983; Mednick & Finello; 1983; Menuck, 1983; Prins, 1986; Klassen & O'Connor, 1988). It is thus possible that the social indicator models described above could also validly predict variation in utilisation of forensic psychiatric services (e.g. special hospital and/or medium-security beds) across geographical areas. However, this hypothesis remains to be tested.

No published study in the UK has yet described use of social indicators to estimate 'need' specifically for MDO services.

Whether or not 'general' or 'special' social indicator models are required for MDO needs assessment, it is of great importance to note the problems involved in using bed utilisation rates as the criterion to determine whether such models are adequately predictive of either general or forensic need. For example, reference to special hospital and medium-security utilisation statistics is likely to create distortions in prediction models, given the significant evidence of over-containment in special hospitals and under-supply of medium-security beds (see Chapters 3 and 4). Hence, a social indicator model of MDO need tested or validated on the basis of whether it adequately predicted either or both types of bed utilisation would be tested against a false measure as regards need. By way of further illustration of this, the substantial unmet need for maximum-security and medium-security beds which has been demonstrated in remand and sentenced prisoner populations would clearly not be reflected in bed utilisation figures.

Conclusions

The social indicator approach is a powerful method for measuring indirectly the need for mental health services across geographical areas (Warheit *et al*, 1977). However, it is very uncertain whether existing social indicator models can be generalised to forensic psychiatric services without substantial modification.

Also, so long as social indicator models are tested against any form of service utilisation, they will be at risk of having been wrongly validated. This is because service utilisation is a poor measure of need. Even worse, if only bed utilisation is used as a proxy for comprehensive service utilisation, then the risk of invalidity is given a further twist. This is because bed utilisation is not necessarily a valid proxy for the comprehensive configuration of services provided within a district (for example, high-, medium- and low-security facilities, open wards, plus specialist and general community mental health interventions). So, it may not be valid to distribute revenue for a complete service simply on the basis of a social indicator model validated solely by reference to bed utilisation. Even were none of these objections to using the social indicator model for revenue allocation to be justifiable, a further problem is bound to remain in practice, namely, that validating social indicator models on the basis of *current* service utilisation of any sort must tend to set resourcing in the present rather than in the proper (needs-based) future.

The development of social indicator models for estimating MDO service 'need' is clearly an area for future exploration, particularly given its natural congruence with NHS commissioning mechanisms and, in particular, its potential for ongoing (re)evaluation of need based on relatively cheaply and easily available statistics. It is also clear that such models are bound to hold attraction to commissioners because they are a relatively cheap form of needs assessment. However, we must caution that it is unlikely that such an approach will offer high validity, even if it addresses specifically MDO need, if it is used in isolation from epidemiological data, survey data and individual needs assessment information. Indeed, only if data from those other sources can be shown to be highly and reliably correlated with given social indicators could they be cast off in favour of such indicators.

6   The key informant approach and the community opinion approach

Introduction

The 'key informant' approach to needs assessment uses the knowledge of individuals assumed to be particularly well informed in order to assist in the identification of local mental health needs (Warheit *et al*, 1977). Information is gathered from 'experts' in the field who are selected on the basis that they are most likely to have knowledge of the mental health needs and service utilisation patterns of a particular community or patient group (e.g. MDOs). Key informants may include mental health service providers and other agencies involved with patients (in the case of MDOs, they may include individuals from the criminal justice system). Key informants may also include service users and their relatives and carers. Indeed, it is government policy that service users (including MDOs) and their relatives and informal carers should be actively involved in the assessment of need. Policy also states that users, relatives and carers should have some influence over the configuration and development of local services (DoH, 1989*a*; DoH, 1992*a;* DoH/ Home Office, 1992).[37] However, as discussed in Chapter 2, there may be conflict and disagreement, sometimes quite profound, between key informants (e.g. between professionals and patients) about what 'needs' exist, and this must obviously be borne in mind when using this, or indeed any other, approach to need.

---

[37] There is a wide literature on user opinion regarding mental health services (e.g. patient satisfaction surveys). See Ruggeri (1996) for a comprehensive review of the literature on patient satisfaction.

The community opinion approach is closely related to the key informant approach, but is primarily concerned with obtaining the opinions of local communities about the needs of the community and about the development of local services (Warheit *et al*, 1977). The opinions of local service users, their families and informal carers, user groups and pressure groups may also be considered, although the opinions of mental health experts are not sought. Hence, the key informant and community opinion approaches can be distinguished in that the former focuses on user and provider groups (i.e. key 'stakeholders') while the latter applies a broader focus on the community in general. The community focus includes the possibility of a 'not in my back yard', or NIMBY, factor, which could serve to block service development, as was commonly witnessed in the late 1970s and early 1980s in relation to the development of medium-security services (see Chapter 1).

The NHS Management Executive (1991) recommended that the key informant approach should be used as one part of its 'hybrid' approach to local needs assessment (i.e. in the form of the 'corporate' approach). Similarly, Fryers & Greatorex (1992) stated that local community opinion should be taken into account in order to ensure local support for decisions about priorities in order to optimise the acceptability of services and to help facilitate health gains.

Information from key informants and community representatives may be gathered through questionnaires or interviews applied to individuals (Warheit *et al*, 1977), as well as stakeholder conferences or focus groups (Hayward *et al*, 1993). Both approaches are, therefore, simple and inexpensive and they allow for the consideration of views from a wide range of sources and perspectives (Warheit *et al*, 1977). The involvement of key informants and of local communities may, in any event, be essential in implementing proposed changes in local service delivery (Rabkin, 1986). Further, the two approaches may represent useful !methods for the preliminary stages of any needs assessment, when researchers wish to explore and identify important issues worthy of exploration by other, more objective means (Rabkin, 1986). They can also provide a qualitative perspective which complements information obtained from quantitative methodologies such as the RUT or epidemiological approaches (Rabkin, 1986; Hayward *et al*, 1993).

A major disadvantage of these approaches is that they are subjective in what they measure or identify and impressionistic in their methods of evaluation. Also, they can clearly only provide 'indirect' and qualitative measures of 'need'. In particular, the views of key informants and community members are likely to reflect their subjective, potentially non-representative position within their organisational or community context. This may not accord with a true representation of the type and extent of actual 'need' in the community (Warheit *et al*, 1977). Hence, provider key informants may have an interest either in protecting current service provision or in preventing the development of new services in order to protect their 'market niche', or they may encourage the development of services in order to expand their 'empires'. Other types of key informant or community member may wish to influence service development so as to avoid local placement of 'unpopular' patient groups, such as MDOs, even if they can see a social benefit to their being contained *somewhere* (but 'not in my backyard'). In summary, therefore, key informants may be inclined to advance their own interests rather than the interests (or 'needs') of service users. Further, key informants may not all have equal power (or confidence) to influence service developments. For example, service providers are likely to be more powerful in their pursuit of influence as key informants than are service users, particularly within mental health services and especially within MDO mental health services. The Home Office is likely to be even more influential than either users or providers (see further below). Some service users may anyway have insufficient technical knowledge to form (or at least express) an informed opinion (Corrigan, 1990), and it may also be difficult (for this and other reasons) to ensure adequate user or community representation (Warheit *et al*, 1977). Certain professions may also have differential power and influence on service planning.[38] Similarly, (non-user) community members are generally unlikely to wield very much power or influence in relation to service development, and in any case their concerns may be over-influenced by stereotypes and sensational media accounts rather than by proper knowledge of the 'needs' of the local mentally ill population. Indeed, it may be those very media accounts that give them any power they do have to wield (an increasing power through the 1990s). To summarise by way of an example, it is acknowledged that 'product champions', 'gatekeepers' and 'blockers' (Stocking, 1985) wielded substantial influence over the early development of medium-security services (see Chapter 1).

There are further considerations regarding, specifically, user involvement in mental health needs assessment. There is considerable debate about the extent to which the mentally ill are *able* validly to assess their needs. Indeed, much of mental health law is justified loosely on the premise that, at times, people who suffer from mental

---

[38] These biases may occur using other methods, too (see Chapter 8).

disorder are unable to know (or, at least, express) what is 'good for them' or for society.[39] Mental health law recognises that third-party intervention may be required in order to protect the patient's own health and safety (and sometimes that of others) from the consequences of his or her illness. This paternalistic/public protectionist approach frequently takes the form of involuntary detention and treatment, which in itself very clearly illustrates a fundamental conflict between perceptions of 'need' on the part of professionals (and society) and of service users. Indeed, it *could* perhaps be argued even that the very presence of mental illness and of a person's consequent involuntary detention makes questionable any valid notion of user involvement in mental health needs assessment. It is certainly essential to recognise that the views that patients hold about their needs are likely to be strongly influenced by the nature of their mental illness and/or by the fact of their detention (Barker *et al*, 1996; Coid, 1993*b*). However, it would be incorrect, and surely unethical, to assume that user opinion is wholly invalidated merely by virtue of their mental illness or of their detention. Albeit both factors must be fully acknowledged when taking a particular user's views into account, they do not necessarily invalidate any approach that incorporates users' views. It may not be appropriate to ask patients about their 'needs' at certain times during their illness (e.g. when they are floridly psychotic), but there will almost certainly be times when they are able to articulate their opinions very clearly (MacDonald *et al*, 1988; Thornicroft *et al*, 1993; Sheppard, 1993). Similarly, it would be wrong to assume that those who are involuntarily detained should not be asked their views about what they 'need', albeit that the fact of their detention, and the impact this must inevitably have on their perceptions of 'need', should be openly acknowledged. Indeed, it can be argued that detained patients should have *particular* attention paid to their opinions, given their powerless and socially marginalised positions.

All of the foregoing considerations are especially important in relation to MDOs, because they are frequently subject to involuntary detention for extended periods and because they are often detained in particularly coercive environments. Coercion must remain inherent to aspects of any forensic mental health care system, and in order for detention to be made as 'tolerable' as possible for the individuals concerned, their opinions should form an important part of the needs assessment process.

---

[39] Of course, strictly, the Mental Health Act 1983 adopts a 'status' test and not a common-law 'incapacity' test for over-riding patient autonomy.

The key informant approach and needs assessment for MDOs

The key informant approach has been used in a number of ways in order to inform needs assessment for MDOs. The Reed review (DoH/Home Office, 1992) was itself clearly based upon the expert opinions of key informants from a range of agencies. Similarly, the individual advisory groups consisted of experts within each field, and the advisory reports were circulated nationally among experts for their comments and advice before the compiling of the composite report. Also, after publication of the Reed report, the Home Office/ DoH (1995) then appointed a committee to advise the government on issues arising from the implementation of the Reed recommendations. This committee was drawn from relevant parts of the health service, social services, criminal justice system, the voluntary sector and government departments.

In a somewhat different vein, well before the Reed report (dating back to the late 1970s), some RHAs appointed regional forensic advisers (consultant forensic psychiatrists given a specific regional remit) to advise them about issues relating to the planning, development and delivery of forensic psychiatric services. These advisers can also be seen as key informants. However, their identification more commonly as 'product champions' serves well to emphasise the general concern about the use and influence of key informants, who necessarily come to their task from a particular standpoint, including sometimes with a formal (and often employed) role. So, can a 'product champion' also be a valid 'key informant'? Perhaps the answer lies in the requirement that key informants be seen necessarily as a *body* of informants who will express, individually, varying views, from varying perspectives, but who, taken *as* a body, can be a useful source of information. Returning to regional forensic advisers as key informants, doctors being referred cases, or even seeking out cases (e.g. in prisons), can clearly be a very useful, even if (sometimes) only anecdotal, source of valid and detailed information about need. They are, perhaps, not only 'product champions' but also 'patient champions'. However, not all key informants are 'equal', either in their perspectives or in their influence and proximity to 'power', and that seems unavoidable. Even the separation of purchasing from provision within the NHS failed to avoid the 'product champion as key informant' problem. When the chips were down, where else was an under-informed purchaser likely (or perhaps even able) to turn for advice, perhaps especially about 'need' (or the proper response to need), than to a clinician who was at the sharp end of responding to such need. In fact, if the purchaser did not so turn, the 'product champion' was likely to bang on the purchaser's door and demand entry, or to precipitate courts to do so in relation to individual need in individual cases under Section 39 of the Mental Health Act 1983.

After Reed, the Home Office/DoH (1995) jointly sponsored, through the Mental Health Foundation, a series of conferences to facilitate inter-agency working in all (then) 14 RHAs in England and Wales. These conferences brought together representatives from all agencies involved with MDOs and allowed for the identification of problems and priorities in relation to service development and delivery via a wide variety of key informants. By thus widening and better balancing the constituency of key informants, they overcame, to some extent, the problem of excessive influence of certain key informants (e.g. forensic advisers). However, ultimately this process seemed as much, if not more, aimed at getting the relevant agencies in each region 'on board' the Reed philosophy as 'key players' as it was aimed at using such a process to consult them as 'key informants'.

The DHAs have also frequently used key informants in order to assist in the planning and commissioning process. As an illustration, the key informant approach was adopted in 1993/94 in South West Thames RHA in the wake of the Reed report. Multi-agency strategy groups were set up within the three main geographical areas of the region.[40] These groups met over a year and used key informants to assist in the development of local strategies for the delivery of services to MDOs. Such key informants included forensic and general psychiatrists, psychologists, social workers, probation officers, police officers, magistrates, public health doctors, researchers, voluntary organisations and user groups. Strategy documents were produced by each group, which were then used to inform purchasing decisions. In parallel with this process, NHS purchasers themselves also set up consortia within the three geographical areas and, again, drew on key informants (e.g. representatives from health and social services, the criminal justice system, the voluntary sector and researchers) in order to assist them in the development of purchasing strategies. Interestingly, however, what this process emphasised ultimately was as much (if not more) the impact of culture incongruence between the various caring and criminal justice agencies as their desire to pursue the Reed philosophy of cooperation. Hence, the problems of lack of congruent data

---

[40] One of the authors (NE) was a 'key informant' to two of the three South West Thames steering groups and writes, therefore, from personal experience.

collection and geographical incoherence in administration described in earlier chapters often appeared, in the context of the steering groups, merely symptomatic of deeper differences in agency purposes, intentions and conceptions specifically of MDOs. This is perhaps best characterised by describing the caring agencies as seeing individual MDOs as problematic because, aside from being mentally disordered, they were also 'offenders'. On the other hand, the criminal justice system found great difficulty accommodating the fact that an individual MDO was not only an offender but was also 'mentally disordered'. Each tended inherently to exclude MDOs, by virtue of their being incongruent with the predominant purpose and culture of the agency. This is not to imply that any agency representative was disingenuous but, rather, that the culture of the agencies they represented was so powerful as to be influential in spite of all the representatives' best intentions. Indeed, such groups nicely represent a microcosm of the national (in fact, international) problem of service provision for a group of people who are both 'mentally disordered' and 'offenders'. Even the conception of 'need' itself may well vary inherently between the various agencies (as discussed in Chapter 2).

The community opinion approach and needs assessment for MDOs

Community opinion and public opinion (the two may be quite distinct) are especially pertinent in relation to service development for MDOs. Communities are frequently in favour of the development of secure services for local MDOs but against such provision locally. Both concerns are fuelled by media coverage of incidents of violence by the mentally ill, although even before the media attention of the 1990s there was resistance to the development of secure units by local communities (Bluglass, 1978). The analogy with provision of prison places is, of course, inescapable. The 'public' wishes there to be more prisons in order to increase public security but no 'community' wishes a new prison to be within its own bounds (this being one example of the distinction between 'public opinion' and 'community opinion').

This latter distinction leads naturally to consideration of the role of pressure groups and the media in *forming* public opinion about (perceived) necessary provision of psychiatric services, secure or otherwise. Indeed, there is much to suggest that a small number of highly publicised 'homicide in the community' cases, most notably

Christopher Clunis' killing of Jonathan Zito (Ritchie *et al*, 1994), have been highly influential in securing additional funding for medium-security services. These cases may have been more influential than a range of other, more obviously valid perspectives grounded in research. The high social and political impact of such cases, and of the subsequent independent inquiries into them (c.f. Peay, 1996) is difficult to ignore. However, when one considers, in cost-benefit terms or cost-need terms, the policy requirement that individual needs be enumerated and also weighed against *other* needs so as to determine national rationing of limited resources, the inappropriateness of such crude political responses to public opinion is made obvious. And yet, political reality may dictate (as, for example, with sick children) a resource allocation response, particularly in a context of public 'moral panic' (Pearson, 1999). Indeed, it could be suggested that a socio-political analysis of the perceived need for secure psychiatric services might better explain (and predict) DoH and health authority decisions about or responses to need than 'properly' conducted 'needs assessment' exercises. Such a public policy analysis does not, of course, deny that the Ritchie report (Ritchie *et al*, 1994), for example, is a good source document regarding MDO need which, together with other such inquiry reports, should be seen as properly informing commissioners about such need. It is just that it should take its place in the group of relevant data on need, not dominate the group.

Conclusions

The key informant and community opinion approaches can provide qualitative information that is extremely valuable both in its own right and also as a complement to needs assessment data obtained using other methods. Indeed, it is government policy that key informant and community opinion approaches should be used when assessing need. However, clearly, what is important is that a combination of qualitative and quantitative needs assessment information is used so as to allow for a convergent analysis which is based upon multiple 'perspectives on need' (see Chapter 8). Also, such 'informant' and 'opinion' data should, because of their sources and very nature, be interpreted with great caution.

7 The definition and measurement of 'ability to benefit' and outcome

Introduction

The 'ability to benefit' from health care interventions is an essential component of the DoH model of need (NHS Management Executive, 1991). This relates to both the population's and the individual's ability to benefit from mental health treatment and care. The model implies that need exists only if there are interventions with proven efficacy and/or effectiveness available to address that need, and that needs for which there are no such interventions should not attract resources. This provides a crude justification for the rationing of NHS resources; only those individuals who have health problems that can benefit from interventions should receive treatment.

The concept of 'ability to benefit' is inextricably linked with the measurement of outcome, since establishing ability to benefit requires that health care interventions are clearly defined and linked with specific benefits or outcomes for specific patient groups. Indeed, it can be argued that knowledge about outcome is a *prerequisite* for the establishment of ability to benefit, since selection of the right patients for the right interventions cannot occur without evidence about outcome. Both outcome and ability to benefit are also highly politicised, since they are bound up with policy concerns such as evidence-based practice and clinical governance, and ultimately with service rationing. Yet, as with the concept of 'need' itself, the notion of 'ability to benefit' is fraught with definitional and conceptual problems. Similarly, the definition and measurement of 'outcome' has long presented theoretical and empirical difficulties in all health and related services research.

There is a vast literature that is relevant to the outcome of MDO treatment, which includes both general mental health and MDO-specific studies. This chapter cannot attempt any sort of comprehensive review of the available literature. Such a review would have to include, for example, studies of recidivism and readmission, which are the most cited studies in relation to MDOs and which have the greatest public policy impact. It would also need to include a wide range of outcome studies that address the broader question of 'what works for whom?' The latter include studies both of the operation of particular types of therapeutic setting or service (for example, therapeutic communities and special hospitals) and of the efficacy of specific therapeutic interventions (such as pharmacological therapy or cognitive-behavioural and psychodynamic psychotherapies).[41]

In the main, this chapter is theoretical in its orientation. It attempts to evaluate definitions and approaches to measuring outcome both generally and in relation to MDOs. It also examines the relationship between different types of outcome measure. It then illustrates how outcome fits into a broader framework that relates to service evaluation. Finally, it attempts to draw together the strands of need, outcome and service evaluation into a coherent framework.

Definition and measurement of outcome

Ovretveit (1995) defines health service outcome as the effect on a person or population that can be attributed to a health treatment, service or intervention. Hence, as with the assessment of need, outcome can be addressed on both an individual and a population level. Establishing outcome in relation to mental health interventions, even in general mental health care, is extremely difficult and hence not well developed. Psychiatric disorders and their associated social disabilities are complex and multi-factorial in their aetiology and manifestations. Baseline information is limited or non-existent, and outcomes are multi-dimensional and difficult to define and measure. There are also difficulties in defining operationally many of the treatments and interventions available. Different treatments may be delivered to the same patient by different professionals, and multi-agency involvement (e.g. health

---

[41] See, for example, Roth & Fonagy (1996) for a critical review of psychotherapy research across a wide range of disorders, albeit not specifically directed to interventions with MDOs.

and social services) complicates the picture even further. As a result, demonstrating valid and reliable *causal* relationships between specific interventions and outcome is extremely difficult. Ovretveit (1995) provides a range of criticisms of outcome measurement. He notes that the measurement of outcome frequently focuses on end-points rather than on health gains made during the treatment process. He is critical of the tendency for outcome measures to fail adequately to include the effects of other services and environments, or other factors that affect health. He also bemoans the tendency of outcome studies to overlook patient views and the quality of service delivery. However, Ovretveit also notes how costly and methodologically difficult it is routinely to measure outcome effectively, as well as warning that commissioners who require providers to measure outcome will pay higher tariffs. Also, the information produced is unlikely to be sufficiently valid and reliable and it could therefore be misleading.

The complexity of outcome measurement in mental health is reflected in a formulation developed by Atkisson *et al* (1992). This model makes useful suggestions about what ought to be measured in outcome research and how measurement should take place. Atkisson *et al* suggest that there are seven major principles of outcome measurement that must be considered for the advancement of research in this area.

Principle 1 is that outcome is multi-dimensional. The authors provide a framework for categorising different measurement areas that ought to be included. This framework contains four domains, and the authors provide suggestions about some of the elements that ought to be included within each:

(a) The clinical domain relates to various aspects of psychopathology and the course of disorders over time. Examples include signs and symptoms, diagnostic entities, amount and severity of psychopathology, and amount and intensity of intervention required to treat the illness. Measures may be categorial (e.g. diagnosis) or dimensional (e.g. severity of thought disorder). Atkisson *et al* also suggest that more general health outcome indicators be included, such as measures of mortality, morbidity, life satisfaction and lifespan.

(b) The rehabilitation domain focuses on adaptation and functional capacity, rather than illness and pathology. Two broad outcome areas are considered important: social functioning (e.g. social skills, frequency of interpersonal contacts, closeness of contacts, involvement in meaningful social networks such as work, family, peer group and community);

and instrumental functioning (e.g. level of education, problem-solving capacities, ability to learn and work, and level of employment).

(c) The humanitarian domain relates to factors such as subjective well-being, consumer satisfaction and quality of life.

(d) The public safety domain is concerned with the appropriate balance between liberty and paternalism that will maximise individual and societal rights to physical safety and well-being. Atkisson *et al* argue that researchers should incorporate public safety and welfare outcome measures into studies of treatment and rehabilitation effectiveness. They suggest that measures of individual, familial and community perceptions of safety should be considered.

The clinical, rehabilitation and humanitarian domains constitute well established 'research industries' in themselves. A wealth of research instruments have been designed to measure various aspects of each. For example, Ferguson & Tyrer (1989) provide an overview of psychiatric rating scales, including measures of general morbidity, diagnostic schedules and diagnosis/symptom-specific rating scales. Similarly, Lehman (1996) provides an overview of scales rating quality of life. Many of the needs assessment instruments described in Chapter 3 could also be used to monitor individual outcomes in each domain if used routinely.

The majority of research on MDO outcomes has focused on the public safety domain. Studies have focused particularly on recidivism, mainly re-arrest and reconviction rates, but also on hospital readmission rates. Many of these studies have been conducted on special hospital populations (e.g. Bailey & MacColloch, 1992*a*, 1992*b*, 1993; Cope & Ward, 1993; Dolan *et al*, 1993; MacCulloch *et al*, 1993). While this domain is obviously very important in relation to MDOs, future research should expand its focus to include other domains.

Principle 2 states that mental health outcomes should be measured from multiple perspectives. Each stakeholder in the system has a different perspective, and each perspective should be taken into account when measuring outcome. This includes perceptions of the patient, family, carers, clinicians and clinical researchers. Much outcome research in mental health tends to focus on clinical perspectives of what constitutes a positive outcome. As with need, different stakeholders within the system may have different views about what constitutes a health gain. This brings us back to the issue of values; values will drive what are viewed as positive outcomes to the same extent that they will drive what is viewed as a need. This leads us naturally to Atkisson *et al*'s third principle.

Principle 3 relates to what Atkisson *et al* describe as 'individual utility differences'. Put simply, this suggests that different individuals and groups may perceive the usefulness (or utility) of mental health outcomes differently. Such 'utility differences' are a source of variability that should be measured and accounted for in outcome studies. For example, Atkisson *et al* argue that culture, age and gender can affect both the course of illness and what is defined by individuals, their families and their communities as desirable outcomes. Once again, the issue of values arises.

Principle 4 is concerned with the standardisation of measures and research designs. Atkisson *et al* argue that progress in the measurement of outcome requires the standardisation of measures across studies so that comparisons are facilitated. An example of such an attempt is the Health of the Nation Outcome Scales (Wing *et al*, 1994). However, Atkisson *et al* note that measures also need to be specific, and that a balance must be established between standardisation and specificity. They also argue for standardisation of design protocols, but recognise the practical obstacles to achieving this. Randomised clinical trials to establish efficacy are frequently not possible, primarily because of their expense, and studies of routine clinical effectiveness often lack generalisability.

Principle 5 relates to longitudinal designs. Atkisson *et al* argue that cross-sectional studies are highly informative, but that longitudinal studies are also essential for studying outcome in mental health, because of the chronic nature of many types of mental disorder. Of course, longitudinal studies tend to be more expensive than cross-sectional studies.

Principle 6 relates to costs as an outcome measure. Atkisson *et al* argue that measures of cost, including the cost to the patient, family and society of the absence (or refusal) of services, must be estimated and factored in. The economic domain in relation to both need and outcome in mental health is not well developed (Beecham & Chisholm, 1995). Many of the difficulties related to measuring costs are discussed at length in Chapter 2.

Principle 7 relates to relevance and impact. Atkisson *et al* suggest that when outcome research is designed and reported, researchers should consider information needs in three spheres: science, clinical practice, policy and legislation.

These seven principles provide a comprehensive framework for outcome measurement. It is self-evident that most researchers will be unable to measure all these areas of outcome or to adhere strictly to all the principles advocated. Nevertheless, the framework is useful, because it forces us to adopt a broad perspective about outcome measurement and to recognise the limitations on what we are able to achieve. It also forces us to acknowledge that we may be choosing only one component of outcome (and a small one at that), neglecting other domains in its favour. As with the assessment of need, public policy, values and resources will partly drive what aspect of outcome is measured, as well as the methods used to achieve this. There must, therefore, be acknowledgement of what we are *not* measuring, and why – we should be able to justify, for example, why it is more important to measure recidivism as an outcome, rather than symptom reduction or quality of life.

Outcome, quality and service evaluation

The measurement of outcome must be placed within a broader framework that relates to the quality of services. According to Glover & Kamis-Gould (1996), outcome is just one type of performance indicator that fits into a more general model of service evaluation. Jenkins (1990) argues that, in order to evaluate any health care system, it is necessary, in general terms, first to measure the baseline health of the population and then to measure the impact of health care upon that baseline. As she puts it, "We need to be able to monitor and evaluate progress towards more effective health care and better health, to evaluate the efficacy of health promotion and illness-prevention programmes, and to improve resource allocation in health care" (p. 500). Jenkins suggests that this can be achieved in a valid and reproducible manner only if specific health indicators are established which apply not only to general 'well-being' but also to specific categories of illness, and if those categories are then related to specific strategies of treatment and prevention. Jenkins defines an indicator as "a measure that summarises information relevant to a particular phenomenon or a reasonable proxy for such a measure" (p. 501). She notes that indicators should be valid and reliable, but argues that this is difficult to achieve. 'Health indicators' are variables that can be measured directly and that reflect aspects of the state of health of a community, and 'health care indicators' are variables that reflect aspects of the state of health care in a community (World Health Organization, 1981, cited in Jenkins, 1990). According to Jenkins, health care indicators can be categorised into 'input', 'process' and 'outcome' (albeit outcome indicators will also be health indicators). Tansella & Thornicroft (1998) refer to this as the 'temporal dimension', since it is concerned with the chronological steps involved in the delivery of health care.[42] 'Input' refers to resources that are put into the mental health care system (Tansella & Thornicroft, 1998). Input variables include type and size of facilities, human resources and characteristics of physical facilities (Tugwell, 1979, cited in Brugha & Lindsay, 1996). 'Process' refers to activities that take place to deliver mental health services (Tansella & Thornicroft, 1998). 'Process' variables include the technical or interpersonal elements that occur during a health intervention (Tugwell, 1979, cited in Brugha & Lindsay, 1996). This may include treatment prescribed, diagnostic and therapeutic procedures and features of the clinician–patient relationship.

The measurement of input, process and outcome is also a part of the clinical audit cycle (Spender & Cooper, 1995). Clinical audit has been defined as "the systematic and critical analysis of the quality of health care, including procedures used for diagnosis, treatment and care, the associated use of resources, and the resulting outcome and quality of life for the patient" (NHS Training Directorate, 1994).

A similar conceptualisation is offered by Donabedian (1980). He divides research about the quality of health care into studies that address structures of care (e.g. provider systems, organisation of systems, characteristics of treating facilities), process (specific clinical interventions) and outcome.

Berwick (1989) outlines four types of health services research that relate to quality of care:

(a) effectiveness of care (what works for whom);
(b) appropriateness of care (using what works);
(c) execution of care (doing well what works);
(d) examination of the purpose of care(values that underlie action).

According to Atkisson *et al* (1992), progress with the paradigms presented by Donabedian (1980) and Berwick (1989) is required to advance research about the quality of care.

Kamis-Gould (further details available from the authors on request) proposes a model of service evaluation that covers two broad aspects of an organisation or system. The first relates to its capacity. Capacity variables include human and financial resources,

---

[42] Tansella & Thornicroft (1998) also refer to the geographical dimension, which interacts with the temporal dimension. Geographical dimensions refer to different levels within the health care system: country/region level, local level (i.e. catchment area) and patient level.

comprehensiveness of the range and quality of clinical facilities, and technical capacity to operate, coordinate and monitor all aspects of organisational functioning. The second relates to the performance of the system. This is concerned with responsiveness and accessibility (e.g. congruence with local needs, cultural sensitivity, promptness and sensitivity of response to clients). Performance is also measured in terms of efficient use of resources (i.e. levels of productivity, cost containment, occupancy rates). It is also concerned with effectiveness; in other words, with individual and system outcomes (e.g. mental health status, patient satisfaction, providers' views about the service and its effectiveness).

According to Jenkins (1990), aspects of service provision that can be most easily measured at present tend to be those which relate to service input and resources rather than service outcome. She notes that input is relatively straightforward to measure, and that process tends to be measured in terms of 'performance' or 'activity' indicators (e.g. occupied bed-days). Process indicators related to the delivery of specific interventions or the nature of therapeutic relationships are both more difficult to measure and unlikely to be routinely available. Jenkins also points out that process indicators are frequently selected on the basis of what is collectable (or already available), rather than on the basis of previously specified key aspects of performance. Indeed, although there may be good *ad hoc* studies relevant to some desirable process measures, there is, in fact, a profound lack of *ongoing* data which could be of use in monitoring process and, in particular, in monitoring the *meeting* of need. This is of particular note given the recent contracting framework for the commissioning of all mental health care. Indeed, we found that in one study there was little interest among commissioners (and certainly not among providers) in one part of a region in extending to their own commissioning the much more detailed contract reporting requirements established by commissioners in another part of the region (Cohen & Eastman, 1996).[43] In fact, not even the much more extensive reporting requirements placed on the main specialist provider in the latter part of the region began to approach the level of detail of process monitoring suggested by some authors (e.g. see Jenkins' indicators outlined below). Rather, such reporting was largely restricted to an RUT approach, with counting of referrals, acceptances and treatment places utilised, including bed-days. There is little to suggest that the situation is substantially different in other regions.

---

[43] It can be argued that commissioners with stretched budgets have a natural interest in how much MDO care they commission and whether they get what they pay for. However, they may have less interest in whether they are commissioning *enough* of such care (set against 'need').

Jenkins notes that the measurement of outcome is much more complex than the measurement of input and process. She points out that input and process indicators are often used as proxy measures of outcome, which, she suggests, is based on the faulty logic that service utilisation (a process indicator) is equal to cure (outcome). So, just as service utilisation is a poor proxy of need, so too is it a poor proxy of outcome.

The measurement of input, process and outcome in forensic mental health

The measurement of outcome for MDOs has some specific problems. As already described at length in Chapter 2, the term MDO itself is difficult to define. Further, MDOs are a heterogeneous group who may fall into any diagnostic category. They are likely to have many needs for treatment and care that are similar to general psychiatric patients. They may also then have additional needs that relate to their special problems. Consequently, establishing the ability to benefit and the measurement of outcome for MDOs must cover an extremely wide range of interventions for a wide variety of problems, including going beyond health outcome narrowly defined. It is not possible, therefore, to provide a single model of 'what works for MDOs'. The additional component specifically relevant to MDOs of offending and related 'challenging behaviour' adds at least two further complicating dimensions to the assessment of outcome. First, offending and 'challenging behaviour' can, and often do, arise from factors unrelated, or only partially related, to the individual MDO's mental disorder. That is, offending is not exclusively or simply a 'symptom' of mental disorder but a concomitant of it, and not always causally linked to it. A wide range of ordinary criminological explanations of offending, both individual to the offender and more broadly societal, can be relevant to an MDO's offending. This introduces not merely one or two additional factors to a clinical model but superimposes upon it a criminological model that is largely unrelated to mental health care services narrowly defined. Second, as already argued in this book, 'ability to benefit' relates, in the specific social policy context we are considering, not only to the patient's ability to benefit but also to the benefits to *society* of detaining, and hopefully treating, individuals who pose a threat to public safety. Indeed, the commonest empirical approach to the measure-

---

[44] See Robertson (1997), who bemoans the lack of attention paid to *mental health* outcome measures in forensic psychiatric research.

ment of MDO treatment outcomes has involved examination of rearrest, reconviction and recidivism rates.[44] Those who are discharged and do not reoffend are considered to represent successful outcomes. This is surely at least partly because one of the central policies and clinical aims of MDO treatment has been, and is perhaps increasingly, minimisation of the risk of reoffending. However, it may also be because reconviction and readmission are *comparatively* easier to measure (both cross-sectionally and longitudinally) than other types of outcome, albeit that there is still a range of methodological problems involved (e.g. poor detection of recidivism). In any event, the use of readmission or recidivism as a measure of outcome is also problematic because many patients remain in hospital and so cannot be tested on this measure of outcome. Additionally, it is difficult to determine whether recidivism is a result of failure of treatment or whether it is a consequence of other factors extrinsic to treatment.

Table 6 provides a conceptual framework for addressing the measurement of input, process and outcome for MDOs, which integrates the different models presented thus far. This framework uses Tansella & Thornicroft's (1998) 'temporal dimension' of input, process and outcome as the building block for the model. It integrates the conceptualisations of Atkisson *et al* (1992), Donabedian (1980), Berwick (1989) and Kamis-Gould (further details available from the authors on request) into the relevant temporal dimensions, and provides examples of the types of variable that may be measured within each dimension. It then superimposes onto this factors that apply, or can be measured, at each of the temporal dimensions (e.g. values, costs). The model also acknowledges that variables at each temporal dimension can be measured at different geographical levels (Tansella & Thornicroft, 1998) and at different levels of the mental health care system (Beecham & Chisholm, 1995).

Jenkins (1990), then Principal Medical Officer in the Mental Health Division of the DoH, provides a system of input, process and outcome indicators related to schizophrenia, affective psychosis, neurosis, dementia, child psychiatry, mental handicap, alcohol and drugs, and forensic psychiatry. However, her approach to outcome indicators for forensic psychiatry requires that reference be made to 'ordinary' mental health outcome measures in relation to mentally ill and learning-disabled MDOs. She presents 'special' indicators only in relation to MDOs with personality disorder, although her rationale for doing so is unclear. She does recognise that the lists proposed may not be conclusive and that they merely serve as pointers to the kind of indicators that may be used.

TABLE 6
A comprehensive conceptual framework for the measurement of outcome, quality and service evaluation for MDOs

Temporal dimension

Input	Process	Outcome
Structures of care • provider systems • organisation of systems • characteristics of facilities • number of facilities Capacity of services Financial resources Human resources Human resource development Service protocols Access criteria Good practice guidelines Information systems Government policy and legislation	Specific clinical interventions • Somatic therapy • Psychotherapy/counselling • Sociotherapy • Assessment • Rehabilitation (e.g. occupational therapy) Relationship between clinician and patient Movement between tiers of services Responsiveness and accessibility Waiting lists and bed blocking Bed utilisation (inflow, length of treatment, outflow) Pathways to and through care Frequency and duration of treatment Patterns of service use CPA monitoring Continuity of care Coercion Execution of care (doing well what works) Efficiency Appropriateness of care (using what works)	Effectiveness and efficacy of care (what works for whom) *Seven principles (Atkisson et al, 1992):* 1. Outcome is multidimensional • Clinical (e.g. symptom reduction) • Rehabilitation (social and instrumental functioning) • Humanitarian (quality of life, patient satisfaction) • Public safety (risk to self/others, recidivism, security, risk assessment) 2. Take account of multiple perspectives 3. Take account of individual utility differences 4. Strive for standardisation of measures and designs 5. Use cross-sectional and longitudinal designs 6. Include measures of cost 7. Consider relevance and impact

Geographical dimension
(micro → macro)
Patient level → local level → regional/country level

Different aspects of input, process and outcome can be measured at different geographical levels.
Adapted from: Tansella & Thornicroft (1998).

As a policy starting point, Jenkins offers a series of health *objectives* specific to MDOs. These are essentially policy objectives and are clearly influenced by *Health of the Nation* targets. Her list is as follows:

(a) to reduce the incidence of MDOs;
(b) to reduce the incidence of personality disorder;
(c) to reduce reoffending rates, and relapse and readmission rates;
(d) to reduce suicide rates;
(e) to reduce premature mortality;
(f) to prevent entry and re-entry into the criminal justice system;
(g) to reduce social handicaps;
(h) to reduce unemployment;
(i) to reduce homelessness.

She then suggests a range of *input, process* and *outcome indicators* that relate to her proposed objectives. The input indicators are as follows:

(a) systems to identify vulnerable people and families, and to deliver social support, health services, probation services, school support and pre-parenthood training;
(b) systems to provide psychiatric services for assessment and advice to courts, police stations, the Crown Prosecution Service, probation services, and to provide early diversion from the criminal justice system;
(c) systems to provide psychiatric services to prisons and to aid transfer of MDOs to hospital;
(d) systems to ensure ongoing support and care from psychiatric and other services on release from prison;
(e) systems to ensure rehabilitation and to facilitate multi-agency management;
(f) access to housing;
(g) adequate employment opportunities.

She then argues that *process indicators* should be established which reflect the activity on all the above *input indicators*.

Finally, Jenkins identifies a number of *outcome indicators*:

(a) numbers of patients detained under Part III[45] of the Mental Health Act 1983, and their admission and readmission rates;

---

[45] We assume that, although this item actually refers to "Section IV" in the published paper, it must intend to indicate Part III of the Act, which refers to the forensic sections.

(b) prevalence of treatable MDOs in the prison population;
(c) numbers of patients diverted from the criminal justice system;
(d) suicide rates in prison;
(e) standardised mortality ratios.

Jenkins' list of objectives and indicators may no longer accurately reflect the equivalent list of the current government, and it is important to note their historical limitations. They were formulated at a time when the objective of diverting MDOs from the criminal justice system was particularly high on the political agenda and before the deliberations of the Reed Committee. The Reed report, in fact, suggests an additional range of objectives and indicators, such as systems to identify and treat patients who no longer require particular levels of security. Similarly, the recent Ashworth inquiry (Fallon *et al*, 1999) and the wealth of national and local inquiries following homicides by the mentally ill also suggest a wide range of potential objectives and indicators (e.g. Sheppard, 1996; National Confidential Inquiry into Suicide and Homicide by People with Mental Illness, 1999). Hence, a new set of input, process and output indicators might now be drawn rather differently. It is important to recognise, therefore, that appropriate objectives and indicators will change over time, according to altered policy considerations, as well as changes in service structure and advances in the ability to measure need and outcome.

A number of criticisms can be levelled at Jenkins' choice of objectives and indicators. One disadvantage of the indicators proposed is that they reflect a strong public health stance that tends to neglect outcome on the individual level. Further, the majority of indicators suggested by Jenkins have no adequate baselines specific to MDOs and are also not routinely measured at a local, regional or national level. Further, it is difficult to envisage how many of these variables could be reliably and validly measured, particularly at a level that would be useful to commissioners. Jenkins' system includes some objectives that are difficult to conceptualise as being legitimate objectives for forensic psychiatry services (e.g. to reduce homelessness). Further, some variables are dependent upon many factors that are beyond the remit of MDO service interventions. Even if they could be measured reliably and validly in a continuous (or even intermittent) fashion, in the aggregate it may be very difficult to link changes in them to specific service interventions or combinations of interventions. For example, Jenkins' objectives 'reduction of the incidence of MDOs' and 'reduction of the incidence of personality disorder' are so dependent upon extra-service factors as to be meaningless as measures of service performance. Even to the extent that service interventions may make a *contribution* to such broad objectives, this must be limited and their effects are probably statistically unmeasurable. Although it may be possible, for example, to identify individuals at risk of becoming MDOs (or of repeating that status), it would be difficult to determine the effectiveness of preventive strategies aimed at that objective. Similarly, it may be possible to reduce the incidence of MDOs by training general psychiatrists better to predict offending behaviour, or by facilitating communication between agencies (such as through the CPA), but such interventions are bound to have limited effects, as well as (again) being difficult to measure in their effects. Attempts to measure the effects of services upon objectives such as reduction in readmission rates or even re-entry into the criminal justice system are likely to be equally problematic, as is the reduction of suicide (which is known to be highly correlated with social factors, including the availability of means).

On the face of it, direct measures of a desired outcome, or even policy objective, must be superior to all indirect or proxy measures. Hence, if an important objective of MDO care is reduced offending or the improved mental health of MDOs, then the direct measurement of those objectives must be the 'gold standard' towards which we should strive. With that in mind, it is noteworthy, for example, that many of Jenkins' suggested outcome indicators fall well short of being direct measures. Thus, the numbers of patients detained under Part III of the Mental Health Act, readmission rates, prevalence of treatable MDOs in the criminal justice system, and the number of patients diverted from the criminal justice system all represent indirect or proxy variables. They carry an assumption that, in relation to the achievement of goals relating to each, 'good will follow' (e.g. that utilisation infers a positive outcome). Of her outcome indicators, only the suicide rate in prison and standardised mortality ratios can be seen as direct outcome variables. Even with those, it is clear that there are determining factors which go well beyond mental health care and the diversion of MDOs from prison.

The criticisms levelled at Jenkins' system, which at face value appears entirely reasonable, illustrate how difficult it is to formulate *any* system. It is very difficult to select objectives and indicators that are reasonable and realistic (e.g. measurable in relation to baselines and outcomes) and that take into account broader policy objectives, as well as clinical and system realities.

Conclusions

It is clear that the measurement of ability to benefit and of outcome is extremely complex and problematic in relation to MDOs. When outcome is placed within a more general context of service quality and service evaluation it becomes still more complex (Table 6). The conceptual models of outcome measurement and service evaluation presented thus far are extremely helpful, but present considerable challenges in practical and methodological terms. Indeed, it is unlikely that we shall see anything which approaches the degree of comprehensiveness suggested by these models in relation to MDOs in the near future, though this should be the gold standard towards which we should strive. As argued earlier, the value of the integrated conceptual framework presented in Table 6 is that it forces us to acknowledge the complexity of what we are attempting to measure. It helps us to recognise the inter-related nature of the concepts we are measuring, and it also makes us acknowledge, and justify, what we are unable, or choose not, to measure.

In summary, the existing mechanisms available for outcome measurement and service evaluation in relation to MDOs verge on being hopelessly inadequate. The situation would seem to look bleak, therefore. At the root of the problem is a lack of knowledge about how given services and individual clinical interventions influence outcome. Indeed, the root of the problem goes back even deeper. Aside from 'ordinary' treatments and services for the mentally disordered, there are no generally agreed service designs and protocols (i.e. inputs) that might be measured in their effects. We return to this crucial concern in the final chapter, since it inhibits not only the determination of appropriate outcome measures but even the definition of 'need' itself. How can we define 'need' if we have little agreement over the details of effective service response to need? Until we can adequately answer questions about input, process and outcome, we cannot properly answer questions about ability to benefit and, hence, about need.

This chapter has been mainly theoretical in nature. The fact that so much of it has been taken up, as was much of the early parts of the book, with definitions, gives the lie to any notion that much is really known about MDO treatment outcome. With little hard and reliable data on input, process or outcome, great attention must be paid to what data are routinely available and how these may be reconstructed or reinterpreted so as to serve as *proxy* measures of outcome, albeit with reservations about validity and reliability. Where outcomes in relation to MDOs *have* been researched, there has been a strong tendency towards measuring recidivism. Although recidivism is a major factor that marks MDOs out from mentally disordered non-offenders, such an approach neglects the clinical, rehabilitation and humanitarian domains of outcome in favour of the public safety domain. It further enforces a separatist approach to research into forensic mental health services and related services. Indeed, such research separatism is merely reflective of a much wider separatism within the arena of service responses to MDOs.

Finally, it has not proved practicable to cross-reference within this chapter the very many studies described in the rest of the book which are relevant to outcome, if only because outcome is currently defined and measured so widely (often by proxy input measures). However, it is hoped that the chapter will, particularly through trying to be clear in its description and definition of different approaches to outcome and its measurement, facilitate reading of other sections of the book *in terms of* outcome. Above all, in relation to outcome just as much as in relation to needs assessment *per se*, we would wish to emphasise that definitions always either have subjective policy assumptions lying covertly or implicitly behind them *or* are explicitly and obviously expressive of such assumptions. Indeed, as will be obvious by now, that is the single most important message of the book as a whole.

8 Theory, research and practice: the need to assess need, and its dangers

Introduction

Much of Chapter 1 of this book was devoted to elaboration of both the logical and the public policy imperatives to conduct needs assessment. After all, how can it be either logical or justifiable to expend public resources on any activity which it has not been shown is needed? Such an approach, however, assumes that need can be both adequately defined and measured. It also assumes either that any definition or measurement can be erected in a value-free way *or* that it can be erected in overt and explicit awareness of agreed values. What makes the latter assumption, which is surely the only tenable one, extremely difficult to effect is that any values inherent in needs assessment are almost always not immediately obvious. Indeed, we would suggest that the main purpose and value of this entire book is so extensively to dissect out the theory and practice of needs assessment that, when the technique is applied to a particular MDO service problem, any implicit public policy objectives will be *made* obvious. This is important, particularly where such policy objectives may not have been intended by the policy makers or where the policy makers were unaware that they were implied by the particular needs assessment method adopted.

The notion of 'invisible' policy objectives immediately presses an alarm bell. If needs assessment can be conducted without its underlying value judgements and policy inferences being evident can it not, therefore, be *mis*used by anyone actually intending covertly to pursue a particular set of policy objectives? For example, cannot 'product champion' clinical entrepreneurs (Stocking, 1985) demonstrate the 'need' for the service they are advocating merely by choosing, consciously or unconsciously, particular definitions and methods of measurement of need which serve to show that the commissioners should commission what they want from them? And if the commissioners are unaware of the methodological sleight of hand, then are they not an 'easy touch', especially if there are political forces, perhaps unrelated to mental health need *per se,* which tend to drive them down a similar course of resource allocation? Indeed, there might even be covert collusion between the commissioner and the product champion, whereby the former either decidedly does not 'inquire' into the underlying assumptions of the model presented, or is aware of them but wishes to use the cloak of public policy respectability offered by the needs assessment process in order to justify, or make more palatable, a decision that has already been made regarding resource allocation. Such collusion might even amount to managerial self-deception ("I am approving extension of medium-secure unit X because there is a demonstrable mental health need for it", *rather than* "the public safety objective is more important than the *Health of the Nation* target for suicide reduction among ordinary patients with schizophrenia, which is, in any event, too expensive to pursue because there are too many such patients at risk"). Now there may be nothing 'wrong' with the particular resource allocation decision itself, but should not only the decision but the (real) reason for the decision be made explicit? And if the decision has been made in advance of conducting the needs assessment then is there any point in conducting it at all?

The latter challenge is perhaps not so nihilistic or Luddite in its implications as, at first sight, it seems to be. In fact, it is not the case that needs assessment is 'useless' even where the policy decision has already been made. Rather, it is that, like analysis of 'cost-benefit' or 'cost-effectiveness', it is only as good as the way it is used and its 'results' are interpreted. It is an analytical tool which may enlighten resource allocation, not a resource allocation tool *per se.* And, like its close cousins from the economist's box of tricks, its usefulness is as good as the resource allocator's understanding of it. In the hands of the uninformed it can, therefore, be even *worse* than useless, since it can lead to misinformed policy decisions, or at least policy decisions based upon misinformed reasoning. Explicitness and understanding are what are required and, without them, resource allocation decisions are at risk of being misdirected. By contrast, even if a particular decision has already been taken to allocate resources (say) to extend a medium-secure unit, needs assessment data and analysis may still be of great value in demonstrating the type and level of need which the new service will meet. What such data and analysis should *not* be used to do, in those predetermined circumstances, is to *justify* the decision. More fundamentally, it is policy which should determine the framework of needs assessment and not the reverse. That is, policy makers and commissioners should set the values and objectives of service responses to MDO need, as well as the weights of different objectives, and needs assessment should then be framed so as best to reflect those values and objectives.

Clearly, different needs assessment methods have different potentials for policy bias, both in their adopted definitions of need and in their methods *per se*. Indeed, put more positively, each may offer a different and valuable 'perspective on need' (a term to which we shall return with some enthusiasm) in addressing a particular 'need problem'. Although it is not possible to know what is the 'true need' for a particular type of health intervention, it *is* possible to view need from a number of perspectives, each of which has its own inherent definitional and policy biases but which, taken together, offer a range of perspectives on true need. Although the range cannot then simply be averaged, so as to describe statistically a balanced picture of need,[46] at least a variety of individual pictures of need can be viewed, sufficient to allow resource allocation decisions to be made in a more informed and enlightened way than might otherwise occur. Thus, even within one category of methodologies (e.g. the survey method), different definitions and methods might be set alongside one another so as to gain a 'range of need' solution. Such a multiple perspective approach to need might then lead to a statement of the form "The need for intervention X seems to lie between n and m based on the range of definitions of need adopted". The same notion of a 'range solution' can properly emerge from use of not just multiple definitions and measurements within one method but also from use of more than one method.

So, it may be that, for at least some of the foregoing reasons, the DoH has itself recommended a 'hybrid approach' to needs assessment which combines information from *all* of the needs assessment methods described in this book, with required acknowledgement of the limitations of each (DoH, 1991). As other writers have put it, such a hybrid approach allows a convergent analysis which can provide both quantitative and qualitative perspectives on need (Warheit *et al*, 1977; Rabkin, 1986; Hall & Royse, 1987). It also recognises implicitly that, ultimately, all policy decisions are subjective in nature and that such subjectivity can arise from the

---

[46] See below concerning the 'arithmetic' of combining perspectives on need which are 'additive' rather than cross-validating.

decisions being based on value-laden data, even when the values are obscured by a numerically reassuring face, or when it is otherwise not obvious.

Methods, definitions and measurement within methods

Even *with* a hybrid approach to needs assessment, any tendency towards inadequate definitions of key terms, differing agency perspectives, loosely posed research questions, uncertainty regarding appropriate methodologies and general uncertainty about *what* is being measured will bode poorly for valid and reliable needs assessment decisions.[47] Hence, earlier chapters of this book have attempted to dissect out each needs assessment method individually so as to encourage MDO needs assessment practitioners to pursue clarity of both the definition and the method of assessment they adopt. That is, at least needs assessment *practitioners* should be aware of which definitions they are applying. Preferably, they should also expressly choose and specify them, including doing so with understanding of the subjectivity of the choice being made.

We do not intend, in this chapter, to offer a detailed summary of all of the methodological categories, and the variations within them, dealt with in the book. What the book as a whole has attempted to do is both to clarify each method and to describe its strengths and weaknesses. What we *will* do, however, is to suggest some broad-brush comparisons of the various methods. However, before attempting to do so, it is important to emphasise that there can be confusion even over the proper categorical definition of the methods themselves and that this, in turn, can cause confusion about what is being measured. Hence, sometimes without careful thought it can be unclear whether a particular study does, or does not, amount to a RUT study, by contrast with amounting, for example, to a survey. Yet, the distinction is important, because the RUT method does not count unmet need (although it may count, or expose, 'absent need' which *is* being met!). By way of specific illustration, consider whether surveys of patients in special hospitals which aim to determine their needs should properly be seen as RUT studies, because the patients *are receiving* treatment. More properly, perhaps they should be seen as amounting to epidemiological

---

[47] The term 'needs assessment decision' is used to emphasise that determining a particular level of need is just as much a 'decision' as any resource allocation decision based upon such assessed need, because it is necessary to 'decide' between perspectives.

surveys, particularly if they measure not what the patients are receiving (on the assumption, for example, that they *need* it), but what they are *not* receiving, that is, their *unmet* need (or inappropriately met need). In the book we have, therefore, categorised *all* such studies as 'surveys', because their ultimate goal is usually to directly measure unmet (or inappropriately met) need and not just to demonstrate service utilisation as a proxy for need.

We have, in the book, also attempted to address definitions of the client group themselves. If we cannot even agree on *whose* needs we are measuring, then can we ever get started? However, even here, definition is intimately linked with who it is among the mentally disordered who are perceived to have special offender need, such that they come within the term 'MDO'. That is, the definition of what is an MDO itself assumes a particular definition of special need.

Comparison of the methodologies

Chapters 3–6 dealt at length with the categories of methodology within needs assessment as a whole, as well as with many examples of empirical studies within each category. It might seem appropriate, therefore, to spend the next few pages summarising comparatively the strengths and weaknesses of each method. However, as we have already emphasised, merely to look at methodological strengths and weaknesses would be to cut across the core thesis of the whole book, which is that each method implies its own policy assumptions and values, both in terms of needs assessment *per se* and in terms of the values attached to different types of information that emerge. That is, each method has potential value assumptions lying behind it and "you pays your needs assessment money (if you have any) and you gets your value choice". This is not to deny that, within each method, there may be examples of both technically good and bad studies. However, clearly, some qualitative and value comparisons can be attempted at a gross level between methods and, clearly also, there may be variation in the extent to which it is possible for values directly to impinge upon methodologies. It is to discussion of such broad qualitative variations, rather than to a detailed technical critique of each method, that we now turn.

Out of a comparative analysis of all of the methods we will also attempt to extract some pointers towards our consideration later of ways in which varying 'perspectives on need' can be integrated, or at least helpfully viewed side by side, to assist in rational and insightful decision-making about resource allocation in relation to need. However, throughout the book we have emphasised the dearth of reliable and valid information about need and outcome in relation to MDOs. So, inevitably, there will be a gap between what should be done in relation to needs assessment and what is practical, or even possible. Further, even if the amount of information about needs, outcome and effectiveness does increase, the capacity to use it appropriately does not necessarily increase at the same rate (Ovretveit, 1995).

The survey approach

It might be argued that the survey approach is the most desirable approach to measuring need, since it allows for direct rather than indirect (or proxy) measurement of need. However, as described in detail in Chapter 3, in practice it is not possible to conduct epidemiological community MDO studies which are similar to epidemiological studies of easily identifiable and measurable physical (or even mental) diseases in the community. Hence, impracticality (see, for example, Hirsch & Jarman, 1993) determines a constraint on survey methods which immediately introduces greater potential bias. Also, and even more fundamentally, the measurement of *need* rather than *disorder* immediately makes the excercise more value-laden by virtue of requiring a decision regarding *which* disabilities and needs flowing from the disorder are considered to be worth counting and responding to.[48] Less fundamentally, but still importantly, the adoption of the 'comparative approach' to needs assessment (DoH, 1991) – an example of what the NHS Management Executive has called a 'pragmatic approach' – whereby unmet need is assumed to be exposed by demonstrating that people with similar needs receive less resources in one place than in another, is clearly merely presumptuous, since it assumes that the better endowed service 'has got it right'.

Of particular relevance to the foregoing debate is the common MDO needs assessment strategy of surveying particular 'pockets' of the community. Within the survey method this has usually focused upon the mental health or security needs of MDOs in prisons or special hospitals. However, whatever they measure, by making measurements *in* the criminal justice system, or specialist forensic psychiatric service portions of the community, such studies potentially systematically omit large swathes of unmet need. Indeed, by virtue of their detention in a facility with available mental health

---

[48] Of course, some would argue that even disorder or diagnosis is inherently value-laden.

care, all such MDOs are, in any event, either receiving some care (at least potentially, even if they are in prison) or are likely to achieve some measure of care if their disorder (and need) is severe enough. By comparison, those who have offended less, or less severely, may be extremely needy in the community and yet go unnoticed. Hence, underlying such surveys, or at least underlying any exclusive policy reliance upon them, is the assumption that serious offending behaviour is more worthy of a resourced mental health service response than is minor antisocial behaviour (of the type, for example, which may well exclude an MDO from generic mental health care but yet be insufficient to warrant specialist forensic mental health care). In summary terms, therefore, all such studies are highly partial in their nature, both in measuring only 'part' of the MDO problem and in being biased towards a *particular* 'part' of the problem. Put simply, what you decide to *measure* demonstrates what you value; or, sometimes, what you *can* measure determines what you *can* value. Similar arguments apply in relation to measuring the needs of special hospital MDOs against those of MDOs in low-security units. Hence, jumping for a moment again to all the difficulties described in Chapter 7, what need you are prepared to spend (more) money on measuring, defines what you value.

More positively, what surveys *can* validly demonstrate is the size of any individual and clearly defined 'need problem'. Hence, if a narrow question is posed, such as "What levels of security are actually needed by current special hospital MDOs?", then demonstration that a sizeable proportion of such patients do not require high, but only medium, security clearly represents knowledge which is useful to policy makers and commissioners. Therefore, assuming that there is no other type of need considered (e.g. the need for an intra-mural rehabilitation infrastructure beyond that usually available in medium-secure units) which conflicts, in its placement implications, with the implications of security need, it may then be rational to reduce the aggregate bed numbers within the special hospitals while increasing those in medium-secure units.

Even though any analysis constructed in this way very clearly amounts to partial needs assessment, rather than multidimensional (or comprehensive) needs assessment, it can still be of direct value in rationally allocating resources. However, even in this example, it is possible for crude political considerations which transcend and contradict needs assessments still to hold sway, in spite of a clear answer being available to a clearly defined and narrow need question. Such political considerations may, for example, be financial, so that, in practice, a cost-need analysis is conducted or they may arise from consideration of political image, for example by way of a decision that the obvious public protection represented by a small number of large high-security hospitals is deemed to be politically required. Indeed, that particular debate about the future of the special hospitals has been waged, including in a manifestly political fashion, for at least the last ten years (see, for example, Bluglass, 1992), in spite of need data pointing strongly towards their reduction, or at least their redefinition. Again, for largely political rather than solely need reasons, the debate is certain to continue in the wake of the report of the Fallon inquiry (Fallon *et al*, 1999). However, what is of ultimate importance is that, if need *is* to be overridden for political purposes (or in the interests of objectives other than patient need), then it should be overridden overtly. Certainly, the approach adopted towards needs assessment should not be adjusted merely in order that it might point to a politically required result.

Many other surveys conducted in settings other than high security have tended to address issues such as 'readiness to move' or 'difficulty to place'. Although such surveys are, in fact, very useful in micro service planning terms (e.g. in determining the (re)development of an NHS service to cater for the current large numbers of extra-NHS or 'out of area' NHS placements), what is required is a much more detailed, and also *individually based*, approach to needs assessment. Indeed, perhaps herein lies a clue to what will, or should, be the main future of MDO needs assessment, that is, individual needs assessment plus the integration of needs assessment into the substance of clinical practice itself (see, for example, Marshall *et al*, 1995). At the very least, perhaps future commissioners should pursue a combination of 'top-down' (i.e. population level) and 'bottom-up' (i.e. individual level) approaches, as recommended by Wing *et al* (1992). Hence, substantial effort should be put into modifying existing mental health needs schedules in order specifically to take account of MDOs' additional and special needs, within a 'bottom-up' approach.

A rather different type of survey dealt with in Chapter 3 is the 'service-linked survey'. In this example, data are collected alongside a prison, court diversion or police station mental health service intervention. This type of study is clearly very 'partial' in its approach. However, what such surveys emphasise is the diversity of usefulness of (very different) types of needs assessment. So, data *from* a service and collected *by* a service can be extremely useful in further *developing* a service. What such data do *not* amount to are data which are sufficiently epidemiological to design a whole comprehensive forensic service based upon them. Again, what is crucial is clarity of purpose in collecting and analysing the data. With clarity the data can be of use; without it the data are worse than useless, in that they will be misleading.

Beyond all these subtleties of proper use of needs assessment surveys lies the question of whether, in fact, much use *has* been made of even the most persuasive of such studies. As regards court diversion data, clearly these have been linked to service development. However, the data generally has *followed* service development. As regards prison surveys, these have demonstrated overwhelming evidence of large numbers of highly needy MDOs in prison, and yet there has still been no adequate policy response (although there have been some measures, such as a Home Office edict to prison doctors some years ago increasingly to invoke Section 48 transfers, which has had some beneficial effect, though perhaps without accompanying adequate resourcing or resource transfers). There are still wholly inadequate forensic mental health remand facilities (within either the health sector or prisons), albeit there does seem to be a more concerted intention to involve the NHS directly in prison mental health through formal partnership with the Prison Service and the adoption of NHS standards, including those contained within the 'national service framework'. Similarly, as regards the need for long-term medium-security beds (required in order to accommodate patients not requiring high security), although the HSPSCB agreed three model schemes in the mid-1990s, the budgetary rigidity of the special hospitals (arising largely from their high overheads) and the inability of the Board effectively to urge district purchasers to 'pick up the tab' after the initial revenue pump-priming period determined that there was little progress. So, however good and convincing the needs assessment data are, they may remain effectively unused in public policy terms. By contrast, if there is the political will, or especially if there is a perceived political imperative, to develop additional services, then such development will probably occur, and quickly. Thus, after the then Secretary of State for Health, Virginia Bottomley, was called to the Old Bailey and to Chichester crown court in the mid-1990s under Section 39 of the Mental Health Act 1983 in order to explain why medium-security beds were not available for two patients from the South (West) Thames Region, there was substantial and rapid expansion of medium-security beds in the whole of the South Thames Region. Further, such expansion appeared to be decided upon even in the absence of much good and carefully interpreted needs data at all![49]

---

[49] The substantial expansion of medium-security beds in South East Thames in the mid-1990s was, to the second author's knowledge, based on very little detailed and validated needs data.

Equally important, if the commissioning mechanisms avoid perverse financial incentives then there is a much greater chance that valid need data will be translated into rational service responses. Thus, the establishment of regional specialist commissioning groups for specialist MDO services is likely to overcome the type of barrier to implementation of the 'model schemes' previously pursued by the HSPSCB; however, specialist commissioning brings its own problems in terms of integration of forensic and general mental health care services, including by way of (different) perverse financial incentives (see below).

Overall, however, what the survey studies in particular demonstrate is the importance of a comprehensive approach to need, comprehensive both in terms of the types of patient and their types of need[50] *and* in terms of implied service responses. Above all, given the dearth of direct true outcome data, described in Chapter 7, what such studies emphasise is the importance of a far more sophisticated approach to assessing need, which goes beyond security needs and includes the clinical, rehabilitation and humanitarian domains.

The RUT approach

The inherent flaw in the RUT approach is that it measures service utilisation as a proxy for need (i.e. it is indirect). For example, returning to special hospital MDOs, enumerating those receiving high-security care on the assumption that this might equate with need would, as we have already shown, be entirely false. There are many MDOs in prison who *require* high-security psychiatric care and many in special hospitals who do *not*. Indeed, as we shall suggest later on, it is only by pursuing a multi-perspective approach, which may include arithmetical integration of data from varying perspectives, that true need can be approached. Hence, still using the high-security example, and by way of a trailer for a core recommendation which we shall make, the aggregate, best estimate of need for high-security care might be calculated on the basis of a 'formula' amounting to:

number of patients in special hospital (i.e. RUT)

minus

number of inappropriately placed special hospital patients (obtained from the 'best' survey data available)

---

[50] This includes 'special groups', such as adolescents, the learning disabled, women and those with antisocial personality disorder.

plus

number of sentenced and remand prisoners who require special
hospital treatment (obtained from the 'best' prison survey data
available)

plus

number of patients in medium and low security who require high
security (obtained from 'best' survey data available).

Although such a heterogeneous analysis cannot give a valid numeri-
cal answer, even though it may *appear* to do so by giving a precise
answer, it can at least approach an answer which is more likely to be
valid than a single-perspective one (irrespective of from which
method, with its own particular faults, it arises).

However, before pursuing this 'combination of perspectives'
approach in more detail, it is worth spending some time discussing
the quality of the RUT approach as a whole. What the approach *can*
offer is a combination of data availability and direct and immediate
relevance to service pressure, particularly if RUT is extended
to include waiting list data (that is, MDOs *'waiting to be* under
treatment'). If one adds into the model, as does Goldberg (1990),
some notion of optimal bed occupancy, then a rather convincing
snapshot of 'needs pressure' can be gained. Optimal bed occupancy
is defined on the basis of achieving an assumed proper balance
between 'use of beds for treatment for appropriately placed current
patients' (met need) and 'availability of beds for appropriately
placed future patients' (need which would go unmet if there was
not a bed immediately available). In fact, 'RUT plus waiting list'
is the sort of definition of need to which commissioners tend
automatically to turn, perhaps both because it avoids facing up to
the financial consequences of unmet need and because immediately
evident need is difficult to resist, albeit responses to immediate need
may sometimes represent a less than fully rational approach. Indeed,
response to need pressure of this sort represents another form of
'partialism', where the need to which the service response is made
is partial not only by virtue of not being comprehensive across types
of MDO and their needs but also by being partial in temporal terms,
that is, in favouring those who immediately need care. This again
emphasises the importance of either *not* being partial in one
direction, that is, at least adopting a number of (partial) perspectives
on need, or, if a singular approach is to be embraced, of the
necessity for explicit recognition of which perspectives are being
wholly ignored.

Nonetheless, evidence that on a particular day there was 99% medium-security bed occupancy nationally (Coid, 1993*a*) does tell us *something* about need. Unless there are data suggesting, for example, that, *across the country*, there are grossly inadequate low-security bed numbers which could account for there being medium-security beds filled *inappropriately* to that percentage, it may be entirely reasonable to assume that the figure strongly suggests high need. Indeed, still on the basis of taking an 'average across the country', if there are also long waiting lists for medium security *plus* other pointers suggesting substantial *un*met need (even if it is not restricted to, or defined specifically in terms of, medium security) arising from surveys of prisons, then the 99% figure is clearly of substantial policy-making value. But resource allocation policy is ultimately not determined for particular types of service (such as medium-security services) nationally but by local commissioning authorities, or, since 1999, by regional commissioning bodies in consultation with local health authorities. So, for the individual commissioner, regional or local, what matters is not the *national* bed occupancy percentage but the *local* percentage. And at that level a local medium-security bed occupancy percentage of 99% is *not* necessarily indicative of the need for more such beds (or even for the existing number) in the way that, given all the 'averaging out' factors that apply nationally, it may be at a national level. Ignoring the need to take more than one time frame, what a local commissioner will need to know is information indicative of whether the percentage is influenced, for example, by inadequacy of low-security beds or by lax (inappropriately low) admission thresholds operating for other reasons (such as the clinical wish to demonstrate the continuing need for the service, or for an expanded service).

Such information implies an approach which is clearly far more comprehensive in its scope, subtle in its definition and also inherently individual (to the patient) than is a crude aggregate service usage percentage. It emphasises again, therefore, two general conclusions to which our work generally in the field of MDO needs assessment has drawn us: first, that partial needs assessment is dangerous in policy terms, especially if it is insightless to its partial nature; and second, that commissioners should increasingly look to an approach which uses not only aggregate need data but also individual patient data, including ensuring that such individual data are embedded in the clinical process. It is important to emphasise, however, that the latter does not amount to handing back to clinicians the untrammelled power to determine admission thresholds. In fact, far from it – what it amounts to is placing a requirement on them to look beyond disorder *per se* and towards a wider conceptualisation of need, as well as towards incorporating the concepts which arise in that way directly into clinical data. Rather than representing a re-takeover of commissioning power by doctors, it represents a profound integration of a proper commissioning perspective into the clinical model. In fact, ultimately it represents proper collaboration between clinicians and commissioners by ensuring that public policy resource allocation perspectives are taken account of and reflected in clinical decision-making. So, rather than clinicians competing with commissioners for (effective) commissioner power, with clinicians pursuing their own particular partisan resource allocation objectives, *or* commissioners striving vigorously to find ways of constraining clinically based decision-making towards the commissioners' own objectives, the two are inherently integrated. Indeed, the 1997 NHS White Paper (DoH, 1997), which emphasises cooperation between providers and commissioners, lays down a structure which is facilitatory of such an approach. Clinician and commissioner are expected by the DoH to collaborate. Of course, this is an approach which is a general one and which goes far beyond consideration of the RUT method of needs assessment. However, for obvious reasons, it is well illustrated by reference specifically to the RUT method.

To put more practical meat on the theoretical bones of what might be meant by a more comprehensive, subtle and individual approach to needs assessment, it may be helpful to work further on the example of the commissioner who is pondering the meaning of a 99% medium-security bed occupancy. Surely the crucial question for the commissioner will be whether the patients 'need' the beds, be it in terms of their treatment or in terms of the level of security the beds represent. Assuming, for the moment, that the commissioner has less input into issues of treatment (which could occur at any level of security) she or he may then best have a dialogue with clinicians about appropriate security. Since it is, indeed, the commissioner and not the individual medium-security service which is responsible for overseeing and commissioning the *whole range* of secure services, only the commissioner *can* reasonably be in a position to hold the ring about particular secure service placement. In fact, the commissioner may, for example, even consciously decide not to commission low-security services at all, for reasons going beyond MDO services *per se* (either financial reasons or reasons related to overall psychiatric service design), and that clearly emphasises the commissioner's crucial role in determining admission criteria. However, how could that role, and the integration of that role with clinical practice, be pursued? One answer is represented by a type of admission schedule such as that developed at St George's Hospital Medical School, that is the Admission Criteria to Secure Services Schedule (ACSeSS). This represents an attempt to identify factors which could be viewed, from a policy and clinical perspective, as properly determining of the security levels of patients' admissions. The schedule is based upon clinical judgements about patient variables presumed relevant to the appropriate level of secure placement. However, the inclusion of items which go beyond the individual patient characteristics which properly lie at its core emphasises that extraneous factors are, in practice, likely to contribute to placement. Items relating to 'lower-order service failure' offer at least a degree of overtness and explicitness about any decision to place a patient into a given level of security when the relevant patient data do not suggest the need for it. Hence, if a commissioner sees, from some aggregation of individual ACSeSS reports for patients from a particular medium-secure unit, that the average ACSeSS scoring is less than that for other similar units, *and* that 'lack of low-security facilities' was a frequent contributor to medium-security admission, then he or she is made clearly aware of the *lesser* weight that should be placed on the 99% occupancy figure as demonstrative of medium-security need than should otherwise be the case. The commissioner may also be made aware of the effect of his or her own decisions, for example not to commission low-security beds, on how medium-security beds are used, that is, inappropriately. Hence, ACSeSS, or a similar schedule, may both better inform as to the meaning of the 99% figure and make explicit the policy *causes* of it. It can, therefore, offer an obvious and sensible basis for clinician–commissioner cooperation. So, such a schedule does not amount solely to commissioner infringement of clinician freedom since it also makes evident the fact, and impact, of what might otherwise remain covert commissioner decisions not to fund particular services, or not to fund them adequately.

ACSeSS can also represent or reflect cooperation between different clinicians and between different providers, since determining criteria for admission to one level of security should not occur without reference to criteria used at other levels of security. To operate otherwise would be automatically to create the possibility of gaps between services. Indeed, it is the historical gap that has existed between high- and medium-security service criteria represented by medium-security services not admitting patients expected to stay for more than 18–24 months which has largely determined the inappropriate detention of many patients in the special hospitals who require only medium security, albeit in the long term.

The RUT approach would be less inherently limited in its implications and value if there were at least data available within the Prison Health Care Service equivalent to the data available within NHS and private mental health services. Hence, if we could be confident that MDO cases were at least identified and given *some* form of treatment in prison (for their special needs), the problem might then be one of determining who should be in which facility, be it prison health care or some level of NHS/private mental health care – that is, determining the potential transfer of patients by demonstration of inadequate meeting of their need (be it transfer from prison to specialist mental health care or from one level of specialist mental health care to another). However, such data congruence between prisons and the NHS does *not* exist. Indeed, as we have emphasised before, each culture is poor at both collecting and dealing with data which are more congruent with the culture of the other. That leads us towards another type of main conclusion of our review, which is that the future of needs assessment, indeed the future of MDO services themselves and of related government policy, should be marked by pursuit of a 'trans-cultural approach'. This should involve congruence of data and of services, and also joint funding between the NHS and the Home Office, particularly since it seems clear that continuation of the alternative of split funding represents, both symbolically and in real terms, perpetuation of a variety of service and research problems relating to MDOs, of which more later.

The latter recommendation of pursuing NHS/prison data congruence gives rise to its own problem. If, particularly for the lower offending end of the MDO hierarchy, there is a need to incorporate into generic mental health data which are specific for MDOs, and for MDO need, is it likely that this can be combined, at the same time, with collecting data within the NHS in a way which is congruent with the criminal justice system? The short answer is, largely, that it cannot. This is because generic mental health services deal with so many patients who are *not* offenders that it is impractical to set up data sets which encompass data linked to criminal justice. However, one practical solution to this problem would involve: first, the Prison Medical Service collecting *adequate* generic mental health data (as if it were, and surely it should be, equivalent to a general practice facility); *and*, second, 'higher offending MDO' data within the NHS being collected so as to be more congruent between specialist forensic mental health facilities and prisons; *and*, third, 'lower offending MDO' data being collected so as to be more congruent between specialist (or special interest, low-security) forensic mental health facilities and generic facilities. This would allow congruence, biased towards the type or level of offending of the MDOs concerned.

In summary, the RUT approach holds great attractions for both clinicians and commissioners because of its accessibility and its obvious immediate value. However, its needs assessment limitations are obvious from its title. It should, therefore, be used only in conjunction with other perspectives on need, even though it is itself a necessary perspective, and, indeed, a necessary foundation for determining need.

The social indicator approach

This approach would seem tantalisingly to offer commissioners their dream – the ability accurately and validly to estimate the need (and demand) for varying services for MDOs on the basis of aggregate statistics which do not even have to be collected specifically for the purpose to which they are then put. This does seem an ideal, and cheap, basis for determining need. However, the advantages of a model should not blur the eye that addresses its validity. Chapter 5 went into some detail in emphasising four important facts: first, doubts remain about the validity of social indicator models for narrow groups of disorder and related problems; second, the doubts worsen the smaller the service subtype; third, there has been, so far, no demonstration that generic mental health models are adequate in predicting specifically MDO need *and* no specialist MDO model has yet been validated/published; and finally, social indicator models so far developed in relation to mental health need in the UK have been validated only in terms of the extent to which they predict psychiatric in-patient bed usage. Leaving aside the first three problems, the final problem remains massively important, in terms which, by now, will have become familiar to the reader. That is, bed utilisation, or indeed any sort of utilisation, cannot validly be used as a basis for assessment of *need*.[51] At least, it cannot be used *on its own* as a basis for assessment of need. So, yet again, we find ourselves concluding that, even if one particular approach to needs assessment is internally valid within its own terms, it cannot, or rather it should not, be used as the sole measure of need. Hence,

---

[51] It is possible, of course, that social indicators which adequately predict bed utilisation also predict some better proxy for need. However, we cannot know this given that it is bed utilisation against which they have often been tested.

like the RUT approach, the social indicator model can offer an approach based on fairly readily available data which can lay a foundation of need. However, whenever the social indicator method is validated solely on its power to predict utilisation, it shares an inadequacy with the RUT approach. This determines that other methods must also be used to add in unmet need (which the two methods will miss) and for inappropriately met need (which the two methods will miscount as if it were appropriately met need). In fact, another general conclusion emerges from the comparative analysis of all the approaches addressed in this chapter. That is, needs assessment practitioners must be particularly alert to the crucial distinction between appropriately and inappropriately met need.

In summary, therefore, like the RUT and survey methods, on its own the social indicator method gives an incomplete view of need. Quite obviously, it also offers nothing towards determining individual patient need.

Key informant and community opinion approaches

If approaches based on epidemiological methods appear to offer the most objective yet least qualitatively detailed perspective on need, the key informant and community opinion approaches together appear to offer the opposite. Here the possibility of needs assessment bias is all but built into the method. However, it is at least also obvious. Indeed, it is the likely overtness of any bias which offers some reassurance, by comparison with the possibility of bias which may be hidden in the detail of the various quantitative methodologies. It is not, of course, that qualitative methods *per se* are inherently biased but rather that, within these two particular approaches, the individual whom you ask about need may determine what is said. Hence, asking a forensic psychiatrist will almost certainly invoke a different response from asking a general psychiatrist (unless perhaps the latter has just had a difficult patient refused by the regional medium-secure unit!). Similarly, asking the Home Office, which does not fund NHS secure services but which is the guardian of public safety, about the need for medium- or high-security beds may, unsurprisingly, gain a different response from asking the DoH, which does fund such services. By contrast, asking the same bodies about the need for better prison mental health care services may elicit responses that are reversed.

The key informant and community opinion approaches were explored in these terms in some depth in Chapter 6. The nub of both methods is, however, that they are difficult to disentangle from the political and administrative process of *responding* to need. Indeed, it can be argued that the Reed Committee itself, which made great use of the key informant approach, tended over its term to pass somewhat imperceptibly from an investigative to a service evangelistic role. There may be little wrong with such a process in terms of the ultimate good of many MDOs and of society but, at the very least, service evangelism can cast a biased interpretive shadow across more objectively conducted needs assessment. In fact, it could be argued that the whole of the Reed process was *intended* to be evangelistic as regards services and that that was bound to cast such a shadow.

However, perhaps the most well focused illustration of both the advantages and dangers arising from gaining highly detailed data by way of the key informant method is represented by the 'regional forensic adviser' role which some regions previously adopted. He (none were women!) was commonly coincidentally a repository of detailed clinical and need knowledge, a spokesman for users (at least, from one perspective) and an advocate for services. Clearly, at their inception in the late 1970s and in the 1980s these advisers represented a necessary 'kick' to an NHS system that was highly resistant to medium-security service development. However, it is questionable whether they retain substantial value in a more diverse, developed and complex system, at least as they were originally conceived. The view of the DoH and the HSPSCB (now HSPSCT) seems to be that, in whatever form, such an advisory function is, if anything, of increasing rather than diminishing importance in the post-1997 White Paper context of commissioner–provider cooperation.[52] However, the function needs now to be not that of 'product champion' (as in the days of new service development) but that of 'product integrator'. That is, there needs to be recognition that a core problem of the *current* stage of service development is not that of 'getting services going' but of 'getting services relating' to one another. The most obvious example of the problem that needs to be addressed in this way is the continuing isolation of the special hospitals. However, the role extends to the relationship between medium-secure and low-secure units and between medium-secure units and generic mental health care services. Indeed, encouraging 'relatedness' amounts to ensuring the

---

[52] Dr Dilys Jones expressed such a view on behalf of the DoH at the first of a series of regular meetings of clinical directors and regional advisers in Stratford-upon-Avon in February 1998.

responsiveness of all mental health services to the variety of MDOs and their needs at various times. Essentially, the function may be seen, therefore, as amounting to an ongoing 'regional Reed', albeit this clearly should not be in one pair of hands or organised uniformly across regions. Hence, for example, the new London Region has established a large committee of forensic clinical directors and trust chief executives who, together, will mutually advise one another and the Region. However, this system ultimately does blur the distinction between advice and action. Indeed, it looks like a return to a planned economy for health care, albeit with trusts still competing *de facto* for their slice of the forensic cake. However, all of this diverts us away somewhat from the 'key informants' approach *per se* and towards more general matters of policy which are better considered toward the close of this final chapter of the book.

Turning to the community opinion approach, this raises a related but somewhat different set of issues. Basing needs assessment on community opinion seems to offer the most 'democratic' methods. Indeed, properly operated it may seem to be at the opposite pole in this regard from the key informant approach, which is by definition potentially sectional and self-interested in its nature. Hence, if society *recognises* particular types of need and highly values service responses to them then they should be provided, so the argument goes. Indeed, this is an argument which sits well in the current political climate, which includes a government which seems heavily to espouse both community and communitarian politics, including in relation to mental health care (Heginbotham & Elson, 1999). However, such politics can allow vent to misinformed public fear of the mentally ill and to calls for irrational and ethically dubious service responses driven even by moral panic (Pearson, 1999). Indeed, this is obviously a true aspect of the post-Clunis politics of mental health service provision. One direction of this effect is, of course, identical to that of the key informant approach, that is, towards greater provision of secure psychiatric services. However, there is a great risk that, in other and important ways, such pressure for services will be very different in its effects. Hence, whereas key informant mental health professionals and users will be likely also to press for service quality, which reflects strongly their perceived need for a response specifically to MDOs' mental health needs, 'the community' may perceive, or at least be prepared to pay for, only security needs. This takes us back, of course, to earlier parts of the book which dealt with the definition of MDO need and, specifically, with the crucial question of 'whose need?'.

Perhaps the danger of a community approach to needs assessment focusing solely on public need is, however, best illustrated by the current public debate concerning the alleged need for new service provisions for those MDOs with 'severe personality disorder'; although, clearly, such an approach *could* also coincidentally give rise to a response to mental health need in respect of severe personality disorder. The Home Secretary's proposal for new forms of legal and service response to need for MDOs with severe personality disorder who also represent "a grave danger" to the public (Home Office/DoH, 1999) includes a heavy emphasis on public safety. Indeed, this is emphasised, in terms of individual patient needs assessment, by the intention that new service responses for those with 'dangerous severe personality disorder' (DSPD) should be provided compulsorily not only to 'patients' who are treatable but to others who are not. In needs assessment terms, then, these latter MDOs do not *themselves* have a health need, because there is no defined beneficial service response to the problem they pose, *for themselves*. The government's proposals, therefore, lay bare the fact that, for MDOs with DSPD, it is public need and not MDO need to which the service response is being applied. This raises profound questions about the social role and function of forensic mental health care services and, in particular, the question of whether such services amount to (ethically valid) 'public health psychiatry', where there is some benefit to the MDOs themselves, or (ethically invalid) solely 'crime prevention' (Eastman, 1999). The former interpretation, however, also gives the clue to the other side of the government's proposals for DSPD.

Alongside legal measures to deal with those with DSPD who are deemed untreatable (as well as those who *are* treatable), the government intends new protocols and services which will, it is argued, begin seriously to address (what amounts to) 'unmet need'. This will occur by virtue of designing new assessment and treatment methods which can respond to problems which, so long as they remain 'untreatable', technically cannot be counted as a health need at all. That cannot, perhaps, be seen as a bad thing. However, the nature of personality disorder as a nosological and moral entity is of particular importance here. Personality disorder sits at the junction of 'madness' and 'badness' and it is unsurprising, therefore, that it is junctional also in terms of how it is properly perceived in needs assessment terms. This leads to the question, 'Do MDOs with personality disorder present only public need or also individual MDO need?' Similarly, the junctional status of personality disorder demands two different potential service responses to the problems it poses – a penal and a health response. For the government, the fact of an MDO's dangerous severe personality disorder *per se* implies a need for a health response, although the recent proposals are clearly intended primarily as a response to the need of the public for protection. Indeed, the latter is suggested not only by the rhetoric but also by virtue of the fact that, for MDOs with DSPD who are not currently convicted of an offence, the only route to preventive detention which does not contravene the European Convention on Human Rights under Article 5(1)(e) is that offered by the individual being of 'unsound mind'. Hence, to *achieve* public protection the government must, for such MDOs, define them legally as having a mental disorder. This automatically invokes mental health services of some sort. However, if such people of 'unsound mind' cannot be helped (other than by being locked up) then they do not have a health need. So, the result can only be the provision of mental health services for MDOs who are defined (in terms of the DoH's own definition given earlier in this book) as having no mental health need. We are back, therefore, to the core issue for services for MDOs, that is, the question 'Are they provided for the MDO or for the public?' That, in turn, pushes the debate into the realms of social and professional ethics which, although they are ultimately central to the definition of MDO need and service response, are beyond the scope of this book in terms of any detailed discussion. More prosaically, the latter discussion does point us, as did the discussion of the key informant approach to needs assessment, to matters of general policy regarding MDO services which will be addressed briefly at the end of the chapter and of the book.

Calculation by combination

We have exhorted several times now acknowledgement of the inherent partial nature of any one needs assessment method and the importance, therefore, of approaching need via concurrent consideration of a number of 'perspectives on need'. However, in what *way* are various perspectives to be viewed together? Answers to this question address, first, the extent of any 'integration' of perspectives *per se* and, second, the extent of any 'arithmetic' integration of data arising from different perspectives. Let us take each of these aspects in turn.

By 'degrees of integration', we mean that, at one extreme, perspectives could simply be placed side by side to demonstrate different answers to different need questions. A policy judgement would then be taken solely on the basis of looking at the need problem from a variety of perspectives, weighting in an unsystematic way the various findings, hopefully in full awareness of what types, or timescales, of need are emphasised, or excluded, by a particular assessment method.

Alternatively, attempts could be made to cross-relate the findings of the various methods in a more systematic way. This would explicitly incorporate value or policy judgements, whereby the relating of the findings one to another would involve some formal weighting of the various approaches. Such differential weighting could be constructed across very broad classes of approach, for example, 'quantitative' (more characteristically, survey, RUT, social indicator) versus 'qualitative' (commonly, key informant and community opinion) or between particular quantitative methodologies. Of course, if some whole class of data is unavailable then automatically the related approach, and its policy biases, will be entirely excluded from the analysis. Indeed, more generally, the fewer resources that are expended on gaining needs assessment data, the more narrow and partial must be both the data available (taken as a whole) and the resource allocation decision taken.

Turning to the arithmetic of integration of a range of need data, we have already offered a trailer of at least one way of approaching this across methodologies. We suggested, for example, that 'need for high-security beds' might be based upon:

number of patients in special hospital (i.e. RUT)

minus

number of inappropriately placed special hospital patients (obtained from the 'best' survey data available)

plus

number of sentenced and remand prisoners who require special hospital treatment (obtained from the 'best' prison survey data available)

plus

number of patients in medium and low security who require high security (obtained from the 'best' survey data available).

However, this is something of a conceptual and arithmetic dog's dinner, since it amounts to adding and subtracting figures which, although all directed towards need, are defined and collected in very different ways. It could be argued, therefore, that conducting such an arithmetic exercise across methods is invalid. Certainly it falls far short of being meta-analysis.[53] However, a crude aggregation

---

[53] Meta-analysis is a term usually reserved for methods of analysing multiple data sources which all address a single question.

such as this is likely to be all that the average NHS resource allocater has available. So, even if allocaters fall short of actually doing the sum, ultimately they are almost bound to use the figures together by adopting some sort of an approach involving at least putting all the figures side by side in their head and coming to a judgement.

There is, of course, another way of collating more than one quantitative estimate of need where the particular sorts of estimate are not inherently 'additive' but do appear clearly to measure roughly the same thing. For example, if an attempt is made to use the result of a social indicator model *alongside* (say) the type of combined or arithmetic approach just described in relation to the need for high-security beds, then the result would amount to two estimates of the same thing, which allows cross-validation. Of course, such cross-validation can be conducted between any two types of method, or any combination of methods, when they all contribute to measuring some particular definition of need. For example, calculating the need for medium-security beds might be approached in a cross-validating way using the following:

number of patients in high-, medium- and low-security beds and prison who require medium security (based on the 'best' survey data available)

and

'indicative bed norms' adjusted for 'capitation mental illness index'.

In fact, it is the latter which has predominated historically as a basis of decision-making, and yet it is hard to see on what evidence the Glancy, Butler or Reed numbers (Reed, for example, suggested an estimate of 15 medium-security beds per million population) are supportable. Further, even if, as an average of figures across the country, a particular figure *can* be supported nationally, the lack of any recognition of the importance of differential morbidity across and within regions makes extrapolation from the national to the local level highly suspect, even when adjusted for any 'capitation mental illness index'. In practice, therefore, certainly the Glancy number was used as much as a political planning slogan as a rational planning aid, while the Reed report was rather coy, in a local needs-oriented world, about offering its national average figure at all.

A different sort of problem of comparison between methods arises when, for example, an attempt is made to use prison figures. Since good prison data are available only from *ad hoc* studies, and since even those data tend not to be available on a disaggregated

basis by NHS authority (district or region) some method of disaggregation is necessary. But how is the disaggregation to be done?
Clearly, disaggregation solely by population is inadequate. Even
using the capitation mental illness index is inadequate since it takes
no account of differential criminological morbidity. One approach
might be to assume that the distribution of special hospital patients
across the country by region is a valid proxy measure for the relative
forensic morbidities of regions for *all* levels of offending (not just
for the level which determines special hospital admission). This
proxy could be justified on the basis that, like angina, it is likely to
be distributed as regards its *severity* (rather than its frequency *per se*)
equally by regions (or districts) *and* that it can be assumed that a
high proportion of those who 'need' high security ultimately actually
get it. However, the method is likely to be invalidated by the effect
of differently available RSU and locked ward facilities between
regions, which must distort the ratios of special hospital patients
by region.

   The latter method of extrapolating from the national to the local
might, by dint of its simplicity and data availability, appear attractive
as a guide to determining a number of NHS service aspects. For
example, in assessing how many low-security beds a district needs,
at least in terms of comparison with *other* districts, the 'high-security
ratio' approach may be crudely sustainable. However, two further
problems exist. First, how is one to determine the *absolute* number
of beds required (rather than the comparative ratio against another
district)? Second, even if that problem could be overcome, the
required number of low-security beds, or (to some extent) any other
beds, depends upon the rest of the service range within which they
sit. Hence, an outreach service within community mental health
teams may, for example, limit the need for low-security beds, which
otherwise would be necessary for badly deteriorated patients (those
who have deteriorated through inadequate outreach). Similarly, a
commissioner may *decide* not to commission many low-security beds
but, rather, to rely upon (mis)use of medium-security beds by way
of a lower admission threshold. Overall, in fact, the further down
the MDO service pyramid (from high to low security), probably the
greater is the potential for more variable, yet still service valid, ratios
of service components between districts. Ultimately, what this
amounts to is that, at lower-security service levels, any notion of
norms or, indeed, any notion of 'need' as separate from the
definition of a particular sort of 'supply', becomes more tenuous.
Indeed, this conclusion will tend to hold even where social indicators are used to determine relative service needs between districts.
Put another way, the further down the service pyramid one gets,

the greater is the range of reasonable flexibility of service design and response, albeit there must be caution that commissioners do not use this principle as an alibi for only *pretending* to respond to MDO need (e.g. by arguing that an open ward can cope with low-security need because of 'special staffing' when there has been no demonstration that this is so).

Putting some of this back together, any needs assessor is likely to have to mix sources and types of information in making a judgement about the need for a particular type, or range, of MDO services. The sources may involve local utilisation data plus waiting list data, *modified* by local survey data, *modified further* by national special hospital data about patients ready to leave, extrapolated down to the district, and *modified yet further* by extrapolation of known (from *ad hoc* studies) national prison data, again somehow extrapolated to the district. Ultimately, what the assessor is then likely to end up with is two or more estimates, each of which may be represented as a 'range estimate'. It will then be in choosing the need level *within that range* that the needs assessor imposes his or her clear policy positions on the data.

A more technical problem which *must* be addressed is that of what level of bed occupancy to assume, or to plan for. Hence, if on any given patient data, there is a need for (say) 30 medium-security beds, in fact there is obviously a need for more than 30 beds, because more than one bed is needed to support one bed-needing MDO. This arises because, first, there is some average time delay between a discharge and an admission into the same bed and, second, there is a need for flexibility by way of availability of beds for remand assessment and emergency readmission purposes. Now, in fact, mainly because of the national shortage of medium-security beds, the occupancy rate for most services is near to 100%. However, that implies a need for more than that same number of beds. Not to apply some 'multiplier' must, in fact, automatically disadvantage certain classes of MDOs, that is, those requiring assessment and emergency readmission. It must, incidentally, also result in more admission errors against admission criteria, through lack of adequate remand assessment before admission, and in bed blocking.

Finally, yet a further problem relates to conditions where the boundary around need is particularly blurred or ambiguous. As already described, this arises most notably in relation to psychopathic disorder. Here, both the disorder and its 'treatability' or 'appropriateness for treatment' (in terms of the Mental Health Act 1983) are poorly defined and it is here too that the widest of 'range estimates' are likely to occur. Indeed, here a nihilistic attitude to rational commissioning almost seems the sensible approach. As already suggested, since need requires a definable and recognised beneficial intervention for it *to be* 'need', psychopathic disorder and needs assessment *per se* hardly seem to sit happily together at all.

In summary, as regards numbers and arithmetic, estimates can be built up from different sources, based on different methods, which will usually mix and modify both *met* and *unmet* need. Cross-validation will sometimes be possible for some aspects of the total assessment of need but sometimes it will not. However, ultimately the resource allocator will need to make a judgement about which figures to rely upon, or which point in a range estimate to rely upon, in determining his or her commissioning decisions. What is crucially important, however, is that, in making the choice, the commissioner is aware of not only the strengths and weaknesses of the available data *per se* but also the policy stances which are inherent to that choice.

Linking needs to services

This heading could introduce a whole book in itself. However, a number of simple points are worth summarising. First, as we have already described, need can sometimes be met in more than one way and that is increasingly justifiably the case the further down the MDO service pyramid one delves. Second, the type of need may itself dictate a particular level of service 'critical mass'. This is most obviously so in relation to long-term medium-security need, where the service, whether on its own or through combination with other services, requires a substantial intra-mural infrastructure. Third, the definition of an appropriate catchment area is often problematic, especially the further up the service pyramid one goes. In particular, although the Reed principle of placing patients as locally as possible will be a guiding factor, service critical mass will be another, and the more specialised the need to which the service responds the wider will the catchment area have to be in order to support a service of sufficient critical mass. This is so because the 'morbidity density' will tend to be less the more specialised is the need to which the service is responding (e.g. female, adolescent or learning-disabled MDOs). Fourth, the notion sometimes used by city planners of a catchment area defined by an 'isochrone', that is, a contour of equal travelling time, may be useful in defining a catchment area. However, the natural isochrone for a complete service on one site may be different for different components of that service (e.g. generic medium-security services against women's personality disorder services).

Before the Thatcher era of competition between health providers and reduction of the significance of NHS bureaucratic boundaries, catchment areas almost defined themselves. Indeed, the establishment of regional medium-secure units is obvious evidence of that in the MDO service context. However, greater fluidity of commissioning and provision resulted in the possibility of a more rational approach to defining catchment areas and service boundaries. Hence, it makes sense for purchasers, first, to combine with one another in order to commission services which have low morbidity density and, second, to spread commissioning across providers in a rational way which matches the spread of a variety of needs, even though ultimately it may still also be rational, for example, to commission generic 'medium-secure units plus outreach' services on a fairly constant model across the country. In fact, the 1997 White Paper specifically envisages medium-secure unit services being bought on a multi-district or regional level, and some services, for example high-security services, will always tend to be commissioned at a high level of commissioner aggregation.[54]

Of really crucial importance, however, is that commissioning should be required to be seamless between different service responses to the range of MDO need *and* based on the absence of any financial disincentives. Hence, commissioning tariffs should reflect provider costs, such that there are no free or cheap services to commissioners. Breaching the latter principle has been best exemplified in the past by effective national 'top-slicing' for high-security beds, with the effect that such a bed is 'free' to the district commissioner, who is theoretically financially responsible for the patient. This determines major distortions in responses to need. Indeed, removal of the disincentive to leave a patient in high security who does not need it, which will largely result from regional commissioning of high- and medium-security services together, will undoubtedly offer the basis for a major assault on the combined problem of inappropriate high-security utilisation and unmet need for long-term medium-security beds. It will also probably encourage, in a general way, greater integration of the special hospitals into the MDO service pyramid. However, there is a risk that the financial perverse incentive could merely be moved further down the pyramid to the interface between medium-security and general mental health care services.

The latter paragraph suggests another point. The DoH seems committed to greater vertical integration of the MDO service

---

[54] Currently all high-security commissioning is intended to be conducted by the regional specialist commissioning groups.

pyramid. Any such integration must be achieved, however, so as to include assessment of need. This *could* give rise to a new and different approach to 'regionalism' in MDO service provision. In particular, there could be ways of ensuring greater seamlessness between services and, therefore, fewer seams into which particular groups of MDOs might fall. Hence, the admission question about an MDO originating from a given region may properly *not* be 'Should we (a particular service, say medium-security) take this patient?' *but* 'Which of us (of all the secure services) should take this patient?' Just how such seamlessness might be achieved is less clear. However, it could obviously be approached on more than one level. For example, there could be a commitment not to design services with admission and operational criteria fault-lines between them. Additionally, there could be 'sectorisation' of (at least) high- and medium-security services so that, again, the choice would concern which element of the services should take the patient, based upon close working relationships between the relevant high- and medium-security teams. Alternatively, or additionally, the medium-security service for a region or sub-region could operate as a data repository for all regional patients at least down to medium-secure unit level and, perhaps, even lower down the system than that. Thus, there would be congruence of data and also agreement on a unified system (albeit this would probably be unworkable if it attempted to delve substantially into generic mental health services, where the MDO dilution effect becomes a major problem). Joint appointments (between high and medium security, or between medium and low security), or vertically integrated services *per se* down the whole of the specialist forensic portion of the MDO pyramid, could be another route. For example, 'forensic trusts' offering all levels of security for a range of patients could be a model worthy of some consideration,[55] although such trusts would tend to isolate MDOs from generic mental health care, which would cut across a core Reed principle.

The disadvantages of the latter proposal leads naturally to consideration of joint health and criminal justice commissioning. This is relevant particularly to the financial disincentive for district health commissioners to move MDOs from prison into the NHS. As already suggested, the DoH/Home Office argument in this arena tends to run like this. The Home Office states, "You, the district

---

[55] The government's intention to place all three high-secure hospitals into related local general mental health trusts represents a partial move in this direction, albeit most medium-security services will be in trusts not containing high-security services.

health authority, have already received capitation payment for any member of your population who happens to be in prison and so you are fortunate if you do not have to look after them while they are cared for in prison". The health authority replies, "Our budgets have been expended always in the knowledge that some members of our population are in prison and so it is unrealistic to expect us to take MDOs out of prison without the money following them". This seemingly unresolvable dispute (apparently carried on even at government department level) leads naturally to the suggestion of joint funding of MDO services *per se*, on a newly established basis. Such joint funding would also probably assist in minimising the 'culture conflict' between health and criminal justice, described earlier in the book, and encourage greater data congruence between the two. However, as with 'forensic trusts', although such joint funding would probably better secure services and funding for MDOs it would also probably isolate them more from the mainstream of mental health care. What this would amount to, therefore, would be cutting off the top of the pyramid from the rest of it and potentially creating greater barriers to moving some individual MDOs back into generic mental health care. The stark choice appears to be, therefore, between more efficient provision for some MDOs against less efficient provision for others. In any event, recent proposals for reform of prison health care with service provision from the NHS, still explicitly leave the funding and departmental responsibilities broadly as they are at present (Home Office/DoH, 1999).

Finally, it seems clear that, as the number of medium-security beds has expanded, so commissioners have become predictably ever more concerned about their total cost. That should encourage both good needs assessment *and* the use of explicit and rational admission criteria, which again emphasises the importance of an approach to needs assessment which is embedded in the clinical process and which, largely, is 'bottom-up' in nature. In a field of health care which tends, because of political forces, to be heavily 'needs led', rational assessment of need is crucially important. Equally important, though, are service definitions and quality. Yet, like outcome (see Chapter 7), these have received relatively little attention. Although detailed discussion of service definitions is beyond the scope of this book, it is within its scope to discuss the mapping of individual patient need on to particular existing, or planned, services. Perhaps the main point worth stressing in this context is the probable inappropriateness of determining the level of secure placement solely on the basis of security need, on the assumption that the mental health care provided by each level of

194 Assessing forensic mental health need

security is identical and, therefore, will properly respond to all the patient's mental health needs. This assumption is false. For example, a large high-security hospital has occupational and rehabilitation facilities far in excess of the average, much smaller, medium-secure unit. By contrast, the latter unit will likely be closer to the patient's home and so be able to offer more 'testing out' in the community, as well as other aspects of rehabilitation. If patients unequivocally require high security, because of the public risk they pose, then that clearly determines their proper placement (unless we are prepared to 'trade off' degrees of risk against other objectives of the patients' mental health care). However, where patients are deemed no longer to require high security, for some it may still be in their best therapeutic interests to continue to place them there if their mental health needs are better met there than in medium security. Hence, the large group of patients identified in the research papers described earlier in the book as no longer requiring high security may look significantly smaller if one takes into account their strictly defined mental health needs and the unavailability (or even impossibility) of providing for them in smaller, medium-secure units. This is not to argue illiberally for excess containment but, rather, to acknowledge that some mental health needs can only be met in larger and/or more centralised facilities, which, perforce, tend to be associated with higher security. There is, therefore, for the patient, a trade-off between optimal containment level and optimal meeting of his or her health needs. Only by designing secure services entirely differently in this country, placing different levels of security on one site, could such a trade-off be avoided, at least for some patients.

Another and more technical way of looking at placement decisions is to suggest that they should be mapped, on a 'best fit' basis, on to existing service definitions. Hence, a judgement would be taken on the basis of a matrix of defined needs where security was just one such need. This would mirror the way in which cost-benefit analysis is used in policy decision-making. The numbers do not determine the decision but, rather, they ground the decision. For some patients even political pressure will properly override other considerations. For others, a 'trade-off' between benefits of different types will be struck, that is, a judgement will be made on the 'need matrix'. Hence, for example, a particular score on ACSeSS would not determine, or even imply, a particular security placement but, rather, would represent one cell in the matrix. Security need, however measured, would then be considered in conjunction with all the other domains of need, represented in the other cells of the matrix, and a judgement made on the matrix as a whole.

The politics of needs assessment

The latter discussion brings us back to the main argument of the book; that is, that needs assessment, and its use in resource allocation, is an inherently value-laden and, ultimately, political activity. As we have said, what need you decide to measure, and how, is determined by what you value, or at least it indicates what you value. Indeed, most obviously, deciding to commission services in the *absence* of any needs assessment is the ultimate value judgement; that is, commissioning on the basis of hunch or, more probably, perceived political imperative.

It is also important to recognise that particular public policy measures can imply a particular view of need. Indeed, they can even set up a service response irrespective of reference to needs assessment. That is, they can by-pass the needs assessment process, perhaps even without it being noticed that they have done so. This can even apply to legal measures. For example, the introduction of 'supervised discharge orders' in the Mental Health (Patients in the Community) Act 1995 set a particular service priority by virtue of the criteria laid down for its imposition (Eastman, 1997c). Such an order also exerts influences by virtue of its terms once it is in place, albeit these are then expressed as an individualised response to the needs of a particular patient through a care plan. Supervision registers can be seen in a similar vein. And certainly any passage into law of some form of 'community treatment order' would also imply its own perspective on need, and of the appropriate service response to it. Indeed, the raft of legal and administrative measures introduced in the government's 'ten-point plan' (DoH, 1993b) set the terms of very particular service responses to need for all mentally disordered people, by virtue of their emphasis on the severely mentally ill and on risk to self and others. Even the mandating of full external inquiries after homicides by psychiatric patients (DoH, 1991) must exert a subtle influence on which needs are afforded service responses.

The automatic stipulation of need and service response arising from legal measures is modified somewhat by the fact that mental health care law can, within the bounds of negligence law, be picked up or discarded by clinicians as they think clinically fit. Indeed, such law is peculiar in that it is 'law without enforcement' (Eastman & Peay, 1999), inasmuch as the clinician has discretion in its use. It may be said, therefore, that the clinician can customise its use according to individual patient need. However, the criteria determining when it can be invoked do set restrictions on the circumstances in which need can be responded to and, even once invoked, its terms set limits on what responses to which needs can be buttressed by its use.

This leads to another point which concerns not the clinical needs of patients but their civil liberty needs. Perhaps in the same way that we can define a person's clinical state in terms of QALYs, we can also think of 'liberty-adjusted life-years', or LALYs (Eastman & Peay, 1999). This notion links naturally with the method of analysis of cost-benefit or cost-utility analysis dealt with earlier in the book in relation to needs.[56] Hence, in determining 'outcome' it may be proper not only to consider patients' clinical or living state but also their 'liberty state'. This sets up a perspective which can be in natural tension with the needs of the public for protection, since it is patients' right to liberty which is infringed by any imposition of treatment or care on them that is driven by the needs of the public for protection. This perspective, in turn, emphasises the hugely important ethical perspective which must properly be applied to all needs assessment. Any tool which purports both to define need and then to allocate resources accordingly sits firmly within the realms of welfare economics, and that branch of economics is itself profoundly ethical both in what underpins it and in its expression.

Perhaps a more obvious illustration of this domain is offered by the introduction of the 'hospital and limitation direction' in the Crime (Sentences) Act 1997. This is a criminal court disposal which hybridises punishment and mental health care, and it expresses its own perspective on both justice and MDO need, as well as on the need of the public to be protected from the MDO. It is also an order which, if it were to be used widely, would have major implications not just for patients and for the service response to their needs but also for the services and service staff themselves (Eastman, 1997d). Indeed, it is an order which has, built within it, the requirement that a health commissioning authority will commonly have to continue commissioning a level of mental health care for a patient who is acknowledged no longer to require it. This will arise where the patient is treated on a hospital and limitation direction in (say) a medium-secure unit in a hospital and who then is ready clinically for discharge to community care. However, if the patient's penal sentence still has time to run then the clinicians will be able only either to continue with that patient's care in hospital (which is not needed) or to return the patient to prison (where the care may not be adequate to meet any residual needs). Given that clinicians may,

---

[55] See Eastman & Peay (1999) for a full discussion of the economic analysis of liberty.

in those circumstances, take the ethical decision to keep the patient in hospital, the commissioning authority will then be left funding an MDO not for health care but solely for custody (Eastman, 1997*d*). This illustration again emphasises the problems that arise from budgets for MDOs being separated between the DoH and the Home Office. As already suggested, there is much in favour of joint health–justice commissioning. However, this ignores another ethical dimension which, in one sense, bedevils MDO care at both a macro and a micro level, namely, the problem of confidentiality. Hence, within a health care model a patient properly has the right to confidentiality of clinical data except where there is a substantial risk of serious harm to others. Yet, at this individual MDO level, a maximally efficient response to need would require that there are no barriers to data transfer. Putting the ethics another way, of course, would result in the conclusion that patient confidentiality is more important than patient need. Or, at least, that patients' consent to breach of confidentiality is more important than their health needs. MDOs should, essentially, make their own choice on the matter.

The future of MDO services

In the last 25 years, forensic mental health services have gone through a period of major growth and development. From a time when the Butler and Glancy reports identified major gaps in secure service provision, and when forensic mental health care was almost synonymous with prison and special hospital care, there has been a relative burgeoning of a far more comprehensive range of services. This has centred on the building of medium-secure units but has gone much beyond it. There is, therefore, much interest not only in developing long-term medium-security care but also forensic low-security care, community forensic care, consultation-liaison roles for specialist forensic clinicians with general mental health care teams, specialist sex offender services and, for some, specialist personality disorder services. This represents making forensic mental health services even more comprehensive, both by covering all levels of secure and community service need and by addressing specialist needs. The effect of the former is, of course, to initiate a debate about 'integration' and 'parallelism'. For some, there will have to be provision of specialist forensic care at all levels of security and within the community, including for example the provision of specialist MDO hostels. Others will still hold to the principle, perhaps even espoused partly by Reed, that the ultimate aim of such specialist care is to return the MDO to general mental health care.

Probably the fully integrated approach is impossible in practice and there will always be some MDOs who require long-term forensic care, even in the community. Indeed, it might be expected that more rather than less specialist expertise would be required to care for an MDO with a history of serious offending and complex psychopathology in the community than in hospital. However, the danger of parallelism is that forensic services will grow too much and that they will often respond to needs that can, and should, properly be responded to by general services. This is particularly a danger in a service context where the number of general mental health care beds is dwindling and where general community mental health care teams are relatively poorly resourced, particularly compared with specialist forensic services. This further emphasises the need for rigorous needs assessment, as well as the importance of clear service definitions. So, integration should be taken (only) to its (proper) limits.

Integration must also include the specialist forensic services themselves. The continued cultural isolation of the special hospitals, which are still indeed 'special', is damaging for both patients and staff. It also runs counter to rational service provision and to the proper meeting of needs. This agenda goes much further, however, than a crude one of emptying the special hospitals of all the patients who do not need to be there. Rather, it requires full service integration. This will be helped by the establishment of regional specialist commissioning of medium- and high-security services together, but will be facilitatory rather than representing a solution in itself. It will abolish the perverse financial incentive to leave patients inappropriately in high security but will not, of itself, achieve service integration. The government has already put in place the necessary legal provisions to allow the special hospitals to become part of ordinary NHS trusts and, clearly, there is a political will to pursue integration. However, if these hospitals are not to be made substantially smaller and if high-security care is not to be made more local through greater numbers of smaller units, then it will take political will and nerve to stick to the integration agenda. In the face of major adverse publicity and inquiries into these hospitals, government has always continued to treat them *as* 'special'. Indeed, 'government' has often meant as much the Home Office as the DoH and there has appeared always to be a political imperative to make special the services that deal with special (and often politically high-profile) patients. However, the number of such patients is very small and their effect disproportionately distorting of policy. Also, making high-security hospitals special is ultimately self-defeating, since the effect is almost wholly negative in terms of staffing and staff morale.

Finally, the most difficult policy trick of all will be to achieve the integration of all specialist forensic services without emphasising their separation from general services and merely re-creating a similar type of barrier to that which Butler, Glancy and Reed all tried to break down.

Another and related danger for the future is that forensic care more generally will continue to dominate the public and political agenda. MDOs represent a small proportion of all mental health need and yet, for at least the last decade, they have driven the political mental health agenda. The forensic tail has definitely wagged the general dog. This is unhealthy, both for services and for mature public and political debate. There is a cascade effect whereby the most dangerous contaminate the care of even the least dangerous. Again, it will take political nerve to lead a mature and informed approach to policy development.

But there is yet another item on the MDO policy agenda that is already upon us. Again, it derives from a particular MDO group. The government's proposals for services for those with 'severe personality disorder' who present a 'grave danger' are both novel and radical in forensic service terms (Home Office/DoH, 1999). As already described in this chapter, they involve not only indeterminate and reviewable sentences but also reviewable and potentially indeterminate civil orders, together with (in so-called 'Option B') the creation of special personality disorder units that would take both 'prisoners' and 'patients'. These proposals are radical both because they would sometimes allow indeterminate preventive detention based on professional risk assessment in the absence of current or past serious offending *and* because they would allow detention of such 'patients' even if they were deemed 'untreatable'. Whichever of the government's two service options is chosen (Option A involves placing people with DSPD either in prison or in hospital units), caring for some such MDOs in circumstances where there is documented therapeutic and justified nihilism will challenge the morale of even the most dedicated mental health professional. Albeit the government has also announced its intention to put substantial service and research resources into such services, which may offer the advancement of knowledge and of therapeutic techniques, that cannot abolish the morale problem. If the high-security hospitals have in the past been 'special', then surely the new services for prisoner-patients with dangerous serious personality disorder will also be so.

The government's new proposals for DSPD represent a shift not only in service thinking but also in psychiatric jurisprudence. This bears a natural relationship to techniques of risk assessment and, therefore, to a particular aspect of needs assessment. Legislating for either indeterminate and reviewable sentences or orders implies that 'adequate' risk assessment is possible. But 'adequate' hides both ethical and service dimensions. The greater is the mismatch between 'real risk' and 'assessed risk' and the lower is the threshold for determining 'sufficient risk', (for indeterminate detention), the greater will be the number of false positive findings. This has ethical implications, in terms of how many 'innocent people' (or rather, non-dangerous people) will be locked up to achieve a given degree of public safety. However, it also has service and cost implications, since more false positive assessments not only have a negative civil rights impact but must also result in substantial unnecessary expenditure on secure services that are not needed.

The mid-1970s offered excitement of a pioneering type, with service champions carving out new regional forensic patches. The new millennium offers very different challenges. The work of those early product champions established in the UK a substantial forensic mental health care system that, while in need of refinement and integration, represents a huge advance on earlier times. However, a second-order challenge is emerging for the second generation of service and academic leaders. It is represented by the question, 'What are forensic mental health services *for*?' That is, 'What is the social role and definition of such services?' Put in the language of this book, 'Whose needs do they address?'

References

ACORN (1986) *An Allowance for Social Factors in RAWP*. Bexhill-on-Sea: South East Thames Regional Health Authority.

ANDERSON, J. B. & PARROTT, J. (1995) Urgent psychiatric transfers from prison in England and Wales: a prison perspective. *Criminal Behaviour and Mental Health*, **5**, 34–40.

ATKISSON, C., COOK, J., KARNO, M., *et al* (1992) Clinical services research. *Schizophrenia Bulletin*, **18**(4), 561–626.

BAILEY, J. & MACCULLOCH, M. J. (1992*a*) Characteristics of 112 cases discharged directly to the community from a new special hospital and some comparisons of performance. *Journal of Forensic Psychiatry*, **3**, 91–112.

—— & —— (1992*b*) Patterns of reconviction in patients discharged directly to the community from a special hospital: implications for aftercare. *Journal of Forensic Psychiatry*, **3**(3), 445–462.

—— & —— (1993) Judgements of dangerousness and release decisions in special hospitals. In *Rights and Risks: The Application of Forensic Psychology* (eds N. K. Clark & G. M. Stephenson), pp. 76–83. Leicester: British Psychological Society.

BALDWIN, S. (1986) Problems with needs – where theory meets practice. *Disability, Handicap and Society*, **1**(2), 139–145.

BANERJEE, S., O'NEILL-BYRNE, K., EXWORTHY, T., *et al* (1995) The Belmarsh Scheme: a prospective study of the transfer of mentally disordered remand prisoners from prison to psychiatric units. *British Journal of Psychiatry*, **166**, 802–805.

BANKS, C. (1978) *A Survey of the South East Prison Population* (Research Bulletin No. 5). London: Home Office Research Unit.

BARKER, D. A., SHERGILL, S. S., HIGGINSON, I., *et al* (1996) Patients' views towards care received from psychiatrists. *British Journal of Psychiatry*, **168**, 641–646.

BARTLETT, A. (1993) Rhetoric and reality: what do we know about the English special hospitals? *International Journal of Law and Psychiatry*, **16**, 27–51.

——, COHEN, A., BACKHOUSE, A., *et al* (1996) Security needs of South West Thames Special Hospital patients: 1992 and 1993. No way out? *Journal of Forensic Psychiatry*, **7**(2), 256–270.

BEBBINGTON, P. E. (1992) Assessing the need for psychiatric treatment at the district level: the role of surveys. In *Measuring Mental Health Needs* (eds G. Thornicroft, C. Brewin & J. Wing), pp. 99–117. London: Gaskell.

BEECHAM, J. & CHISHOLM, D. (1995) Mental health economics. In *Measurement for Mental Health: Contributions from the College Research Unit* (ed. J. K. Wing), pp. 55–65. London: College Research Unit, Royal College of Psychiatrists.

—— & KNAPP, M. (1992) Costing psychiatric interventions. In *Measuring Mental Health Needs* (eds G. Thornicroft, C. Brewin & J. Wing), pp. 163–183. London: Gaskell.

BELL, R. A., GOLDSMITH, H. F. & LIN, E. (1988) A clinician's perspective on the measurement of the need for mental health services: complete or incomplete, right or wrong. In *Needs*

Assessment: Its Future (ADM 88–1550) (ed. H. F. Goldsmith), pp. 17–21. Washington, DC: US Government Printing Office.

BERWICK, D. M. (1989) Health service research and quality of care: assignments for the 1990s. *Medical Care,* **27,** 763–771.

BEVERIDGE, W. (1942) *Social Insurance and Allied Services.* London: HMSO.

BIRMINGHAM, L., MASON, D. & GRUBIN, D. (1996) Prevalence of mental disorder in remand prisoners: consecutive case study. *British Medical Journal,* **313,** 1521–1524.

BLOM-COOPER, L., BROWN, M., DOLAN, R., *et al* (1992) *Report of the Committee of Inquiry into Complaints about Ashworth Hospital* (Cm 2028-I). London: HMSO.

BLOOM, B. L., GOLDSMITH, H. F. & LIN, E. (1988) Indirect indicators of need. In *Needs Assessment: Its Future* (ADM 88–1550) (ed. H. F. Goldsmith), pp. 25–32. Washington, DC: US Government Printing Office.

BLUGLASS, R. (1978) Regional secure units and interim security for psychiatric patients. *British Medical Journal, i,* 489–493.

—— (1985) The development of regional secure units. In *Secure Provision: A Review of Services for the Mentally Ill and Mentally Handicapped in England and Wales* (ed. L. Gostin), pp. 153–175. London: Tavistock.

—— (1992) The special hospitals should be closed. *British Medical Journal,* **305,** 323–324.

—— & BOWDEN, P. (1990) *Principles and Practice of Forensic Psychiatry.* London: Churchill Livingstone.

BOWLING, A. (1992) Assessing health needs and measuring patient satisfaction. *Nursing Times,* **88**(31), 31–34.

BRABBINS, C. J. & TRAVERS, R. F. (1994) Mental disorder amongst defendants in Liverpool magistrates' court. *Medicine, Science and the Law,* **34**(4), 279–283.

BRADSHAW, J. S. (1972) A taxonomy of social need. In *Problems and Progress in Medical Care: Essays on Current Research (7th series)* (ed. G. McLachlan). London: Oxford University Press.

BREWIN, C. & WING, J. K. (1989) *MRC Needs for Care Assessment: Manual for Version Two/2.* London: Institute of Psychiatry.

BROOKE, D., TAYLOR, C., GUNN, J., *et al* (1996) Point prevalence of mental disorder in unconvicted male prisoners in England and Wales. *British Medical Journal,* **313,** 1524–1527.

BROWN, P., MCKENNA, J. & TOMENSON, B. (1996) Waiting for a bed at a regional secure unit. *Journal of Forensic Psychiatry,* **7**(3), 634–640.

BRUGHA, T. S., WING, J. K., BREWIN, C., *et al* (1988) The problems of people in long-term psychiatric day care: an introduction of the Camberwell High Contact Survey. *Psychological Medicine,* **18,** 443–456.

—— & LINDSAY, F. (1996) Quality of mental health service care: the forgotten pathway from process to outcome. In *Mental Health Outcome Measures* (eds G. Thornicroft & M. Tansella), pp. 93–109. Heidelberg: Springer-Verlag.

BUTLER, J. (1992) *Patients, Policies and Politics: Before and After 'Working for Patients'.* Buckingham: Open University Press.

BYNOE, I. (1990) Rampton revisited. *Open Mind,* **45,** 4.

—— (1992) *Treatment, Care and Security. Waiting for Change.* London: MIND.

CAGLE, L. T. & BANKS, S. M. (1986) The validity of assessing mental health needs with social indicators. *Evaluation and Program Planning,* **9,** 127–142.

CALDICOTT, F. (1994) Supervision registers: the College's response, and reply from Mrs Bottomley. *Psychiatric Bulletin,* **18,** 385–388.

CALMAN, K. C. (1995) Letter to the Editor. *British Medical Journal,* **310,** 1530.

CARR-HILL, R. A., SHELDON, T. A., SMITH, P., *et al* (1994) Allocating resources to health authorities: development of method for small area analysis of use of inpatient services. *British Medical Journal,* **309,** 1046–1049.

CIARLO, J. A. & TWEED, D. L. (1992) VI. Implementing indirect needs-assessment models for planning state mental health and substance abuse services. *Evaluation and Program Planning,* **15,** 195–210.

—, SHERN, D. L., TWEED, D. L., *et al* (1992*a*) II. The Colorado social health survey of mental health service needs: sampling, instrumentation, and major findings. *Evaluation and Program Planning*, **15**, 133–147.

—, TWEED, D. L., SHERN, D. L., *et al* (1992*b*) I. Validation of indirect methods to estimate need for mental health services: concepts, strategy and general conclusions. *Evaluation and Program Planning*, **15**, 115–131.

CLIFFORD, P., CHARMAN, A., WEBB, Y., *et al* (1991*a*) Planning for community care: the Community Placement Questionnaire. *British Journal of Clinical Psychology*, **30**, 193–211.

—, —, —, *et al* (1991*b*) Planning for community care: long-stay populations of hospitals scheduled for rundown or closure. *British Journal of Psychiatry*, **158**, 190–196.

COHEN, A. & EASTMAN, N. (1996) *A Study of the Feasibility of a Standardised Minimum Data Set for Forensic Psychiatry Services and a Standardised Approach to Needs Assessment in South Thames Region* (Report to Health Authorities of South Thames (West) Region). London: Section of Forensic Psychiatry, St George's Hospital Medical School.

COID, J. (1988) Mentally abnormal offenders on remand. I. Rejected or accepted by the NHS? II. Comparison of services by Oxford and Wessex Regions. *British Medical Journal*, **153**, 635–644.

— (1991*a*) 'Difficult to place' psychiatric patients. *British Medical Journal*, **202**, 603–604.

— (1991*b*) A survey of patients from five health districts receiving special care in the private sector. *Psychiatric Bulletin*, **15**, 257–262.

— (1993*a*) *A Survey of Occupancy in Medium Security, 21st November, 1993* (discussion paper for the Department of Health, 21.12.93). London: Department of Forensic Psychiatry, Hackney Hospital.

— (1993*b*) Quality of life for patients detained in hospital. *British Journal of Psychiatry*, **162**, 611–620.

COMMANDER, M. J., SASHI DHARAN, S. P., ODELL, S. M., *et al* (1997) Access to mental health care in an inner-city health district. I: Pathways into and within specialist psychiatric services. *British Journal of Psychiatry*, **170**, 312–316.

COPE, R. (1993) A survey of forensic psychiatrists' views on psychopathic disorder. *Journal of Forensic Psychiatry*, **4**(2), 215–235.

— & NDEGWA, D. (1991) Ethnic differences in admission to a regional secure unit. *Journal of Forensic Psychiatry*, **1**, 365–378.

— & WARD, M. (1993) What happens to special hospital patients admitted to medium security? *Journal of Forensic Psychiatry*, **4**(1), 13–24.

CORRIGAN, P. W. (1990) Consumer satisfaction with institutional and community care. *Community Mental Health Journal*, **26**(2), 151–165.

COTGROVE, A. J., BELL, G. & KATONA, C. L. (1992) Psychiatric admissions and social deprivation: is Jarman underprivileged area score relevant? *Journal of Epidemiology and Community Health*, **46**, 245–247.

COURTNEY, P., O'GRADY, J. & CUNNANE, J. (1992) The provision of secure psychiatric services in Leeds. Paper II: A survey of unmet need. *Health Trends*, **24**(2), 51–53.

CRIPPS, J., DUFFIELD, G. & JAMES, D. (1995) Bridging the gap in secure provision: evaluation of a new local combined locked forensic/intensive care unit. *Journal of Forensic Psychiatry*, **6**(1), 77–91.

CROWN, J. (1991) Needs assessment. *British Journal of Hospital Medicine*, **46**, 307–308.

DE GRAAF, V. (1967) *Theoretical Welfare Economics*. London: Cambridge University Press.

DELL, S. (1980) Transfer of special hospital patients to the NHS. *British Journal of Psychiatry*, **136**, 222–234.

— & ROBERTSON, G. (1988) *Sentenced to Hospital*. Oxford: Oxford University Press.

—, —, JAMES, K., *et al* (1993*a*) Remands and psychiatric assessments in Holloway Prison. I: The psychotic population. *British Journal of Psychiatry*, **163**, 634–640.

—, —, —, *et al* (1993*b*) Remands and psychiatric assessments in Holloway Prison. II: The non–psychotic population. *British Journal of Psychiatry*, **163**, 640–644.

204   References

DEPARTMENT OF THE ENVIRONMENT (1983) *Urban Deprivation. London: Inner Cities Directorate* (Information Note No. 2). London: Department of the Environment.

DEPARTMENT OF HEALTH (1989a) *Caring for People: Community Care in the Next Decade and Beyond* (Cm. 849). London: HMSO.

—— (1989b) *Working for Patients* (Cm. 555). London: HMSO.

—— (1990) '*Caring for People*'. *The Care Programme Approach for People with a Mental Illness Referred to the Specialist Psychiatric Services* (HC(90)23/LASSL(90)11). London: Department of Health.

—— (1991) *Stephen Dorrell Announces Inquiry into Homicides Committed by Discharged Psychiatric Patients* (H91/498). London: Department of Health.

—— (1992a) *The Health of the Nation* (Cm 1986). London: HMSO.

—— (1992b) *Press Notice H92/38* (27 January 1992).

—— (1993a) *Legal Powers on the Care of Mentally Ill People in the Community: Report of the Internal Review.* London: Department of Health.

—— (1993b) *Legislation Planned to Provide Supervised Discharge of Psychiatric Patients* (press release H93/908). London: Department of Health.

—— (1993c) *Health of the Nation Key Area Handbook: Mental Illness.* London: HMSO.

—— (1995) *The Health of the Nation: Building Bridges – A Guide to Arrangements for Inter-agency Working for the Care and Protection of Severely Mentally Ill People.* London: HMSO.

—— (1996) *Health of the Nation: The Spectrum of Care – Local Services for People with Mental Health Problems.* London: HMSO.

—— (1997) *The New NHS: Modern, Dependable.* London: HMSO.

DEPARTMENT OF HEALTH/HOME OFFICE (1992) *Review of Health and Social Services for Mentally Disordered Offenders and Others Requiring Similar Services: Final Summary Report* (Reed report) (Cm 2088). London: HMSO.

—— (1993a) *Review of Health and Social Services for Mentally Disordered Offenders and Others Requiring Similar Services. Vol. 2. Service Needs: The Reports of the Community, Hospital and Prison Advisory Groups and an Overview by the Steering Committee.* London: HMSO.

—— (1993b) *Review of Health and Social Services for Mentally Disordered Offenders and Others Requiring Similar Services. Vol. 3. Finance, Staffing and Training: The Reports of the Finance and Staffing and Training Advisory Groups.* London: HMSO.

—— (1993c) *Review of Health and Social Services for Mentally Disordered Offenders and Others Requiring Similar Services. Vol. 4. The Academic and Research Base: The Reports of the Academic Development and Research Advisory Groups.* London: HMSO.

—— (1993d) *Review of Health and Social Services for Mentally Disordered Offenders and Others Requiring Similar Services. Vol. 5. Special Issues and Differing Needs: The Reports of the Official Working Group on Services for People with Special Needs.* London: HMSO.

—— (1994a) *Review of Health and Social Services for Mentally Disordered Offenders and Others Requiring Similar Services. Vol. 7. People with Learning Disabilities (Mental Handicap) or with Autism.* London: HMSO.

—— (1994b) *Review of Health and Social Services for Mentally Disordered Offenders and Others Requiring Similar Services. Vol. 6. Race, Gender and Equal Opportunities.* London: HMSO.

—— (1994c) *Report of the Department of Health and Home Office Working Group on Psychopathic Disorder.* London: Department of Health/Home Office.

—— (1994d) *Report of the Working Group on High Security and Related Psychiatric Provision.* London: Department of Health.

DEPARTMENT OF HEALTH AND SOCIAL SECURITY (1971) *Hospital Services for the Mentally Ill.* DHSS memorandum, December.

—— (1974a) *Revised Report of the Working Party on Security in NHS Psychiatric Hospitals* (Glancy report). London: HMSO.

—— (1974b) *Security in NHS Hospitals for the Mentally Ill and the Mentally Handicapped* (HSC(15)61). London: HMSO.

—— (1976) *Sharing Resources for Health in England. Report of the Resource Allocation Working Party.* London: HMSO.

—— (1988) *Review of Resource Allocation Working Party Formula. Final Report by the Management Board.* London: DHSS.

DILLNER, L. (1992) Special hospitals under review. *British Medical Journal,* 305, 334.

DINITZ, S. & CONRAD, J. P. (1978) Thinking about dangerous offenders. *Criminal Justice Abstracts,* 10, 99–130.

DOHRENWEND, B. & DOHRENWEND, B. (1969) *Social Status and Psychological Disorder: A Causal Enquiry.* New York: Wiley.

DOLAN, B. & COID, J. (1993) *Psychopathic Disorder and Antisocial Personality Disorders.* London: Gaskell.

DOLAN, M., COOREY, P. & KULUPANA, S. (1993) An audit of recalls to a special hospital. *Journal of Forensic Psychiatry,* 4(2), 249–260.

—— & SHETTY, G. C. (1995) Transfer delays in a special hospitals population. *Medicine, Science and the Law,* 35, 237–244.

DONABEDIAN, A. (1980) *Explorations in Quality Assessment and Monitoring: The Definition of Quality and Approaches to its Assessment.* Ann Arbor, MI: Health Administration Press.

DONALDSON, C. & MOONEY, G. (1991) Needs assessment, priority setting, and contracts for health care: an economic view. *British Medical Journal,* 303, 1529–1530.

DOOLEY, E. (1990) Prison suicide in England and Wales, 1972–87. *British Journal of Psychiatry,* 156, 40–45.

EASTMAN, N. L. G. (1993) Forensic psychiatric services in Britain: a current review. *International Journal of Law and Psychiatry,* 16, 1–26.

—— (1995) Anti-therapeutic community mental health law. *British Medical Journal,* 310, 1081–1082.

—— (1996a) Hybrid orders: an analysis of their likely effects on sentencing practice and on forensic psychiatric practice. *Journal of Forensic Psychiatry,* 7(3), 481–494.

—— (1996b) Inquiry into homicides by psychiatric patients: systematic audit should replace mandatory inquiries. *British Medical Journal,* 313, 1069–1071.

—— (1996c) Towards an audit of inquiries: enquiry not inquiries. In *Inquiries after Homicide* (ed. J. Peay), pp. 147–172. London: Duckworth.

—— (1997a) Hybrid justice: proposals for the mentally disordered in the Crime (Sentences) Bill: the ethical, legal and health service cost implications. *Psychiatric Bulletin,* 21(3), 129–131.

—— (1997b) Psychopathic disorder and therapeutic jurisprudence. In *Challenges in Forensic Psychotherapy* (ed. H. van Marle), pp. 89–94. London: Jessica Kingsley.

—— (1997c) The Mental Health (Patients in the Community) Act 1995. A clinical analysis. *British Journal of Psychiatry,* 170, 492–496.

—— (1997d) Hybrid orders: an analysis of their likely effects on sentencing practice and on forensic psychiatric practice and services. *Journal of Forensic Psychiatry,* 7(3), 481–494.

—— & BELLAMY, S. (1998) Admission criteria to secure psychiatric care: the AcSeSS Schedule (unpublished paper for South Thames Regional Office of NHS Executive and High Security Psychiatric Services Commissioning Board). London: St George's Hospital Medical School.

—— & PEAY, J. (1998) Sentencing psychopaths: is the 'Hospital and Limitation Direction' an ill-considered hybrid? *Criminal Law Review,* February, 93–108.

—— & —— (1999) Afterword: Integrating mental health and justice. In *Law Without Enforcement: Integrating Mental Health and Justice* (eds N. Eastman & J. Peay), pp. 197–218. Oxford: Hart Publishing.

EXWORTHY, T. & PARROTT, J. (1993) Evaluation of a diversion from custody scheme at magistrates' courts. *Journal of Forensic Psychiatry,* 4(3), 498–505.

FALLON, P., BLUGLASS, R., EDWARDS, B., *et al* (1999) *Report of the Committee of Inquiry into the Personality Disorder Unit, Ashworth Special Hospital* (Cm. 4195). London: HMSO.

FARIS, R. E. L. & DUNHAM, H. W. (1939) *Mental Disorders in Urban Areas.* Chicago, IL: Hafner.

FAULK, M. & TAYLOR, J. C. (1986) Psychiatric interim regional secure unit: seven years' experience. *Medicine, Science and the Law*, **26**, 17–22.

FENNELL, P. (1996) *Treatment Without Consent: Law, Psychiatry and the Treatment of the Mentally Disordered Since 1845.* London: Routledge.

FERGUSON, B. & TYRER, P. (1989) Rating instruments in psychiatric research. In *Research Methods in Psychiatry* (eds C. Freeman & P. Tyrer), pp. 148–175. London: Gaskell.

FORD, J., YOUNG, D., PEREZ, B. C., *et al* (1992) Needs assessment for persons with severe mental illness: what services are needed for successful community living? *Community Mental Health Journal*, **28**(6), 491–503.

FOSTER, K., MELTZER, H. & HINDS, K. (1996) *Adults with a Psychotic Disorder Living in the Community* (OPCS Surveys of Psychiatric Morbidity in Great Britain, Report 8). London: HMSO.

FRYERS, T. (1979) Estimation of need on the basis of case register studies: British case register data. In *Estimating Needs for Mental Health Care: A Contribution of Epidemiology* (ed. H. Häfner), pp. 52–63. New York: Springer-Verlag.

—— & GREATOREX, I. (1992) Case registers and mental health information systems. In *Measuring Mental Health Needs* (eds G. Thornicroft, C. Brewin & J. Wing), pp. 81–98. London: Gaskell.

GALLWEY, P. L. G. (1990) The development of a district-based psychiatric service for difficult and offender patients. *Journal of Forensic Psychiatry*, **1**, 53–71.

GILL, B., MELTZER, H., HINDS, K., *et al* (1996) *Psychiatric Morbidity among Homeless People* (OPCS Survey of Psychiatric Morbidity in Great Britain, Report 7). London: HMSO.

GLOVER, G. R. (1990) The official data available on mental health. In *Indicators for Mental Health in the Population* (eds R. Jenkins & S. Griffiths), pp. 18–24. London: HMSO.

—— (1996) The Mental Illness Needs Index (MINI). In *Commissioning Mental Health Services* (eds G. Thornicroft & G. Strathdee), pp. 53–57. London: HMSO.

—— & KAMIS-GOULD, E. (1996) Performance indicators in mental health services. In *Commissioning Mental Health Services* (eds G. Thornicroft & G. Strathdee), pp. 265–272. London: HMSO.

——, ROBIN, E., EMAMI, J., *et al* (1994) *The Distribution of Need for Mental Health Services: A Study of the Sociodemographic Predictors of Prevalence of Psychiatric Hospital Admission in a London Region.* London: Department of Health.

GOFFMAN, E. (1961) *Asylums.* New York: Doubleday.

GOLDBERG, D. (1990) Filters to care – a model. In *Indicators for Mental Health in the Population* (eds R. Jenkins & S. Griffiths), pp. 30–37. London: HMSO.

—— & HUXLEY, P. (1980) *Mental Illness in the Community: The Pathway to Psychiatric Care.* London: Tavistock.

GOODMAN, A. B., SIEGAL, C., CRAIG, T., *et al* (1983) The relationship between socio-economic class and prevalence of schizophrenia, alcoholism and affective disorders treated by inpatient care in a suburban area. *American Journal of Psychiatry*, **140**, 166–170.

—— & HAUGLAND, G. (1994) Mental health service needs assessment. *Administration and Policy in Mental Health*, **21**(3), 173–197.

GREENHALGH, N. M., WYLIE, K., RIX, K. J. B., *et al* (1996) Pilot mental health and assessment scheme for an English metropolitan petty sessional division. *Medicine, Science and the Law*, **36**(1), 52–58.

GREENLAND, C. (1978) The prediction and management of violent behavior: social policy issues. *International Journal of Law and Psychiatry*, **1**, 205–222.

GRIFFITHS, R. (1988) *Community Care. Agenda for Action.* London: HMSO.

GROUNDS, A., SNOWDEN, P. & TAYLOR, P. J. (1993) Forensic psychiatry in the National Health Service of England and Wales. In *Forensic Psychiatry: Clinical, Legal and Ethical Issues* (eds J. Gunn & P. J. Taylor), pp. 691–731. Oxford: Butterworth-Heinemann.

GUDJONSSON, G. H. & MACKEITH, J. A. C. (1983) A regional interim secure unit at the Bethlem Royal Hospital – the first fourteen months. *Medicine, Science and the Law*, **23**(3), 209–219.

References 207

GULEVICH, G. D. & BOURNE, P. G. (1970) Mental illness and violence. In *Violence and the Struggle for Existence* (eds D. N. Daniels, M. F. Gilula & F. M. Ochberg). Boston: Little, Brown & Co.

GUNN, J., ROBERTSON, G., DELL, S., *et al* (1978) *Psychiatric Aspects of Imprisonment*. London: Academic Press.

——, MADEN, T. & SWINTON, M. (1991*a*) Treatment needs of prisoners with psychiatric disorders. *British Medical Journal*, **303**, 338–341.

——, —— & —— (1991*b*) *Mentally Disordered Prisoners*. London: Home Office.

—— & TAYLOR, P. J. (1993) *Forensic Psychiatry: Clinical, Legal and Ethical Issues*. Oxford: Butterworth-Heinemann.

HÄFNER, H. (1979) Estimation of needs by epidemiological instruments. In *Estimating Needs for Mental Health Care: A Contribution of Epidemiology* (ed. H. Häfner), pp. 1–17. New York: Springer-Verlag.

HALL, O. M. & ROYSE, D. (1987) Mental health needs assessment with social indicators: an empirical case study. *Administration in Mental Health*, **15**(1), 36–46.

HALLECK, S. L. (1975) A multi-dimensional approach to violence. In *Violence and Criminal Justice* (eds D. Chappell and J. Monahan), pp. 33–47. Massachusetts: Lexington Books.

HAMILTON, J. (1990) Special hospitals and the state hospital. In *Principles and Practice of Forensic Psychiatry* (eds R. Bluglass and P. Bowden), pp. 1363–1373. London: Churchill Livingstone.

HANSSON, L., BJORKMAN, T. & SVENSSON, B. (1995) The assessment of needs in psychiatric patients: interrater reliability of the Swedish version of the Camberwell Assessment of Needs instrument and results from a cross-sectional study. *Acta Psychiatrica Scandanavica*, **92**, 285–293.

HAYWARD, P., PECK, E. & SMITH, H. (1993) Qualitative and quantitative approaches to needs assessment in mental health: creating a common currency. *Journal of Mental Health*, **2**, 287–294.

HEGINBOTHAM, C. & ELSON, T. (1999) Public policy via law: practitioners' sword and politicians' shield. In *Law Without Enforcement: Integrating Mental Health and Justice* (eds N. Eastman & J. Peay), pp. 59–74. Oxford: Hart Publishing.

HER MAJESTY'S CHIEF INSPECTOR OF PRISONS FOR ENGLAND AND WALES (1990) *Report of a Review of Suicide and Self-harm in Prison Service Establishments in England and Wales* (Cmnd 1383). London: HMSO.

HIGGINS, J. (1981) Four years' experience of an interim secure unit. *British Medical Journal*, **282**, 889–893.

HILLIS, G. (1992) Diverting tactics. *Nursing Times*, **89**(1), 24–27.

HIRSCH, S. (1988) *Psychiatric Beds and Resources: Factors Influencing Bed Use and Service Planning*. London: Gaskell.

—— & JARMAN, B. (1993) Changing approaches to determining mental health service resource needs. In *Principles of Social Psychiatry* (eds D. Bhugra & J. Leff), pp. 517–525. Oxford: Blackwell Press.

HOGG, L. I. & MARSHALL, M. (1992) Can we measure need in the homeless mentally ill? Using the MRC Needs for Care Assessment in hostels for the homeless. *Psychological Medicine*, **22**, 1027–1034.

HOLCOMB, W. R. & AHR, P. R. (1986) Clinicians' assessments of the service needs of young adult patients in public mental health care. *Hospital and Community Psychiatry*, **37**(9), 908–913.

HOLLOWAY, F. (1994) Need in community psychiatry: a consensus is required. *Psychiatric Bulletin*, **18**, 321–323.

HOLZER, C. E., GOLDSMITH, H. F., JACKSON, D. J., *et al* (1988) Indirect indicators for mental health services: comments and an independent formulation. In *Needs Assessment: Its Future* (ADM 88–1550) (ed H. F. Goldsmith), pp. 33–46. Washington, DC: US Government Printing Office.

HOME OFFICE (1964) *Report of the Working Party on the Organisation of the Prison Medical Service* (Gwynne report). London: HMSO.

—— (1986) *Report of the Working Group on Suicide Prevention*. London: HMSO.

208   References

—— (1990a) *Provision for Mentally Disordered Offenders* (circular no. 66/90). London: Home Office.

—— (1990b) *Report of a Review by Her Majesty's Chief Inspector of Prisons of Suicide and Self-harm in Prison Service Establishments.* London: HMSO.

—— (1991) *Prison Disturbances: Report of an Inquiry by the Rt Hon. Lord Justice Woolf (Parts I and II) and His Honour Judge Stephen Tumin (Part II).* London: HMSO.

—— (1994) *Statistics of Mentally Disordered Offenders England and Wales 1992* (Home Office Statistical Bulletin 04/94). London: Home Office Research and Statistics Department.

—— (1996) *Mentally Disordered Offenders: Sentencing and Discharge Arrangements* (discussion paper on a proposed new power for the courts). London: HMSO.

HOME OFFICE/DEPARTMENT OF HEALTH (1995) *Mentally Disordered Offenders: Inter-agency Working.* London: HMSO.

—— (1999) *Managing Dangerous People with Severe Personality Disorder: Proposals for Policy Development.* London: Joint Home Office/Department of Health.

HOME OFFICE/DEPARTMENT OF HEALTH AND SOCIAL SECURITY (1974) *Interim Report of the Committee on Mentally Abnormal Offenders* (Cmnd 5698). London: HMSO.

—— (1975) *Report of the Committee on Mentally Abnormal Offenders* (Butler report) (Cmnd 6244). HMSO: London.

HOSTICK, T. (1995) Research design and methodology for a local mental health needs assessment. *Journal of Psychiatric and Mental Health Nursing,* **2**, 295–299.

HUDSON, D., JAMES, D. & HARLOW, P. (1995a) *Psychiatric Court Liaison to Central London: A Report on the Service at Horseferry Magistrates' Court April 1994–March 1995.* London: Riverside Forensic Services, Riverside Mental Health Trust.

——, ——, ETHERINGTON, D., *et al* (1995b) *Psychiatric Intervention at the Police Station: A New Preventative Service to Central London.* London: Riverside Forensic Services, Riverside Mental Health Trust.

JACOBS, D. (1983) Evaluation and management of the violent patient in emergency settings. *Psychiatric Clinics of North America,* **6**, 259–269.

JAMES, D. & HAMILTON, L. W. (1991) The Clerkenwell scheme: assessing the efficacy and cost of a psychiatric liaison scheme to a magistrates' court. *British Medical Journal,* **303**, 282–285.

——, CRIPPS, J., GILLULEY, P. L., *et al* (1997) Abolishing remands to prison for psychiatric reports? A new court-focused model of forensic psychiatry provision to central London. *Journal of Forensic Psychiatry,* **8**, 390–405.

——, —— & GRAY, N. S. (1998) What demands do those admitted from the criminal justice system make on psychiatric beds? Expanding local secure services as a development strategy. *Journal of Forensic Psychiatry,* **9**(1), 74–102.

JARMAN, B. (1983) Identification of underprivileged areas. *British Medical Journal,* **286**, 1705–1709.

—— (1984) Validation and distribution of scores. *British Medical Journal,* **289**, 1587–1592.

——, HIRSCH, S., WHITE, P., *et al* (1992) Predicting psychiatric admission rates. *British Medical Journal,* **304**, 1146–1151.

JENKINS, R. (1990) Towards a system of outcome indicators for mental health care. *British Journal of Psychiatry,* **157**, 500–514.

JOHNSON, S., THORNICROFT, G., PHELAN, M., *et al* (1996) Assessing needs for mental health services. In *Mental Health Outcome Indicators* (eds G. Thornicroft & M. Tansella), pp. 217–226. Heidelberg: Springer-Verlag.

JONES, D. & DEAN, N. (1992) Assessment of need for services for mentally disordered offenders and patients with similar needs. *Health Trends,* **24**(2), 48.

JOSEPH, P. & POTTER, M. (1993a) Diversion from custody. I: Psychiatric assessment at the magistrate's court. *British Journal of Psychiatry,* **162**, 325–330.

—— & —— (1993b) Diversion from custody. II: Effect on hospital and prison resources. *British Journal of Psychiatry,* **162**, 330–334.

References 209

JUDGE, K. & MAYS, N. (1994) A new approach to weighted capitation. *British Medical Journal*, **309**, 1031–1032.

KAMMERLING, R. M. & O'CONNOR, S. (1993) Unemployment as predictor of rate of psychiatric admission. *British Medical Journal*, **307**, 1536–1539.

KENNEDY, J., WILSON, C. & COPE, R. (1995) Long-stay patients in a regional secure unit. *Journal of Forensic Psychiatry*, **6**(3), 541–551.

KLASSEN, D. & O'CONNOR, W. (1988) A prospective study of predictors of violence in adult male mental patients. *Law and Human Behaviour*, **12**, 143–158.

KLERMAN, G. L., OLFSON, M., LEON, A. C., *et al* (1992) Measuring need for mental health care. *Health Affairs*, **11**(3), 23–33.

KNAPP, M. & BEECHAM, J. (1990) Costing mental health services. *Psychological Medicine*, **20**, 893–908.

KROLL, J. & MACKENZIE, T. B. (1983) When psychiatrists are liable: risk management and violent patients. *Hospital and Community Psychiatry*, **34**(1), 29–37.

LAGOS, J., PERLMUTTER, K. & SAEXINGER, H. (1977) Fear of the mentally ill: empirical evidence for the common man's response. *American Journal of Psychiatry*, **134**, 1134–1137.

LEHMAN, A. F. (1996) Measures of quality of life among persons with severe and persistent mental disorders. In *Mental Health Outcome Indicators* (eds G. Thornicroft & M. Tansella), pp. 75–92. Heidelberg: Springer-Verlag.

LEHTINEN, V., LINDHOLM, T., VEIJOLA, J., *et al* (1989) The prevalence of PSE–CATEGO disorders in a Finnish adult population cohort. *Social Psychiatry and Psychiatric Epidemiology*, **25**, 187–192.

LEIGHTON, D. C., HARDING, J. S., MACKLIN, D. B., *et al* (1963) Psychiatric findings of the Stirling County Study. *American Journal of Psychiatry*, **119**, 1021–1026.

LELLIOTT, P. (1995) Mental health information systems. In *Measurement for Mental Health: Contributions from the College Research Unit* (ed. J. K. Wing), pp. 89–101. London: Royal College of Psychiatrists.

—— & WING, J. (1994) A national audit of new long-stay psychiatric patients. II: Impact on services. *British Journal of Psychiatry*, **165**, 170–176.

——, —— & CLIFFORD, P. (1994) A national audit of new long-stay psychiatric patients. I: Method and description of cohort. *British Journal of Psychiatry*, **165**, 160–169.

——, JARMAN, B., BAJEKAL, M., *et al* (1996) Commentaries on: An Index of Need for psychiatric services based on in-patient utilisation. *British Journal of Psychiatry*, **169**, 317–321.

LESAGE, A. D., MIGNOLLI, G., FACCINCANI, C., *et al* (1991*a*) Standardised assessment of the needs for care in a cohort of patients with schizophrenic psychoses. In *Community-based Psychiatry: Long-term Patterns of Care in South-Verona* (ed. M. Tansella), *Psychological Medicine*, monograph supplement 19, pp. 27–33.

——, COPE, S. J. & PEZESGHI, S. (1991*b*) Assessing the needs for care of non-psychotic patients. *Social Psychiatry and Psychiatric Epidemiology*, **26**, 281–286.

——, CLERC, D., URIBE, I., *et al* (1996) Estimating local-area needs for psychiatric care: a case study. *British Journal of Psychiatry*, **169**, 49–57.

LEVIN, G., WILDER, J. F. & GILBERT, J. (1978) Identifying and meeting clients' needs in six community mental health centers. *Hospital and Community Psychiatry*, **29**, 185–188.

LYALL, I., HOLLAND, T., COLLINS, S., *et al* (1995) Incidence of persons with a learning disability detained in police custody: a needs assessment for service development. *Medicine, Science and the Law*, **35**(1), 61–71.

LYNCH, M. M. & KRUZICH, J. M. (1986) Needs assessment of the chronically mentally ill: practitioner and client perspectives. *Administration in Mental Health*, **13**(4), 237–248.

MACCARTHY, B., LESAGE, A., BREWIN, C., *et al* (1989) Needs for care among the relatives of long-term users of day care: a report from the Camberwell High Contact Survey. *Psychological Medicine*, **19**, 725–736.

MACCULLOCH, M., BAILEY, J., JONES, C., *et al* (1993) Nineteen male serious reoffenders who were discharged direct to the community from a special hospital: I. General characteristics. *Journal of Forensic Psychiatry*, **4**(2), 237–248.

210 References

MACDONALD, L., SIBBALD, B. & HOARE, C. (1988) Measuring patients' satisfaction with life in a long-stay psychiatric hospital. *International Journal of Social Psychiatry*, **34**(4), 292–304.

MADEN, A., CURLE, C., MEUX, C., *et al* (1993) The treatment and security needs of patients in special hospitals. *Criminal Behaviour and Mental Health*, **3**, 290–306.

——, SWINTON, M. & GUNN, J. (1994*a*) Psychiatric disorder in women serving a prison sentence. *British Journal of Psychiatry*, **164**, 44–54.

——, —— & —— (1994*b*) Therapeutic community treatment: a survey of unmet need among sentenced prisoners. *Therapeutic Communities*, **15**(4), 229–236.

——, TAYLOR, C., BROOKE, D., *et al* (1995) *Mental Disorder in Remand Prisoners*. London: Home Office.

MANN, A. (1990) Public health and psychiatric morbidity. In *Indicators for Mental Health in the Population* (eds R. Jenkins & S. Griffiths), pp. 6–17. London: HMSO.

—— (1993) Epidemiology. In *Principles of Social Psychiatry* (eds D. Bhugra & J. Leff), pp. 25–35. Oxford: Blackwell Press.

MARSHALL, M. (1994) How should we measure need? Concept and practice in the development of a standardised assessment schedule. *Philosophy, Psychology, Psychiatry*, **1**(1), 27–36.

——, HOGG, L. I., GATH, D. H., *et al* (1995) The Cardinal Needs Schedule – a modified version of the MRC Needs for Care Assessment Schedule. *Psychological Medicine*, **25**, 605–617.

MASON, P. & WILKINSON, G. (1996) The prevalence of psychiatric morbidity: OPCS survey of psychiatric morbidity in Great Britain. *British Journal of Psychiatry*, **168**, 1–3.

McCLURE, G. M. G. (1987) Suicide in England and Wales 1975–1984. *British Journal of Psychiatry*, **150**, 309–314.

McCRONE, P. & WEICH, S. (1996) Mental health care costs: paucity of measurement. In *Mental Health Outcome Indicators* (eds G. Thornicroft & M. Tansella), pp. 131–142. Heidelberg: Springer-Verlag.

McMURRAN, M., CLERKIN, P. & ROSENBERG, H. (1996) Assessment of female patients in a secure psychiatric hospital. *Psychology, Crime and Law*, **3**, 15–19.

MEDNICK, S. A. & FINELLO, K. M. (1983) Biological factors and crime: implications for forensic psychiatry. *International Journal of Law and Psychiatry* **6**, 1–15.

MELTZER, H. & JENKINS, R. (1994) The national survey of psychiatric morbidity in Great Britain. *International Review of Psychiatry*, **6**, 349–356.

——, GILL, B., PETTICREW, M., *et al* (1995*a*) *OPCS Surveys of Psychiatric Morbidity in Great Britain, Report 1. The Prevalence of Psychiatric Morbidity Among Adults Living in Private Households.* London: HMSO.

——, ——, ——, *et al* (1995*b*) *OPCS Surveys of Psychiatric Morbidity in Great Britain, Report 2. Physical Complaints, Service Use and Treatment of Adults with Psychiatric Disorders.* London: HMSO.

——, ——, ——, *et al* (1995*c*) *OPCS Surveys of Psychiatric Morbidity in Great Britain, Report 3. Economic Activity and Social Functioning in Adults with Psychiatric Disorders.* London: HMSO.

——, ——, ——, *et al* (1996*a*) *OPCS Surveys of Psychiatric Morbidity in Great Britain, Report 4. The Prevalence of Psychiatric Morbidity Among Adults Living in Institutions.* London: HMSO.

——, ——, ——, *et al* (1996*b*) *OPCS Surveys of Psychiatric Morbidity in Great Britain, Report 5. Physical Complaints, Service Use and Treatment of Residents with Psychiatric Disorders.* London: HMSO.

MENTAL HEALTH ACT COMMISSION (1989) *Third Biennial Report 1987–1989* (laid before Parliament by the Secretary of State for Health pursuant to section 121(10) of the Mental Health Act 1983). London: HMSO.

—— (1991) *Fourth Biennial Report 1989–1991* (laid before Parliament by the Secretary of State for Health pursuant to section 121(10) of the Mental Health Act 1983). London: HMSO.

—— (1993) *Fifth Biennial Report 1991–1993* (laid before Parliament by the Secretary of State for Health pursuant to section 121(10) of the Mental Health Act 1983). London: HMSO.

MENUCK, M. (1983) Clinical aspects of dangerous behavior. *Journal of Psychiatry and Law*, **15**, 277–304.

MILMIS PROJECT GROUP (1995) Monitoring inner London mental illness services. *Psychiatric Bulletin*, **19**, 276–280.

MIND (1997) *MIND's Policy on People with Mental Health Problems and the Criminal Justice System*. London: MIND.

MINISTRY OF HEALTH (1961) *Special Hospitals: Report of a Working Party* (Emery report). London: HMSO.

MITCHISON, S., RIX, K. J. B., RENVOIZE, E. B., *et al* (1994) Recorded psychiatric morbidity in a large prison for male remanded and sentenced prisoners. *Medicine, Science and the Law*, **43**(4), 324–331.

MOHAN, D. J., MURRAY, K., TAYLOR, P. C., *et al* (1997) Developments in the use of regional secure unit beds over a twelve year period. *Journal of Forensic Psychiatry*, **8**(2), 321–335.

MONAHAN, J. (1981) *The Clinical Prediction of Violent Behavior* (ADM 81–921). Washington, DC: US Government Printing Office.

—— & STEADMAN, H. J. (1983) Crime and mental disorder: an epidemiological approach. In *Crime and Justice: An Annual Review of Research, Vol. 4* (eds M. Tonry & N. Morris), pp. 145–188. Chicago: University of Chicago Press.

MOONEY, G. (1994) *Key Issues in Health Economics*. London: Harvester Wheatsheaf.

MOXLEY, D. P. & FREDDOLINO, P. P. (1991) Needs of homeless people coping with psychiatric problems: findings from an innovative advocacy project. *Health and Social Work*, **16**(1), 19–26.

MULLEN, P. E. (1997) Assessing risk of interpersonal violence in the mentally ill. *Advances in Psychiatric Treatment*, **3**, 166–173.

MULVIHILL, D. J. & TUMIN, M. M. (1969) *Crimes of Violence, Vol. 12*. Washington, DC: US Government Printing Office.

MURPHY, E. (1992) The effects of NHS reorganization on forensic psychiatry services. *Journal of Forensic Psychiatry*, **3**(1), 13–31.

MURRAY, K. (1996) The use of beds in NHS medium secure units in England. *Journal of Forensic Psychiatry*, **7**(3), 504–524.

——, RUDGE, S., LACK, S., *et al* (1994) How many high security beds are needed? Implications from an audit of one region's special hospital patients. *Journal of Forensic Psychiatry*, **5**(3), 487–499.

——, AKINKUNMI, A., LOCK, M., *et al* (1997) The Bentham Unit: a pilot remand and assessment service for male mentally disordered remand prisoners. I. Clinical activity in the first year, and related ethical, practical and funding issues. *British Journal of Psychiatry*, **170**, 456–461.

MURRAY, V., WALKER, H. W., MITCHELL, C., *et al* (1996) Needs for care from a demand led community psychiatric service: a study of patients with major mental illness. *British Medical Journal*, **312**, 1582–1586.

NAISMITH, L. J. & COLDWELL, J. B. (1990) A comparison of male admissions to a special hospital 1970–1971 and 1987–1988. *Medicine, Science and the Law*, **30**(4), 301–308.

NATIONAL CONFIDENTIAL INQUIRY INTO SUICIDE AND HOMICIDE BY PEOPLE WITH MENTAL ILLNESS (1999) *Safer Services: National Confidential Inquiry into Suicide and Homicide by People with Mental Illness*. London: Department of Health.

NEMITZ, T. & BEAN, P. (1995) Discrepancies and inaccuracies in statistics for detained patients. *Psychiatric Bulletin*, **19**, 28–32.

NHS EXECUTIVE (1994a) *Guidance on the Discharge of Mentally Disordered People and Their Continuing Care in the Community* (HSG(94)27)). London: Department of Health.

—— (1994b) *Implementing the Infrastructure for Information Management and Technology in the NHS*. London: Department of Health.

—— (1995a) *High Security Psychiatric Services: Changes in Funding and Organisation*. London: HMSO.

—— (1995*b*) *Home Office Circular on Provision for Mentally Disordered Offenders: Interagency Working* (circular no. 12/95). London: Department of Health.

NHS MANAGEMENT EXECUTIVE (1990) *Services for Mentally Disordered Offenders and Difficult to Manage Patients* (EL90/190). London: Department of Health.

—— (1991) *Assessing Health Care Needs: A DHA Discussion Paper.* London: Department of Health.

—— (1992*a*) *Services for Mentally Disordered Offenders and Patients with Similar Needs* (EL(92)6). London: Department of Health.

—— (1992*b*) *Assessment of Need for Services for Mentally Disordered Offenders and Patients with Similar Needs* (EL(92)24). London: Department of Health.

—— (1993*a*) *Assessment of Need for Services for Mentally Disordered Offenders and Patients with Similar Needs* (EL(93)68). London: Department of Health.

—— (1993*b*) *Priorities and Planning Guidance 1994–95* (EL(93)54). London: Department of Health.

—— (1993*c*) *Managing the New NHS: A Background Document.* London: HMSO.

—— (1994) *Introduction of Supervision Registers for Mentally Ill People from 1 April 1994* (HSG(94)5). London: Department of Health.

NHS TRAINING DIRECTORATE (1994) *Getting Ahead with Clinical Audit: A Facilitator's Guide.* Bristol: NHS Training Directorate.

ODEGARD, O. (1932) Emigration and insanity: a study of mental disease among Norwegian born population in Minnesota. *Acta Psychiatrica Neurologica Scandinavica*, supplementum 4.

O'GRADY, J. (1990) The complementary role of regional and local secure provision for psychiatric patients. *Health Trends*, **22**, 14–16.

O'LEARY, D. & WEBB, M. (1996) The needs for care assessment – a longitudinal approach. *Psychiatric Bulletin*, **20**, 134–136.

OVRETVEIT, J. (1995) *Purchasing for Health.* Buckingham: Open University Press.

PARKER, E. (1985) The development of secure provision. In *Secure Provision: A Review of Services for the Mentally Ill and Mentally Handicapped in England and Wales* (ed. L. Gostin), pp. 15–65. London: Tavistock.

PEARSON, G. (1999) Madness and moral panic. In *Law Without Enforcement: Integrating Mental Health and Justice* (eds N. Eastman & J. Peay), pp. 159–172. Oxford: Hart Publishing.

PEAY, J. (1996) *Inquiries after Homicide.* London: Duckworth.

PHELAN, M., SLADE, M., THORNICROFT, G., *et al* (1995) The Camberwell Assessment of Need: the validity and reliability of an instrument to assess the needs of people with severe mental illness. *British Journal of Psychiatry*, **167**, 589–595.

PORTER, R. (1987) *Mind-Forg'd Manacles: A History of Madness in England from the Restoration to the Regency.* London: Penguin.

POWELL, R. B., HOLLANDER, D. & TOBIANSKY, R. I. (1995) Crisis in admission beds: a four-year study of the bed state in Greater London's acute psychiatric units. *British Journal of Psychiatry*, **167**, 765–769.

PRINS, H. (1986) *Dangerous Behaviour, the Law, and Mental Disorder.* London: Tavistock.

—— (1990) Dangerousness: a review. In *Principles and Practice of Forensic Psychiatry* (eds R. Bluglass & P. Bowden), pp. 499–505. London: Churchill Livingstone.

PRYCE, I. G., GRIFFITHS, R. D., GENTRY, R. M., *et al* (1991) The nature and severity of disabilities in long-stay psychiatric patients in South Glamorgan. *British Journal of Psychiatry*, **158**, 817–821.

——, ——, ——, *et al* (1993) How important is the assessment of social skills in current long-stay in-patients? An evaluation of clinical response to needs for assessment, treatment, and care in a long-stay psychiatric in-patient population. *British Journal of Psychiatry*, **162**, 498–502.

RABKIN, J. G. (1986) Mental health needs assessment: a review of methods. *Medical Care*, **24**(12), 1093–1109.

REED, J. (1994) *Survey of Requirements for Long Stay Care for Patients Currently in Medium Secure Units*. London: Department of Health.

—— (1996) Psychopathy – a clinical and legal dilemma. *British Journal of Psychiatry,* **168,** 4–9.

REID, A., LEA, J. & WALLACE, D. (1982) Rehabilitation on Elton Ward, an interim secure unit: a description after four and a half years. *Nursing Times,* **78,** 20–32.

REID v. THE SECRETARY OF STATE FOR SCOTLAND (1998) 1 ALL ER 481.

RENNIE, Y. (1978) *The Search for Criminal Man: A Conceptual History of the Dangerous Offender*. Lexington, MA: Lexington Books.

RENSHAW, J. (1994) The Audit Commission's review of mental health services. *Psychiatric Bulletin,* **18,** 421–422.

REVOLVING DOORS AGENCY (1994) *The Management of People with Mental Health Problems by the Paddington Police*. London: Revolving Doors Agency.

RICHMAN, A., BOUTILIER, C. & HARRIS, P. (1984) The relevance of sociodemographic and resource factors in the use of acute psychiatric in-patient care in Atlantic provinces of Canada. *Psychological Medicine,* **14,** 175–182.

—— & BARRY, A. (1985) More and more is less and less: the myth of massive psychiatric need. *British Journal of Psychiatry,* **146,** 164–168.

—— & BRITTON, B. (1992) Level of care for deinstitutionalized psychiatric patients. *Health Reports,* **4**(3), 269–275.

RITCHIE, J. H., DICK, D. & LINGHAM, R. (1994) *The Report of the Inquiry into the Care and Treatment of Christopher Clunis*. London: HMSO.

ROBERTSON, G. (1997) Research in forensic psychiatry. *Journal of Forensic Psychiatry,* **8**(3), 501–503

——, GROUNDS, A., DELL, S., *et al* (1994) A follow-up of remanded mentally ill offenders given court hospital orders. *Medicine, Science and the Law,* **34**(1), 61–66.

——, PRESTON, R. & GIBB, R. (1996) The entry of mentally disordered people to the criminal justice system. *British Journal of Psychiatry,* **169,** 172–180.

ROBINSON, J. & ELKAN, R. (1996) *Health Needs Assessment: Theory and Practice*. London: Churchill Livingstone.

ROTH, A. & FONAGY, P. (1996) *What Works for Whom: A Critical Review of Psychotherapy Research*. New York: Guilford Press.

ROWLANDS, R., INCH, H., RODGER, W., *et al* (1996) Diverted to where? What happens to the diverted mentally disordered offender? *Journal of Forensic Psychiatry,* **7**(2), 284–296.

ROYAL COLLEGE OF PSYCHIATRISTS (1980) *Secure Facilities for Psychiatric Patients: A Comprehensive Policy* (Council Report 1). London: Royal College of Psychiatrists.

—— (1989) *Guidelines for Good Medical Practice in Discharge and Aftercare Procedures for Patients Discharged from In-patient Psychiatric Treatment* (Council Report 8). London: Royal College of Psychiatrists.

—— (1996) *Response to the Home Office/Department of Health Mentally Disordered Offenders Sentencing Arrangements. A Discussion Paper on a Proposed New Power for the Courts*. London: Royal College of Psychiatrists.

ROYAL COMMISSION ON THE LAW RELATING TO MENTAL ILLNESS AND MENTAL DEFICIENCY (1957) *Report* (Percy report) (Cmnd 169). London: HMSO.

ROYSE, D. & DRUDE, K. (1982) Mental health needs assessment: beware of false promises. *Community Mental Health Journal,* **18**(2), 97–106.

RUBIN, B. (1972) Predictions of dangerousness in mentally ill criminals. *Archives of General Psychiatry,* **27,** 397–407.

RUGGERI, M. (1996) Satisfaction with psychiatric services. In *Mental Health Outcome Indicators* (eds G. Thornicroft & M. Tansella), pp. 26–51. Heidelberg: Springer-Verlag.

SCHINNAR, A. P., ROTHBARD, A. B. & HADLEY, T. R. (1992) A prospective management approach to the delivery of mental health services. *Administration and Policy in Mental Health,* **19**(4), 291–308.

SCOTT, P. D. (1970) Punishment or treatment: prison or hospital. *British Medical Journal,* ii, 167–169.

—— (1974) Solutions to the problem of the dangerous offender. *British Medical Journal,* iv, 640–641.

SCULL, A. T. (1979) *Museums of Madness: The Social Organization of Insanity in Nineteenth Century England.* London: Alan Lane.

SEDGWICK, P. (1982) *Psychopolitics.* London: Pluto Press.

SHAPIRO, S., SKINNER, E. A., KRAMER, M., et al (1985) Measuring need for mental health services in a general population. *Medical Care,* **23**, 1033–1043.

SHAW, J., McKENNA, J., SNOWDEN, P., et al (1994a) The North West Region. I: Clinical features and placement needs of patients detained in special hospitals. *Journal of Forensic Psychiatry,* **5**(1), 93–105.

——, ——, ——, et al (1994b) The North West Region. II: Patient characteristics in the research panel's recommended placement groups. *Journal of Forensic Psychiatry,* **5**(1), 107–122.

SHEAFF, R. (1996) *The Need for Health Care.* London: Routledge.

SHEPHERD, M. (1957) *A Study of Major Psychosis in an English County* (Maudsley Monograph No. 3). London: Chapman and Hall.

SHEPPARD, D. (1996) *Learning the Lessons: Mental Health Inquiry Reports Published in England and Wales between 1969 and 1996 and their Recommendations for Improving Practice* (2nd edn). London: Zito Trust.

SHEPPARD, M. (1993) Client satisfaction, extended intervention and interpersonal skills in community mental health. *Journal of Advanced Nursing,* **18**, 246–259.

SHORTER, E. (1997) *A History of Psychiatry: From the Era of the Asylum to the Age of Prozac.* New York: Wiley.

SINGLETON, N., MELTZER, H., GATWARD, R., et al (1998) *Psychiatric Morbidity among Prisoners in England and Wales.* London: HMSO.

SLADE, M. (1994) Needs assessment: involvement of staff and users will help to meet needs. *British Journal of Psychiatry,* **165**, 293–296.

——, PHELAN, M. THORNICROFT, G., et al (1996) The Camberwell Assessment of Need (CAN): comparison of assessments by staff and patients of the needs of the severely mentally ill. *Social Psychiatry and Psychiatric Epidemiology,* **31**, 109–113.

SMITH, P., SHELDON, T. A., CARR-HILL, R. A., et al (1994) Allocating resources to health authorities: results and policy implications of small area analysis of use of inpatient services. *British Medical Journal,* **309**, 1050–1054.

——, —— & MARTIN, S. (1996) An index for psychiatric services based on inpatients' utilisation. *British Journal of Psychiatry,* **169**, 308–316.

SNOWDEN, P. R. (1983) The regional secure units programme: a personal appraisal. *Bulletin of the Royal College of Psychiatrists,* **143**, 138–140.

—— (1985) A survey of the regional secure unit programme. *British Journal of Psychiatry,* **147**, 499–507.

—— (1990) Regional secure units and forensic services in England and Wales. In *Principles and Practice of Forensic Psychiatry* (eds R. Bluglass & P. Bowden), pp. 1375–1386. London: Churchill Livingstone.

SOLOMON, P. & BECK, S. (1989) Patients' perceived service needs when seen in a psychiatric emergency room. *Psychiatric Quarterly,* **60**(3), 215–226.

SPECIAL HOSPITALS SERVICE AUTHORITY (1991) *SHSA Review 1991.* London: SHSA.

—— (1993) *Report of the Committee of Enquiry into the Death in Broadmoor Hospital of Orville Blackwood and a Review of the Deaths of Two Other Afro-Caribbean Patients: 'Big, Black and Dangerous'.* London: Special Hospitals Service Authority.

SPENDER, Q. & COOPER, H. (1995) The hinterland between audit and research. *ACPP Review and Newsletter,* **17**(2), 65–73.

STEADMAN, H. J. & COCOZZA, J. J. (1978) Public perceptions of the criminally insane. *Hospital and Community Psychiatry,* **29**(7), 457–459.

STEERING COMMITTEE OF THE CONFIDENTIAL INQUIRY INTO HOMICIDES AND SUICIDES BY MENTALLY ILL PEOPLE (1996) *Report of the Confidential Inquiry into Homicides and Suicides by Mentally Ill People.* London: Royal College of Psychiatrists.

STEVENS, A. & GABBAY, J. (1991) Needs assessment needs assessment.... *Health Trends,* **23**(1), 20–23.

—— & RAFTERY, J. (1992) The purchasers' information requirements on mental health needs and contracting for mental health services. In *Measuring Mental Health Needs* (eds G. Thornicroft, C. Brewin & J. Wing), pp. 42–61. London: Gaskell.

—— & —— (1994) Introduction. In *Health Care Needs Assessment: Epidemiologically Based Needs Assessment Review* (eds A. Stevens & J. Raftery) (vol. 1, pp. 11–30). Oxford: Radcliffe Medical Press.

STOCKING, B. (1985) *Initiative and Inertia.* Oxford: Nuffield Hospital Trust.

STRATHDEE, G. & THORNICROFT, G. (1992) Community sectors for needs-led mental health services. In *Measuring Mental Health Needs* (eds G. Thornicroft, C. Brewin & J. Wing), pp. 140–162. London: Gaskell.

STUART, R. B. (1981) Violence in perspective. In *Violent Behavior: Social Learning Approaches to Prediction, Management and Treatment* (ed. R. B. Stuart), pp. 3–30. New York: Brunner/ Mazel.

SWANSON, J. W., BORUM, R., SWARTZ, S., *et al* (1996) Psychotic symptoms and disorders and the risk of violent behaviour in the community. *Criminal Behaviour and Mental Health,* **6**, 309–329.

TANSELLA, M. & THORNICROFT, G. (1998) A conceptual framework for mental health services: the matrix model. *Psychological Medicine,* **28**, 503–508.

TAYLOR, P. & GUNN, J. (1984) Violence and psychosis. I: Risk of violence among psychotic men. *British Medical Journal,* **288**, 1945–1949.

——, BUTWELL, M., DACEY, R., *et al* (1991) *Within Maximum Security Hospitals: A Survey of Need.* London: Special Hospital Services Authority.

——, MADEN, A. & JONES, D. (1996) Long-term medium-security hospital units: a service gap of the 1990s? *Criminal Behaviour and Mental Health,* **6**, 213–229.

TENNENT, G., PARKER, E., MCGRATH, P., *et al* (1980) Male admissions to the English special hospitals – 1961–1965, a demographic survey. *British Journal of Psychiatry,* **136**, 181–190.

THOMPSON, C. (1995) New powers for the mentally ill. *The Times,* 23 March.

THORNICROFT, G. (1991) Social deprivation and rates of treated mental disorder: developing statistical models to predict psychiatric service utilisation. *British Journal of Psychiatry,* **158**, 475–484.

——, GOOCH, C., O'DRISCOLL, C., *et al* (1993) The TAPS project 9: The reliability of the Patient Attitude Questionnaire. *British Journal of Psychiatry,* **162** (supplement 19), 25–29.

TOCH, H. (1969) *Violent Men: An Inquiry into the Psychology of Violence.* Chicago: Aldine.

TREASADEN, I. H. (1985) Current practice in regional interim secure units. In *Secure Provision: A Review of Services for the Mentally Ill and Mentally Handicapped in England and Wales* (ed. L. Gostin), pp. 176–207. London: Tavistock.

TWEED, D. L. & CIARLO, J. A. (1992) IV: Social-indicator models for indirectly assessing mental health service needs: epidemiologic and statistical properties. *Evaluation and Program Planning,* **15**, 165–179.

——, ——, KIRKPATRICK, L. A., *et al* (1992) V: Empirical validity of indirect mental health needs-assessment models in Colorado. *Evaluation and Program Planning,* **15**, 181–194.

VAN HAASTER, I., CYR, M. & TOUPIN, J. (1994*a*) Problems and needs for care of patients suffering from severe mental illness. *Social Psychiatry and Psychiatric Epidemiology,* **29**, 141–148.

——, LESAGE, A. D., CYR, M., *et al* (1994*b*) Further reliability and validity studies of a procedure to assess the needs for care of the chronically mentally ill. *Psychological Medicine,* **24**, 215–222.

WAISMANN, L. C. & ROWLAND, L. A. (1989) Ranking of needs: a new method of assessment for use with chronic psychiatric patients. *Acta Psychiatrica Scandanavica,* **80**, 260–266.

WARHEIT, G., BELL, R. A. & SCHWAB, J. (1977) *Needs Assessment Approaches – Concepts and Methods* (ADM 88–1550). Rockville MD: National Institutes of Mental Health.

WATT, F., TOMISON, A. & TORPY, D. (1993) The prevalence of psychiatric disorder in a male remand population: a pilot study. *Journal of Forensic Psychiatry*, **4**(1), 75–84.

WEAVER, T., TAYLOR, F., CUNNINGHAM, B., *et al* (1997) The Bentham Unit: a pilot remand and assessment scheme of mentally disordered offenders. II. Report of an independent evaluation. *British Journal of Psychiatry*, **170**, 462–466.

WESSELY, S. (1997) The epidemiology of crime, violence and schizophrenia. *British Journal of Psychiatry*, **170** (supplement 32), 8–11.

WING, J. K. (1990) Meeting the needs of people with psychiatric disorders. *Social Psychiatry and Psychiatric Epidemiology*, **25**, 2–8.

—— (1993) Defining need and evaluating services. In *The Mentally Disordered Offender in an Era of Community Care: New Directions in Provision* (eds W. Watson & A. Grounds), pp. 90–101. Cambridge: Cambridge University Press.

—— (1994) Mental illness. In *Health Care Needs Assessment: Epidemiologically Based Needs Assessment Review* (eds A. Stevens & J. Raftery), vol. 1, pp. 202–304. Oxford: Radcliffe Medical Press.

—— (1995) The informatics of need. In *Measurement for Mental Health: Contributions from the College Research Unit* (ed. J. K. Wing), pp. 1–16. London: Royal College of Psychiatrists.

——, BREWIN, C. & THORNICROFT, G. (1992) Definitions and targets for needs assessment. In *Measuring Mental Health Needs* (eds G. Thornicroft, C. Brewin & J. Wing), pp. 1–17. London: Gaskell.

——, CURTIS, R. & BEEVOR, A. (1994) Health of the nation: measuring mental health outcomes. *Psychiatric Bulletin*, **18**, 690–691.

WOLFGANG, M. E. (1975) Contemporary perspectives on violence. In *Violence and Criminal Justice* (eds D. Chappell & J. Monahan), pp. 1–13. Lexington, MA: Lexington Books.

WRIGHT, J., WILLIAMS, R. & WILKINSON, J. (1998) Development and importance of health needs assessment. *British Medical Journal*, **316**, 1310–1313.

ZAUTRA, A. & SIMONS, L. S. (1978) An assessment of a community's mental health needs. *American Journal of Criminal Psychology*, **6**, 351–362.

Index

Compiled by NINA BOYD